THE FOOTBALL BUSINESS

The football business

Fair game in the '90s?

David Conn

MAINSTREAM
PUBLISHING PROJECTS

First published in Great Britain in 1997 by
MAINSTREAM PUBLISHING PROJECTS
Edinburgh

ISBN 1 85158 916 3

A catalogue record for this book is available from the British Library

Typeset in Bembo
Printed and bound in Great Britain by Butler and Tanner Ltd, Frome

CONTENTS

ACKNOWLEDGEMENTS

Obtaining interviews with people in the upper level of professional football involves a gruelling obstacle course: letters, faxes and constant reminder phone calls which are rarely even acknowledged. Despite its massive media profile, Premier League football seems determinedly reticent of explaining itself. The contrast could not be greater at other levels of the game, amongst supporters and the grass-roots; in preparing for this book, all attempted brush-offs from Premier League press offices have been outweighed many times over by enlightening, often inspiring conversations with people whose involvement in football springs from their love of it.

I would like to thank those from the Premier League who did provide the interviews related in this book, and collectively thank everybody quoted in the book for their help. I am grateful to the following people for the generosity with which they gave their time: Andy Walsh, Kevin Miles, Mike Heckles, Lucy Milton, Nigel Todd, Dolly Potter, Peter Greenwood, Maureen Bateson, Derek Howarth, Bill Jeffries, Steve Bell, Ray Nulty, Paul Loftus, Dr Milton Jeffries, Alan Watts, Greg Dyke, Jeff Farmer, Simon Johnson, Kate Hoey MP, Patrick Caveney, Tony King, Tony Tighe, Chris Hull, Irving Scholar, Mike Glancy, Damian Sanders, Darryl Keys, Tony Simpson, John de Quidt, Mike Appleby, John Bowler, Bryan Gray, Steve White, Ron Noades, Gordon Taylor, Paul Power, Mick McGuire, Jon Holmes, Leroy Whale, Dave Merrington, Jimmy Armfield, Peter Lorimer, John Williams, Mick Johnstone, Sheila Spiers, Dave Wallace, Don Price,

John Barnwell, Alex Fynn, Dave Thomas, Kath Marah, Graham Craggs, Chris Armstrong, Shaun Teale, Des Murphy, Evan Bryson, Tony Pickerin, Chris Winne and the players of Rusholme Argyle FC, Ron Halfacre, Fred Harris, Graham Kelly.

In addition I would particularly like to thank the following people: Professor Eric Dunning of Leicester University for his time and for sharing his awesome knowledge of the development of the game of football; Allen Wade for his reminiscences and insights; Brian Lomax for his uplifting reflections on football support; John Morton and Malcolm Berry of the ESFA for their extensive help over the last couple of years; Gary Blumberg for his background explanations and encouragement; Ian Muter for allowing me to cover his brave, solitary supporters' campaign and Phil Redmond for help beyond the call of duty.

Phil and Hilda Hammond spared a long night in a busy period for them discussing the Hillsborough disaster and the tragic loss of their son Philip. I hope that my account of Hillsborough does at least no further injustice to the memories of those who died and the families' continuing struggle.

I am grateful also to Colin Moneypenny and Jimmy McGovern for their help with the Hillsborough chapters, and would like to express particular thanks to Ann Adlington for sparing so much of her hard-pressed time.

The help and advice of the following fellow journalists have been invaluable: Mark Edmonds, Frances Gibb, David Meek, Eric Paler, Peter Montellier, John May, Andrew Head, Andrew Mourant, Juliette Wills, Michael Crick, Steve Brauner, Tim Rich, Brian McNally.

I owe a particular debt to Rex Nash and Sam Johnstone of the Football Research Unit, Liverpool University, for providing so generously, and rapidly, the benefit of their expert knowledge and insight.

Many people gave practical help and moral support over the course of researching and writing the book; I owe a large debt to my mother for crucial support at critical times; to Aunties Sharon and Ruth for their help; to Mark Pinder, Deborah Frieze and Jez Berman for allowing me completely to abuse their hospitality with frantic working visits; Newsco Publications in Manchester for assistance ranging from expert advice to a chair to sit on; Faiz Naqvi for his unfailing, daily cheerfulness and generosity.

My friend Sean Thorpe was an immense help all the way through, particularly in the latter stages of writing. It is frightening to imagine the state I or the book would have been in without Sean's wise and unstinting support.

I will always be grateful to the following people for showing faith in my work from the beginning: Frances Gibb, Matthew Kalman, all at Newsco Publications, Martin Regan, Andy Lyons, Mark Edmonds and in particular Peter Freedman.

I would also like to thank Jo and Neil for lending me their computer . . .

Finally, but most of all, only my partner Sarah knows the gory reality of the research and writing of this book – unfortunately for her. It is literally impossible to thank her enough for her support and love – and tolerance.

1

WHEN SKY FELL IN

Alan Sugar may have his detractors but there surely can be no question that he is a remarkable character. Having been born into a poor, working-class Jewish family in Hackney in 1947, father in the rag-trade, brother Derek a taxi-driver, Sugar must have had something unique to have achieved what he did. His is an amazing record, almost incomprehensible to ordinary people; the story of how a man managed to grow up, from that background, at that time, so totally uninterested in the game of football.

Tottenham Hotspur's reputation as the Jewish-supported football club is an oversimplification – all football clubs close to large Jewish communities draw a proportion of that support. Arsenal's chairman, David Dein, is Jewish. West Ham are still followed by the grandchildren of Jewish immigrants who crowded into the East End around the turn of this century. They toiled, mostly in the rag-trade, eventually to make their way north to semi-detached respectability in Redbridge, Ilford, Gants Hill. And it is true that in these North-East London hinterlands, pale lives of suburban graft, in cab-driving, or market-trading, have traditionally been leavened by Spurs.

Derek Sugar, older by 12 years, grew up Spurs-mad, never missing a game. He was 26 in 1961, a good age to savour the Double, won by Bill Nicholson's elegant, great side. As much as the Double itself, the first of the twentieth century, Tottenham's style played its way into football legend. Generations of North-East London kids would grow up hearing about the team: Dave Mackay, Bobby Smith, John

White, the cool, graceful captaincy of Danny Blanchflower.

It was Blanchflower who eloquently expressed football's beauty, how and why it so captures the heart, a famous comment, clasped by Spurs fans as their club motto: 'The great fallacy is that the game is first and last about winning. It's nothing of the kind. The game is about glory. It's about doing things in style, with a flourish.'

Alan's father, Nathan, took him to White Hart Lane as a kid. Alan was unmoved. He couldn't see the point. Even as a child, he never had much time for enjoying himself. Much younger than twins Derek and Daphne, Alan grew up sickly and solitary. His earliest memory is of having his adenoids out in Hackney Hospital. He never played football out with the other kids, developed few interests to enrich his life. Overexposed to the adult miseries of poverty and insecurity, he grew up obsessed by money. He was always thinking about it. When Spurs were doing the Double, 14-year-old Alan Sugar was, famously, boiling beetroot to sell to a local greengrocer, or making ginger beer to sell at school, undercutting Tizer.

Since the Eighties, businessmen have been worshipped in Britain, held up as models of achievement, portrayed as admirable self-starters, strivers, natural leaders. But this is to look superficially on the bright side of complex individual stories. Sugar, the teenage moneyspinner, became a businessman of barely repressed anger, casting himself as an avenging hero, the champion of cheap suburban taste fighting a snobby and complacent establishment.

His view of humanity is spelled out at length in *Alan Sugar: The Amstrad Story*, by journalist David Thomas, who painted Sugar's scowling, railing vulgarity as some kind of way forward for the nation. Starting out at 19, buying and selling car aerials out of the back of a Mini-van, the driven Sugar formed a limited company out of his initials, AMS Trading – Amstrad – in 1968. Two years later he broke out of pure trading by manufacturing his first product, a plastic covers for turntables.

From the beginning he based his approach on undercutting products already on the market; he was a 'pile-it-high-sell-it-cheap' philistine, and proud of it. He reckoned quality hi-fi manufacturers were wankers, appealing to only 5 per cent of the population, who were 'snooty'. Amstrad's hi-fi punters were characterised as 'the truck driver and his wife'. He reckoned they made up 95 per cent of the population: 'They want something that makes a noise and looks good.'

Sugar's products were based on looking better than they actually were and being as cheap as possible. Calling British manufacturing 'crap', Margaret Thatcher's favourite entrepreneur subcontracted everything, having components and even his instruction manuals made cheaply in the Far East, to be assembled back in London and have the Amstrad name tacked on.

The word-processor, which feathered Amstrad's heyday, originated as a plan to save manufacturing costs on a computer by incorporating the printer. The result, the 'PCW8256', filled the gap between expensive, quality, Apple and IBM office computers, and basic games machines for homes. So Amstrad undercut its way into a part of human progress, making computers accessible to ordinary people, word-processing possible in domestic back rooms and little offices across middle England.

Sugar began then to give the world the benefit of his wisdom. Having made money, it seemed to prove that his attitude, scornful of culture, quality, institutions, was right. A manufacturer of electronic goods, he boasted of his complete lack of scientific knowledge. He had his finger on the cheapo pulse of the nation and his sole aim in business, profit, was all the philosophy anybody needed.

This was Thatcher's heyday, around the time of her famous, chilling comment that there was 'no such thing as society'. In the social strife of the time, the destruction or privatisation of industry, the assault on institutions like the unions, the professions, the universities, the health service, men like Sugar were being presented as the new heroes. In April 1987 he was invited to lecture to City University Business School. He summed it up like this:

'Pan Am takes good care of you.
Marks and Spencer loves you.
IBM says the customer is king . . .
At Amstrad – We want your money!'

It is a sad reflection of the times that this was then considered cheeky-chappie, iconoclastic stuff worth listening to. In 1997 Amstrad would fold after years of losses and troubles, Sugar finally giving up on the brand he named after himself, which he failed to develop after the ephemeral success of his word-processor. The other three boring, misguided companies appear to be still in business.

In June 1988, Sugar agreed to make receiving dishes for Rupert Murdoch's planned Sky Television. He had not, unsurprisingly, clinched the deal by offering to be the best: 'I felt the whole thing was contingent on getting a supplier at a low price,' said Murdoch. They did a deal: very large numbers of dishes, to sell at £199. Sugar, working on low profit margins, thought he could find a 'dustbin-lid manufacturer in Birmingham' to make them.

Murdoch and Sugar liked each other; they were both obsessive, bottom-line Eighties men with scarcely a single interest in life outside their businesses. Murdoch had built a newspaper and television empire on sharp takeovers and ruthlessness in his deals and towards employees. He rarely missed an opportunity to lambast 'the establishment' in Britain, by which he tended to mean, mainly, educated people with a broader view of life merely than making a profit.

Murdoch had been substantially responsible for what is now called the 'dumbing down' of the British media; the demise of investigative journalism, which was replaced by an obsession with trivia and sensationalism. A landmark in this process, less explosive than his 1986 cracking of the print and journalists' unions at Wapping, was the gradual undermining of Harold Evans, editor of *The Times*, who was pushed into resigning in 1982. In his 14 previous years as editor of *The Sunday Times*, Evans had become one of the most distinguished journalists of his generation, winning awards in 1973 for revealing the scandal of Thalidomide. Murdoch introduced Page Three to the nation, and *The Sun* was the jewel in his crown. He brought this approach to *The Times*. Evans, in his memoirs, recalls Murdoch's view of *The Times*' double-page coverage of martial law in Poland, in 1982, at the time of Solidarity's emergence: 'Murdoch flicked open a copy of *The Sun*. "There," he said, "that's all you need on Poland", and he put his hand on a few paragraphs of his *Sun*.'

Murdoch's journalism undercut the traditions of investigation and inquiry, of newspapers as upholders and guardians of integrity in public life. He was a purveyor of infotainment, his tabloid newspapers featuring birds, stars, sport, scandal, there to be looked at, not to be read. This, he said, deriding the liberal culture of the British media, was what people wanted. A high priest of the bottom line, Murdoch always supported Margaret Thatcher's project with his battery of newspapers, and she helped him in return. He thought sport was a waste of his time, although he stuffed his newspapers full of it. Alan Sugar had found a soulmate.

Amstrad's terminal decline started the following year, 1989, Sugar struggling to move upmarket with the PC2000 and suffering losses at Spanish and German subsidiaries. Amstrad's brief flowering as the embodiment of everything Britain should stand for withered with a 52 per cent fall in profits and plummeting share price. From £150m profits in 1988, Amstrad made just over £10m in 1991. In 1992 it recorded its first losses: £70m. 'I haven't been able to find any new blockbusters,' Sugar mourned, admitting his failure to grow the company into maturity.

Murdoch's Sky was doing even worse, disastrously. It launched on Sunday, 5 February 1989, at a cost of £100m, with the slogan a 'new world of freedom' and a dire bill of fare. The channel had managed to include the recognised ingredients of pay television: entertainment, news, movies, sport, but the content was a joke. Highlight of the first night was *Dolly*, a chat show hosted by Dolly Parton, on Sky One. The sports channel, Eurosport, opened with Davis Cup tennis, Italy v. Sweden, followed by skiing, autocross and bobsleigh. This, though, was only a taster for the sporting highlight of the first week, Tuesday at 7 p.m., when excited viewers could take the phones off the hook and settle down eagerly to Baltic Cup Handball.

In fact, however, there weren't many viewers. Sky's technical deliberations had delayed manufacture of dishes, so Sugar was not able to produce them in time for the launch. The shops, Dixons and Rumbelows, had one each, for demonstration only. By June, Sky was costing News Corporation, Murdoch's media leviathan, £2m a week, £75m since the launch.

Despite relentless hyping in Murdoch's tabloids, *News of the World* and *The Sun*, featuring Page Three girls holding sizzling dishes, Sky's first chink of light was not to come until 1990, when it landed England's Ashes series in Australia. Cricket fans, accustomed to half an hour of Richie Benaud on BBC2, paid in some numbers for the chance to stay up all night, watching it ball by ball.

In November 1990 Sky merged with the embryonic, bloated opposition, BSB, to give themselves half a chance of survival. Really a Sky takeover, it left Murdoch's NewsCorp with 40 per cent of BSkyB. For a while, the joint operation was losing £10m a week, the biggest drain on NewsCorp, which was in very real danger of going bust. Only a tough, strict $8bn refinancing package, imposed by 146 banks worldwide in February 1991, saved Murdoch at the brink of ruin. One, the Pittsburgh National, had come within minutes of putting NewsCorp into receivership. Sluggish dish sales were damaging Amstrad too, which was then moving into lossmaking. Sugar and Murdoch, both struggling in the recession, used to share their troubles, talking on the phone twice a week.

Sport, it was becoming clear to BSkyB executives, was the only kind of television which could bring in enough of an audience to give Sky a hope of survival. And not just any sport. As David Hill, Sky's Australian head of sport, was to say in 1992, in Britain, which nurtured, devised, then gave the beautiful game to the world, it was one sport alone: 'Here it's football first, second and third,' he said. The English television companies already knew that. It was one of the few things BSB had done right, a joint deal with the BBC, £30m to show five years of FA Cup and England matches.

'It's a guaranteed bringer of an audience,' explains Jeff Farmer, current head of football at ITV. 'It's a great sport, great television, and it has very many diehard fans who will always want to watch their clubs. That is why it is so big a prize to television.'

The fans, in other words, cannot do without football. They are practically addicted to the game, they watch it wherever it appears. If Sky could get hold of football exclusively, take it off terrestrial television, football supporters would then have no choice but to fork out for a dish and a subscription. Sky came to see football supporters as a 'captive market', just about the only group in Britain who could be made to pay to watch television. Greg Dyke, then managing director of London Weekend Television, knew this very well, and had foreseen that satellite, fighting for its life, would try to pay the top football clubs enough for them to agree to take the game off free television. In 1988, Dyke had only just managed to snatch the live rights to First Division matches away from BSB, preserving ITV's live Sunday afternoon matches and Saint and Greavesie's soon-to-wear-thin buffoonery. This contract was to run out in 1992. Planning ahead, Dyke invited the then Big Five football clubs over for dinner at LWT in November 1990.

This dinner was the beginning of the Premier League breakaway. Martin Edwards, chief executive and major shareholder in Manchester United, was there, along with Noel White and Peter Robinson from Liverpool, David Dein of Arsenal, Irving Scholar, then chairman of Spurs, and Philip Carter of Everton. Dyke made it clear to them he was only interested in showing the top clubs. 'We believed we could get a better deal from the big clubs only,' explains Dyke.

Irving Scholar recalls that Dyke put no precise figure on how much ITV would pay for exclusive rights, but, if the top clubs could break away, it was obvious there was going to be plenty of cash for them: 'Even if we only got the same money as 1988, we would each get more because, after breaking away, we would not be sharing the money out with the other, smaller football clubs.'

The big clubs, savouring this idea after the dinner with Dyke, sent David Dein and Noel White 'for a quiet word' with the Football Association, to see if the FA would back their plan to break away from the Football League. The FA, to its shame, betraying its historic role as regulator, controller of commercialism for the wider good of football, was to put its name to the breakaway, which would make a fortune for the owners of the big clubs and open up enormous inequality in football. The big five were to carve the television money up between them, no longer to have to share it, as they had always previously done, with the other professional clubs.

Spurs was still one of the Big Five at that time. Following a brief visit to the Second Division in 1977-78, the glory club had returned, under manager Keith Burkinshaw, to unveil Osvaldo Ardiles and Ricardo Villa, fresh from Argentina's victory in the 1978 World Cup. The next Spurs generation watched football to cherish; solidity at the back, Steve Perryman's consistency, Garth Crooks and Steve Archibald up front. Ossie. And Glenn Hoddle. Spraying the memories around the park.

Spurs managed to retain their flairful reputation throughout the Eighties, David Pleat's diamond formation of 1986-87 giving way to rough diamond El Tel, who, despite the club's financial problems, still managed to lay on Chris Waddle, Paul Gascoigne, Gary Lineker.

At the end of the Eighties, Tottenham was in trouble, bottom of the Stock Exchange, seeking re-election. Irving Scholar had mingled his support for Spurs and business practices into a float in 1983 and a disastrously diversified series of schemes. The East Stand, replacing the elegant Shelf of terracing with two strips of executive boxes, had cost £10m compared to the original estimate of £4.8m. Scholar had had a loan for this underwritten by Robert Maxwell, who was then developing an appetite for football clubs, having swallowed a couple of small fry for hors d'oeuvres.

El Tel, Cleverest Man in Football, too sharp, too clever, too crafty to be a football manager all his life, had his eye on taking over a club completely. No longer just working for a club, but getting his hands on the lot. He saw his chance then to put together a bid to take over Tottenham himself, snatch it from the large jaws of Maxwell. With Venables casting around for support, who should come riding to the rescue one day in 1991, ringing him up, but Alan Sugar, the UK's Greatest Living Entrepreneur, who, after a lifetime's complete obliviousness to football, had discovered a sudden interest in Spurs? It was an irresistible team: scowling, swearing Sugar and chirpy, chewing El Tel: Essex man and Dagenham man, come to save the Spurs. The 'dream ticket', combining Alan Sugar's knowledge of football with Terry's financial acumen. Or was it the other way round?

Sugar and Venables bought Scholar and his partner Paul Bobroff out, 35.8 per cent of Spurs, for £2.73m. They also bought 21 per cent from other shareholders, mainly City institutions taking the chance to bail out of the stricken football company, leaving Sugar and Venables with 57 per cent between them, at a cost of £4.3m. Sugar was dipping into small change. Tel was borrowing like crazy to keep up.

In December 1991 Tottenham had a rights issue, to be financed more by Sugar than Venables. When it closed on 20 January 1992, it had raised £7m in total. Sugar, for a total investment of £8m, ended up with 47.8 per cent of Spurs. Tel had 22.1 per cent. Amstrad shares dropped 3p, City dealers not seeing this as any kind of dishy potential for the company. The newspaper back pages were more welcoming, though, except for *The Mirror*, Maxwell's paper. Murdoch's titles had backed the Sugar campaign throughout. Sugar was not given much of a quizzing about his takeover by any part of the media. Nobody ever got to the bottom of why Sugar, who had never been interested in

Spurs, even when he'd been taken to White Hart Lane as a post-adenoidal child, should suddenly want to buy the club. He was simply welcomed, as businessmen routinely are on the sports pages, as a saviour. He dutifully vowed to turn Spurs round.

Sky was still struggling, even with *The Simpsons*. Dishes had sprouted on only 2.87m homes by then, 13 per cent of British television homes. Exclusive rights to world cup cricket from Australia in February 1992 had dragged 26,000 nightowl cricket anoraks in, taking Sky to its first ever trading profit. But this was a drop in an ocean of £1.52bn of debt, stock and investment.

With the top clubs fighting their greedy way out of the footballing community, backed by the FA, Sky was desperate to land the Premier League television rights. Sam Chisholm, the pugnacious, hard-nosed Aussie chief executive of BSkyB, took Rick Parry, 'chief executive' of the Premier League, to Scotland to see Sky's operation. There, he whispered some magic words to Parry: pay per view. The future prospect of making fans, who currently watched football free, pay for each game. Parry, his job to get as much money as possible for the 22 football club chairmen, loved the idea.

Greg Dyke, seeing Sky, and Murdoch, fighting for their very survival, decided to increase ITV's offer to the big clubs. He and Trevor East, ITV's executive director of football, were there to greet the 22 Premier League representatives when they gathered to award themselves millions of pounds at London's Royal Lancaster Hotel on 18 May 1992. They handed over ITV's final bid, believed to be £262m for five years, confident it would keep football on ITV and perhaps mean the end of Sky in Britain. East was walking through the lobby of the hotel at around 9.45, when he saw Alan Sugar on a payphone, beside himself. 'You don't seem to understand what I'm talking about,' Sugar was screaming. 'These are the figures.' Screaming. 'Take them down. You better get something done. You better get somebody down here quickly. Blow them out of the water.'

Sugar admitted later he was ringing Sky, telling them to come down and make sure they put in a higher bid than ITV. He, of course, stood personally to benefit if Sky got the football, because it would mean dish orders for Amstrad. Nobody has ever found out whether the ITV deal, with its guarantee from Dyke to show the Big Five regularly, would have been better for Tottenham.

Sugar admitted his personal financial interest at the meeting. Sky produced a bigger offer − £305m for five years − but it turned out that Rick Parry had himself already phoned Sam Chisholm before Sugar did. David Dein argued Sugar should abstain, but the other clubs let him vote. A two-thirds majority was required. The smaller clubs, led by Chelsea and Crystal Palace, supported Sky because ITV had favoured the big clubs. Herbert Douglas Ellis, chairman of Aston Villa, voted with the big clubs, as did Leeds. Of the Big Five, only A.M. Sugar voted for Sky. Two clubs abstained. That made it 14–6, two-thirds. Sugar's vote had been crucial. Football went to Sky, exclusively, together with the hour-long terrestrial meteorite of *Match of the Day*, for which the BBC paid £44m of licence-payers' money.

Dyke immediately took the Premier League to court, arguing that Parry's leaking of the ITV bid to Chisholm, and Sugar's phone call, amounted to a breach of confidence, but he failed. The Premier League football clubs were breaking away from the rest of football and now they had sold out to Sky. They were happy to vote themselves the higher offer on the table, and so to force 87 per cent of their supporters to pay for something they had always had free.

If the £305m was to make the football club chairmen and owners a fortune, for Sky it was to be money well spent. Sky gave football the Murdoch treatment, hyping it near-orgasmically from the word go. Sky always gives the impression that it invented football, rather than merely paid to take it off free television. 'A Whole New Ball Game', they called it, immediately putting the sports channel on subscription, £5.99 a month.

Still, the take-up was slow, for matches sandwiched between fireworks and dancing girls, only 500,000 people watching the first live game between Nottingham Forest and Liverpool on 23 August 1992, compared to 7,000,000 who had watched ITV's live games. Gradually, though, football fans found they couldn't do without the game. In Holland in 1996, a similar transfer of football on to the subscription channel Sport 7 failed after widespread popular protests backed by strong political opposition. Here, football fans have not historically been natural rebels. They had, after all, put up for years with the foul conditions at grounds which had led to the Hillsborough disaster. Such an accepting bunch as these were not going to march in the streets protesting about the Sky deal. As expected, the reaction was quite the opposite. Grudgingly, gradually, football addicts put down the remote control, got off the couch, switched off their *Match of the Day: Best of the Eighties* videos, and trudged down to Comet with their credit cards.

Sixty-seven Labour MPs, in the days when Labour used to try to stand up to Murdoch, signed a motion in the House of Commons, condemning the grabbing of the people's game by a subscription channel. The party's leader, Neil Kinnock, repeated a promise that if Labour won the election Murdoch's media dominance, his ownership of so many newspapers and a television channel, would be curtailed.

The following month, on the day of the general election, *The Sun* ran its notorious front cover, lampooning Kinnock and urging its readers not to vote for him. 'It was *The Sun* what won it,' Murdoch's tabloid would boast, after Kinnock lost to the Tories again.

Sky subscriptions rose dramatically every year after it got hold of football exclusively. Immediately, in 1993, Sky's loss of £47m was turned into a £62m profit. It has massively increased profits every year since, to £170m in 1994, £237m in 1995. In 1996 it reached five million subscribers, earning £1bn, making profits of £315m, on which the company paid little tax. Sam Chisholm, who announced his retirement from Sky in June 1997, said that the football had been the 'turning point' for Sky, revealing that Murdoch had been prepared to pay double what he did pay, to ensure Sky grabbed the football.

There has always been speculation that this was Sugar's reason for contacting El Tel in the first place, that the Tottenham deal presented a way of getting on the inside, and seeing football on to Sky. 'Nonsense,' says Nick Hewer, Sugar's faithful spokesperson. 'He'd have had to have been a genius, to foresee all that.' One has to wonder about that. It was common knowledge in the football and television worlds that in 1992 the TV deal was up for renewal, and that Greg Dyke then had the Big Five sewn up for ITV. And Sugar, talking to Murdoch twice a week, would have been aware how vital football was to Sky's prospects. Hewer's alternative explanation for Sugar's motives is anything but convincing. 'It was a nice thing he wanted to do. Something to do on Saturdays with the family.'

What happened to the dream ticket of Sugar and Venables is well documented and the subject of several other books. Four years on, it is still not over. Sugar has trounced Venables several times over in court, but still El Tel is coming back for more, now in the form of a libel action, rumbling on against Sugar. But amongst all the fallout, Sugar sacking Venables on 14 May 1993, Venables' subsequent hopeless, doomed court battle to be reinstated 'for the good of the company', the important point is this: Sugar won.

It was a key, symbolic event in English football's recent history, the world of business colliding with the world of football, played out at the High Court on the Strand, in front of snarling, chanting, pro-Venables Tottenham fans, Sugar spat upon as he emerged from his car. A hard-faced entrepreneur, product of the Eighties, against the cleverest man in football. Venables was widely admired in football, even if he had never won much domestically. He had had the 'Team of the Eighties' (Crystal Palace, remember) and managed Barcelona. When he was in Catalonia, not only did he win the league, he even, the football world gasped in awe, learned some Spanish. And he was a writer, co-author of *Hazell*, and a businessman, with his famed karaoke nights at Scribes, his own club. Too clever to be a mere football manager all his life.

If Terry Venables could only have seen the limitations of his worldliness, the tininess of the pond in which he shimmered, he might have realised the true balance of power when he went swimming in the big financial ocean. If he'd have held on, been nice to Alan, looked after the football team, kept his job and 22 per cent of Spurs, it would have been worth, at the time of writing, £22m. Instead, taking Sugar on, he was devoured without much effort, Sugar wiping the spittle off his own suit before spitting El Tel out on the Strand.

So Sugar wiped the floor with Venables, who ended up selling his 22 per cent back to institutions on the Stock Market. The lawyers grew rich on the caseload, but the facts of the Sugar–Venables split are that Tottenham Hotspur plc is now Alan Sugar's main business and El Tel is national coach in Australia and owner of Portsmouth.

Sugar, who'd managed to grow up a Jewish boy in Hackney yet remain totally ignorant of Spurs, struggled to learn his new business. 'I am not a fanatic,' he said, 'but I have a certain affection for Spurs.' It took him some time to work out what you said. 'Double? What Double?' he was caught in one interview.

He found it a strange business; the supporters not like normal customers. They were immensely loyal, but hard to please. But then Sugar brought in Ossie Ardiles as manager in June 1993 and even the phlegmiest gozzers on the Strand could not help but be pleased. All the players who had threatened to leave stayed, except Neil Ruddock, who insisted on leaving, but not before his agent Eric Hall had negotiated a loyalty bonus. But the season was not a success, Spurs winning only four home games, struggling all year. And this Sugar did understand: you were not supposed to lose. So he put Ossie on notice that he expected better from his employees.

In the close season of 1994, Sugar got mad, stung by swingeing penalties from the FA for irregular payments to players made by Scholar, which Sugar himself had reported to the FA. Suddenly, there they were in the sunshine, on Sugar's yacht in Monte Carlo: Alan and Jurgen, the sailor and the diver, a marriage to melt Spurs fans' hearts. Klinsmann, doing it 'for the challenge of English football', was said to be on £24,000 a week. Vilified in the World Cup for diving, Klinsmann was given the sternest interrogation by the British sporting media: 'Do you, er, dive, Jurgen?' he was asked on *Football Focus*.

'I never heard this even said before,' he smiled, and that was it. Klinsmann was not a diver, he was a world-class player, come to grace English football.

And looking somehow right in a Spurs shirt. Sugar did some good PR at this time. Journalists watched matches with him and wrote that he'd been 'bitten by the football bug', 'become a fan'. In love with football, he bought Ossie a couple of Romanians as well. But there was barely a defender in sight. Ossie's team seemed to revert to the Fifties, pre-Dave Mackay, 2-3-5, and on 1 November 1994, Sugar sacked him.

Gerry Francis came in on 15 November, and led Spurs to an enjoyable if trophyless season, Klinsmann rampaging in the FA Cup, to which the FA had reinstated Spurs after mutterings of legal action. Klinsmann, a truly world-class footballer, exploded Spurs out of all those years of shady, litigious, fly-by-nightery. Popescu didn't fancy it, Dumitrescu didn't cut it, but Jurgen formed a cerebral, athletic partnership with Sheringham. Anderton gambolled into top form on the wing. Spurs suddenly looked like Spurs again. For many younger fans, Klinsmann was the greatest experience of their supporting lives;

for the older ones it was a welcome return to football as pleasure, not trauma.

Then Klinsmann left. He had a get-out clause and, at the end of the season, he fancied going back to Germany so he dived off to Bayern Munich. Sugar's reaction was to foam at the mouth, famously cursing that he 'wouldn't wipe his car (a Rolls Royce AMS 1) with Klinsmann's shirt'.

Klinsmann, he fumed, had just been a mercenary. That was it for Sugar; he'd tried to learn this football business, buy star players, but it had all just confirmed his view of the world. Quality was to be mistrusted. The bottom line was the most important thing. The fans wanted only short-term success, they didn't understand the need to balance the books. Tottenham Hotspur, a 113-year-old football club, associated with some of the game's most beautiful moments, became the next focus for the philosophy of the Amstrad undercutter.

The irony of a man coming into football, without any previous interest in the game, calling lifelong fans 'short-term' appeared to be as lost on AMS 1 as the barefaced cheek of his calling players mercenaries.

When Arsenal signed Dennis Bergkamp from Inter Milan for £7.5m in August 1995, Sugar scorned the signing in *The Sun*: 'Arsenal got him because they needed a bit of cosmetic marketing,' he spouted. 'I don't think Spurs would ever sign a superstar like a Klinsmann or a Bergkamp again. These guys are floaters. They'll go anywhere, play for anyone who pays them the most.'

This throwback to the Amstrad outbursts of the Eighties was not merely depressing, philistinism unleashed on the beautiful game, Sugar was wrong in business terms too. David Dein has been one of the most successful chairmen of the fat-cat age. An Arsenal fan himself, he has gone about his job with some relish, aware of Arsenal's traditions, the Herbert Chapman, marble-hall traditions, not the boring, boring ones, and he has made the most of the inrush of money. He has built a superb ground, the North Bank Stand one of the few notable post-Taylor stands. He has accepted that the players will fight hard for money in their free market, and that if you want the best, you have to pay for the best. Yet he has managed to keep Bergkamp, keep him loyal, look after him, he has brought in Arsene Wenger, a proper coach, outshining most of the English self-taught managerial wheeler-dealers. And thinking big makes money. Bergkamp gets Arsenal on television, sells tickets, sells shirts. People watch Arsenal because of him. And Bergkamp gets them into Europe, further in cups, brings some success, which also has financial rewards. Dein has not railed against the world, criticised fans, players. He has embraced the current age of money with his eye on the long term, nurtured his club into an era, if not of greatness, certainly of health and prosperity. It is Spurs, at the moment, which is boring, boring, Arsenal becoming the glory club.

In an interview with *The Guardian* in early 1997, seeking to give the world the benefit of his don't-spend-money approach to football, Sugar made a comment which stands as a direct negation of the values in Blanchflower's famous glory remark: 'We still have a lot to do marketing the club. Building the brand image. And we have to do that initially by winning things.'

The supporters, out of the Scholar into the Sugar, are jaded by their succession of businessmen, the use of Tottenham in an exercise in financial philosophies. Football is a game, more than a profit and loss account. In 1997 I interviewed dozens of Spurs fans before Tottenham's home match against Nottingham Forest. They spoke with amazing unanimity. Only one was happy with the current Spurs regime, and he was drunk. All, without exception, acknowledged the importance of balancing the books. They had, after all, suffered the shame and pain of the Scholar period. But they thought Sugar did not understand what football was. That a club must be run in a business-like manner, but that it was more than a business. That it was about the team, the game, glory. This, they thought, he could not understand. He couldn't feel it.

Nearly all of them quoted Danny Blanchflower. They'd loved Klinsmann, thought Sugar had embarrassed himself, giving a man a get-out clause then crying like a baby when he got out. One or two even hankered for El Tel. At least they'd always had some decent players then. Even with the shares suspended in 1991, they'd won the FA Cup.

Sugar, when he bought into football, whatever his reason, happened to buy the glory club. If he wants to talk brands, that's his brand. Not sticking the badge on things; that's the crest. The brand is style. With a flourish. At Spurs, few adults wear replica shirts. Vestments of belonging in Newcastle, here, in the metropolis, that's kids' stuff. The kids wear them. Adults go to Spurs for pleasure, for the beautiful game, not to express their identity.

The ground's a shocker. The Shelf vulgarised with boxes. An exercise in making as much money out of as little aesthetic as possible. The North Stand is being developed next year – it needs it. It looks like the back end of a garden centre.

They've got these screens for action replays. A.M. Sugar, sitting in his stubble in the West Stand, probably reckons they really impress the punters, look flash and show a picture. But they look cheap. The whole ground looks functional and cheap. There is no grandeur, no sense of pride.

The Tottenham crowd has never, even in the glory, glory days, been the most vocal. At the Forest game, it was almost silent, all game. Dean Saunders scored a good goal for Forest after 17 minutes. Nobody even bothered to boo. The second half was spent chucking the ball long for Sheringham to nod on. Iversen, foreign-but-young, so qualifying under the no-mercenaries rule, could have scored a few. But he's only 19 and he can't have the traditions of a great club riding on his frail Norwegian shoulders. Increasingly desperate, Spurs brought on Dozzell. Then Ronnie Rosenthal, a tryer, a bull in a china shop.

'Spurs used to be so important to me,' moaned Juliette Wills, a journalist and lifelong Spurs fan whom I met at the game. 'I used to love it, standing on the Shelf, in the Paxton Road Stand. Now all these stands, they're just anonymous, North, South, sponsored by McDonald's, I don't even know what they're called. There's this failed business aura about everything at White Hart Lane.

'Something's gone now. I never enjoy it any more. Even the players don't look like they enjoy it any more. I'm determined to wean myself off Tottenham now. It's like some really nasty divorce.'

Spurs lost. Dismally. We walked out of the West Stand. The first thing we saw was a Jaguar XK8, a prowling, preening image of wealth, parked next to a Porsche Carrera, two Rolls-Royces covering behind.

'This is what I hate,' said Juliette. 'You spend £20 watching that and when you come out the carpark just laughs at you.'

All today's FA Carling Premiership carparks are exhibitions of ostentation, field studies of inequality. But Spurs' is top of the league. The servile stewards in a cluster, taking the keys off the well-heeled, scampering to bring their cars to them. All around, the fans streaming out, silent, heads down.

I waited in the carpark for a while afterwards. There, at Spurs, where the corporate clientele is clearly so rich, I took the opportunity to talk to a few of them as they came out of the boxes. Half were attending their first ever football match. They'd all enjoyed it very much, thank you. Three South Africans on a corporate hospitality ticket, invited by a client, said they were rugby people really but, yes, it had been great. I spoke to a man who turned out to be the group treasurer of Tesco, Bob Howell. Yes, thanks, enjoyed it. Tesco, he said, used the box to entertain suppliers, but it was really an unnecessary business expense and always a close call whether to renew it. It would be a factor this time that Tottenham were playing so badly.

Another group came out. One of them was Richard Sharp, 38. An IT manager, he'd been invited to a box by a client for a treat. He was a Spurs fan in exile, working in Manchester. 'The thing is,' he said, the evening darkening, the cold tightening its grip, 'I used to come here as a kid. I saw Jimmy Greaves and Alan Gilzean play here.' His eyes were watery. He sighed. 'I just can't believe how bad that was.'

Suddenly, amid the showy chrome and personalised flashery of the carpark, the corporate first-timers and their pleasant afternoons, I realised this was a football fan.

'There was just no atmosphere,' he said, shaking his head. He looked bereft, like he might cry. 'It was so . . . soulless.'

This is Tottenham under Alan Sugar.

'He's said,' says Nick Hewer, 'that if he doesn't win something in two years he'll let another brain surgeon take it on.' This, in 1997, was the first statement from Sugar that he might sell Spurs in the near future. He bought in for £8m, introduced some financial discipline, rode the boom of the Sky money, raised ticket prices in line with the rest of football. At the time of writing, Tottenham Hotspur plc is valued by the city at £100m. Sugar's share, 50 per cent, is £50m. This is a capital gain of £42m in six years. If he does sell, it will have been good business.

His legacy to football will be Sky TV, whether that was his original intention or not. 'One of the great corporate romances,' says Sam

Chisholm of the relationship between the Premier League and Sky, walking off to the sunset together, immeasurably richer, off the backs of the fans. The truth is it's been more Page Three than romance. The beautiful game, slapped all over a Murdoch medium between the adverts, hyped relentlessly, appreciated only for its surface. Andy Gray screaming at a pitch of constant near-orgasm. Spend an evening with Sky and it's as if they're trying to sell you something, not just in the adverts. They're trying to sell you an idea, that there is nothing wrong with football having been taken off the terrestrial screen and given to them, supporters having to pay Murdoch to watch England's national game. They're trying to sell you the idea that the football clubs did nothing wrong, turning the game, of which they were custodians, into a commodity, selling it to the highest bidder, Alan Sugar screaming on a payphone in the corridor. And it turned Sky round; English football is now to be a 'battering ram' for the march of the Murdoch empire into Asia and the rest of the world.

But Sky's revival was not enough to save Amstrad. Sugar announced he was breaking his company up in June 1997, the same day he announced Sheringham could leave Tottenham, real quality dispensed with at Sugar's latest business interest. With Amstrad gone, Spurs is now Sugar's monument, which he is recreating in his image. Occasionally, appearing to cave in to pressure from supporters, he contradicts his own principles by suddenly spending big, overpaying for Les Ferdinand or buying David Ginola. Many find Sugar's approach heartbreakingly wrong for the traditions of football's glory club, the club of Hoddle, style and flourish. Supporters are tearing themselves away, nasty divorces are taking place. The carpark is full of luxury saloons and White Hart Lane is losing its soul. When it finally leaves, it will be a silent farewell, the terminal moment of the glory, glory club, shown in action replay on two cheap screens.

2

GLORY, GLORY, MAN UNITED

Old Trafford on a match day is a magnet. People hurry, scurry, heads down, to join the human river pouring down Sir Matt Busby Way, to where the ground sits, wreathed in a floodlight halo. This is only a midweek game against Wimbledon, but the streets are flooded with cars, bumper to bumper, intent on seeing the Champions: the red shirts of Giggs, Beckham, Keano. It's every man for himself, in the urgent push to get inside that ground before kick-off. Behind the ground the streets are a nightmare; all dead ends and one ways and no parking, clumps of supporters rushing through the warren. A man with beard and woolly hat, at a pub charging £3 for parking, pulls a chain across the entrance

'Sorry mate,' he shakes his head. 'Capaci'y.'

I end up leaving the car miles away, down some side street, ages after kick-off. Cursing, muttering, I walk through the empty streets, along Chester Road. Nothing blocks a clear view of the ground from there; the gleaming floodlights, the red neon MANCHESTER UNITED sign, the over-the-top new tier on the North Stand, stuck on what was a perfect bowl. I'm waiting now for the first roars, to rub in the sense of exclusion. So far, there's nothing. Nearer the ground is the debris of the rushing hordes: cans and chip papers crumpled outside the Lou Macari Fish Bar, swagmen taking a break. A policeman sweeps up the bollards. A few disappointed fans are coming the other way: 'Any spares?' says one, without hope.

Still, even here, there's no noise. Even down Sir Matt Busby Way, then past the shuttered superstore, to right under the bowels of the main stand, not a sound. 55,000 people are sitting on the other side of the wall and you could hear a programme drop.

It is eerie. Old Trafford, whether the team is in a successful period or not, has always thundered with noise. It's the home of the legendary football club, the folklore of great names and historical monuments; of the Busby Babes, dancing to championships in 1956 and 1957, before being cut down, shockingly, in 1958, in the slush of Munich. Busby, damaged, rebuilding for a decade, Best, Law and Charlton, marching almost grimly to Wembley '68.

Anti-climax after that, going down in 1973-74, to the outrageous fortune of a flick from Denis Law in a Manchester City shirt, before they came up again under Docherty. Old Trafford was always loud. The Stretford End had the reputation in the Seventies as the scrappers' end, but really the fighters went in the United Road or the Scoreboard Paddock, next to the away fans. The Stretford End was amiable, passionate, tremendous. And it was cheap; you could pay on the day at the turnstiles. There was even a reduced fee turnstile for under-16s: 90p. Ninety pence. To watch Coppell and Pearson and Martin Buchan, later Bryan Robson and Ooh Aah Paul McGrath.

The 90p queue was always Old Trafford's longest, overseen haplessly by one mounted policeman, trying to spot those over-age. Dozens of men with deep adult voices, some with beards, hemmed in to pass themselves off as 16. The only ones who ever really seemed to test the copper were those trying to take their kids in with them.

'Terry!' a man shouted once, really loud. 'Bring the nipper!'

Inside, United wasn't sarcastic wags, a football crowd of sullen pessimists, hard to impress like at Maine Road. It was thousands singing and chanting in unison, rousing anthems of optimism and expectation: 'Glory, glory, Man United, Glory, glory, Man United, Glory, glory, Man United, As the Reds go marching on, on, on,' to waves of clenched fists punching the air.

There was always a hint of danger, the Red Devils swaggering in the roar. Away fans struggled to raise a whimper in the bowl of noise.

'Follow, follow, we are United's boys,' went another of the songs of the time; 'Follow, follow, we are United's boys, And if you are a City fan surrender or you'll die, We will follow United.'

The locals from Salford and Manchester were always swollen at Old

Trafford by pilgrims from around the country, Ireland, and abroad, come to be part of the legend. And for years, surveying all of this, his large frame inseparable from the Old Trafford bowl, was Louis Edwards. United had been his life's passion, then his obsession. He had begun by supporting United, like the other pilgrims. Gradually he'd wanted to rise above them, be involved in the heart of the club. Later, he'd had to own it, the club, with all its glory, the human magnet, have it belong to him.

He'd grown up in the Twenties and Thirties in Salford, close to Old Trafford, feeling in his blood the intense thrill of football, the incomparable escape it allowed from the grey, dreary streets. Robbed of his teenage-hood, Louis was put to work at 14, alongside his father, a butcher. He spent his whole working life in the business, Louis C. Edwards and Sons. He and his brother Douglas took it over in 1943, when their father died. They made money through the post-war grip of rationing, expanding their shops, winning wholesale meat contracts. Looking to extend their provincial influence, Douglas found an outlet in Conservative politics. Louis, though, wanted a piece of what really moved the people: United.

He began to court Matt Busby, having met him round Manchester through a mutual friend. To Louis' delight, Matt would occasionally invite Louis and his wife to watch a game from the directors' box. They first took their son Martin in 1952, United against Wolves, when he was seven.

Louis wanted a piece of the football glamour. He liked to be seen with the players, the Busby Babes; it earned him a hangers-on touch of fame, reflected glory, as 'Champagne Louis'. By the late Fifties, his business reaching its peak, he had positioned himself to replace the ageing directors in United's boardroom.

Many believed that the preferred candidate to join the board, certainly for Busby, was another businessman, Willie Satinoff. But Satinoff's closeness to the team meant he was on the plane coming back from the European Cup quarter-final in Belgrade in 1958. He was one of the 23 who died, including eight of the Busby Babes, when the frozen plane failed to take off after its refuelling stop at Munich. With the board utterly shocked and grief-stricken, Louis Edwards was made a director the day after the disaster. It was a dream come true for Louis, and for four years he was happy with that. He never looked to spread his tentacles on ownership of the club. From 1958 to 1962, he played an increasing role in club affairs, but never had more than 17 shares, out of a total of 4,132.

Then Louis Edwards & Son floated on the Stock Exchange, making Louis a cash fortune and giving him more time to devote to United. He embarked then on a single-minded campaign to take control of the club. His quest, to feed a massive ego, was relentless, the methods justifying the end. His pursuit of United shares was revealed 20 years later, in January 1980, by *World in Action*, uncovering bullying and underhand dealings, along with revelations of corruption in the meat business. 'Champagne Louis' had a fixer, conservative councillor Frank Farrington, tramp the streets of Manchester for him, knocking on the doors of minor United shareholders.

One shareholder featured was Alice Rowbotham. She had inherited 100 shares from her Uncle Albert, who had been given them in exchange for helping the club out of a financial crisis in the Thirties. Such football club shares were never seen as investments, to be bought and sold. The club hadn't started out as a company; it was formed, as Newton Heath, in 1878, by men of the Lancashire and Yorkshire Railway who wanted to play the great new game of football, which was sweeping through the industrial north at the time.

Newton Heath began paying their players in 1885, as soon as it was legal, competition in the emerging game having brought widespread under-the-table payments, impossible to stamp out. In 1892, Newton Heath joined the professional Football League First Division, four years after the league was formed. Only then did they form themselves into a limited company. The football club had grown into a substantial expense now, with players' wages, and the cost of enclosing a ground, installing turnstiles for the paying gate. Forming a company was a protection for the founders, making the club a separate body in law. The liability of the founders to pay the club's debts would now be limited only to the amount they had put in in shares. Forming a company was a defensive measure, not an investment in the hope of selling the shares on at a profit one day. The Football Association guarded against the clubs being used as tradeable, speculative companies by insisting on rules which would preserve their status as football clubs.

New shares were usually issued only during tough times. In 1932, the cash had come in after a desperate appeal by United to their supporters. The benefactors, like Alice Rowbotham's Uncle Albert, might be entitled to a season ticket, or a Cup final ticket, but the shares were of sentimental, not financial, value, certificates of supporters' small part in the histories of their football clubs.

Alice Rowbotham and her husband Norman were not rich. They lived in a terraced house, Norman paying the bills by working in a local ICI factory. One evening Frank Farrington came knocking, offering them £500 cash for their United shares. A minutely researched book, *Manchester United: The Betrayal of a Legend*, by journalist Michael Crick and David Smith, former chairman of the Manchester United Supporters Club, relates the finer details of this and Louis' other captures. The Rowbothams went to meet Louis at his meat company headquarters. Alice was asked to leave the room. Louis paid cash to Norman. Farrington, for setting up the deal, wanted £50. The Rowbothams were given a bag of meat, the standard Edwards thank you in the gloomy early Sixties.

Louis acclerated his campaign, writing to people on the United share register, describing United as his 'life's ambition', offering £15 a share, a testament to his 'devotion' to the club. Many people, suddenly offered money for sentimental heirlooms, sold. By early 1963, Louis was the club's biggest shareholder, although he did not have a personal majority. The two other big shareholders, Alan Gibson and chairman Harold Hardman, then forbade share dealing by the three of them, to preserve some democracy at the club, prevent United coming under the control of one man, who could then do what he wanted with the club.

Louis, undaunted, had his brother, Douglas, and brother-in-law, Denzil Haroun, write to shareholders instead. They amassed over 300 shares. Gradually, the long, scrawly list of United's historic benefactors was coalescing into the control of Louis Edwards.

In September 1963 Alan Gibson sold out. He was the son of James Gibson, United's greatest backer in the 1930s crisis, partner in a clothing firm, who had paid the players' wages, sunk another £2,000 into the club, then, as chairman, built the great pre-war stadium at Old Trafford.

'Champagne Louis' paid Gibson's son £25 each for 500 shares. The directors, despite the club's rules to protect the club against takeover, gave up their resistance. By January 1964, in only 14 months, Edwards had accumulated 2,223 shares, 54 per cent, personal control, of Manchester United. Crick and Smith estimate the whole grim, pathetic exercise cost him only £31,000 to £41,000. In June 1965, when Harold Hardman died, Louis Edwards had no opposition to his election as chairman.

United had just won the Football League, their first Championship since the sweet-bitter memory of the Busby Babes' 1957 victory. Denis Law had arrived, for £115,000, a British transfer record. Bobby Charlton had been through the Munich mill and was playing like a man possessed. A scrawny lad called George Best, spotted in Belfast by the weathered eye of United scout Bob Bishop, was dribbling his way into every football hall of fame.

Louis had big plans for his United. In 1964 a long-term plan had been drawn up to redevelop Old Trafford, foreseeing it as a fully cantilevered bowl. It was to take 30 years to complete, culminating finally in 1994 in the post-Taylor Report sedating of the Stretford and Scoreboard Ends. The first phase, the new United Road Stand, was completed in time to host three qualifying matches in the 1966 World Cup, incorporating 'executive boxes', staring glassily at an English football pitch for the first time.

However much his rule, at the club and in his business, was to curdle later on, at this time, flush with cash, Louis Edwards' heart was in United. Mixed with everything else, football was in his blood. In 1967, United won the League again. The following year, 1968, they finally won the European Cup, at a charged, tearful Wembley, in which the living paid an exhausting, committed tribute to the memory of the dead. Brian Kidd, 19 that day, was overcome with the weight of it, so much more than a football match.

A sustained anti-climax followed. Matt, now Sir Matt, retired almost immediately and was irreplaceable. Tommy Docherty, manager from 1972-77, personifies the era. Jekyll and Hyde. He brought United back up and to the FA Cup with a dashing team. Behind the scenes, though, relations were fractious.

Louis was beginning to have financial problems, the meat business having lurched uncomfortably past its peak. *World in Action* revealed bribery in this local empire, gifts of meat to buyers in local authorities, sweetening them to buy tons of Edwards' meat for school dinners. And there was worse rottenness. A report by Manchester City Council in 1966, the year 'Champagne Louis' was hosting World Cup matches at the executive box-bloated Old Trafford, found his company was supplying poor quality meat for Manchester school dinners, the worst being supplied to the areas with the poorest children. Twelve years later the company was fined for bad, fatty meat supplied for Cheshire school meals.

The wholesaling struggled, the shops faded from popularity with the emergence of better quality and more choice. By 1975 the company was making a loss. In 1978, it lost £340,000. It was now, with Louis strapped for cash, that the failure of United's directors to protect the club from Edwards over a decade before came home to roost. In adversity, Manchester United looked less like a passion and more like an asset to the Edwards family. They looked now, for the first time, at making money out of United, changing it, according to Crick and Smith, 'from a football club into a business'.

Edwards had to work round FA rules, still in place, preventing profit being made out of clubs. The payment of dividends was restricted to only 5 per cent of the £1 face value of each share, namely five pence a year. Louis could not therefore vote himself money out of the club. Flotation of the club on the Stock Exchange was not then a realistic option. Unlike today, the City had barely heard of football then, the working-man's game.

The idea which emerged from Louis and his adviser, Professor Roland Smith, was to increase the dividend payments simply by multiplying the five pences. They would have a rights issue, giving every shareholder the right to buy 208 £1 shares for every one he held. The club would stay under the Edwards' control, and they would have 209 times the numbers of shares.

Blatantly not the best way to raise money for United, because it did not invite money in from outside, it was bitterly opposed by supporters. An increasingly disillusioned Sir Matt Busby and secretary Les Olive stood up against it, arguing it paved the way for money to be leaked out of the club.

Martin Edwards, now 33, was becoming involved. He had grown up with United, but, away from the urban crush which had seeped football into his father's blood, Martin's experience of it was more remote. Martin had always known money and space, at the family home in Cheshire's loamy commuter land. He was sent to a minor public school, Cokethorpe in Oxfordshire. There he was one of the lads, keen on rugby. At 19 he went into the family business, working in shops and meat counters for ten years, then becoming retail/ wholesale controller. Martin was never a United fan like his father; he was second generation. Even when he became a United director in March 1970, aged 24, he hardly went to Old Trafford, still played rugby on Saturdays, for Wilmslow.

In late 1977, Louis and Martin embarked on another round of share buying, echoing that of the Sixties. One who sold was Beryl Norman. She had inherited 51 shares from her uncle, Walter Crickmer, United's former secretary who had died at Munich. Louis paid £9,900.

Martin bought out Alan Gibson's remaining 1,138 shares for £172.70 each, a total of £196,545. Martin's money came from the bank, a £200,000 overdraft. The Edwards family shareholding grew to 74 per cent of United. Already planning the rights issue, they were buying shares cheap, knowing they would shortly be worth more. This amounted to insider trading, which was not then a criminal offence.

Martin increased his overdraft to £600,000 to pay for the 208–fold increase of the rights issue. That, £600,000, is the sum total of his 'investment' in United, ever. The rights issue cost the Edwards family, in total, £740,000. As Les Olive had feared, money immediately began to be paid out of the club in dividends.

In 1978, only £312 had been paid out in dividends. After the rights issue, there were suddenly over a million shares. Immediately, in 1979, the board announced a dividend of £50,419. The following two years saw similar amounts paid out, £80,000 going to the Edwards family. In 1981 the FA raised its maximum dividend to 15 per cent, to encourage outside investors to put their money into football clubs. United immediately paid this maximum out, £151,284, Martin receiving £77,319. He was still working for the meat company. By 1987, total dividends since the rights issue totalled £500,000. Martin's portion was £233,684.

In 1980, Louis Edwards died, only four weeks after *World in Action* had revealed the darkness behind his 'Champagne Louis' lustre. Martin took over as chairman. The following year, the FA changed another of its old rules protecting the amateur sporting ethos. A compromise with a more commercial age, clubs were allowed for the first time to have a paid director, as long as he genuinely worked full time. The meat business had been sold by then to Argyll Foods; Martin had left in 1980 and wasn't working. He became one of English football's first full-time chief executives.

The club, controlled by the Edwards family shareholding, did not stint on Martin's salary. He started on £30,000, rising to £75,000 in 1985, £88,000 in 1988, £96,000 in 1989, breaking the £100,000 barrier in 1990.

He ruled over a decade in which recovery stalled into frustration. Ron Atkinson, taking over from Dave Sexton in 1981, brought United FA Cup wins in 1983, Ray Wilkins curling the beginning of Brighton's decline; 1985, Whiteside and Hughes getting a grip against Everton after the injustice of Kevin Moran's sending-off. But Atkinson never instilled the steel necessary to capture the League. United finished third in 1982 and '83, fourth in '84, '85 and '86 when, having started with ten straight wins, the team of Whiteside, Strachan, Robson and Hughes stuttered to a lazy, dismal spring.

At other clubs, Wembley wins are the stuff of once-in-a-lifetime anecdote. At United they were inadequate consolation prizes. The fans became enraged at Merseyside's blanket league dominance. United v. Liverpool games in the Eighties crystallised all this intensity into 90 searing minutes, United tending to beat Liverpool, real hatred poisoning Matt Busby Way, and Liverpool still usually strolling away with the title.

Martin Edwards was frustrated too. Crick and Smith say Martin was still complaining in 1988 about being saddled with his overdraft. United was his only full-time business interest. Throughout the decade, he was a leading voice calling for the First Division clubs to break away, no longer to share their money with the rest of the Football League. The 'Superleague' idea rumbled on, as did the idea of floating United, particularly after Edwards' breakaway soulmate, Irving Scholar, had put Tottenham on the Stock Exchange in 1983. After meetings, though, they dismissed the idea, Martin going instead into negotiations to sell United to Robert Maxwell, then still a major magnate, developing a taste for football clubs. He talked seriously with Edwards, the figure of £10m was aired, but, with Maurice Watkins advising, the deal fell through.

Watkins was a partner in James Chapman & Co, a stolid set of Manchester solicitors, whose main work is defendant personal injury. Manchester United was a client. Maurice Watkins inherited their moderate amount of work in 1977, also becoming Martin Edwards' solicitor. Seven years later, with Edwards sweeping the old guard off the United board, Watkins was made a director. To go on the board, he had to buy 50,000 shares, probably for one to two pounds each.

Just before the first match of the 1989-90 season, with United due to play Arsenal, an overweight, mustachioed 40-year-old with a bouffant hairdo burst on to Old Trafford's sun-kissed pitch wearing United training kit and juggling a football. He paused, drinking in the cheers of adoring fans. Smiling hugely, he then dribbled the ball towards the massed red bank at the Stretford End, lashing the ball into the empty net.

This is the only incident now capable of bringing a blush to the self-satisfied faces of the men in charge at Manchester United plc. The more often it is shown on television, the more cringemaking it is, Michael Knighton (for it was he), like a Dad acting one-of-the-kids at a children's party, short pants and all.

That United fans greeted this unknown, portly show-off with cheers says more about the desperation of their hopes than their grip on reality. Knighton was completely unknown and, by his own frank admission, small-time. A geography and PE teacher, he had run St David's, a private school for kids of the middle-ranking rich, and spent the holidays trying to get rich himself. For him the Eighties, the Thatcher years of easy credit and fantastical property prices, were a godsend. He was not a property developer; he just bought houses, waited for the price to rise, then sold. When the music stopped, Knighton had stopped playing, made enough to relax with a few million tax-free in the Isle of Man.

Part frustrated footballer, having played in his youth, part glory seeker, Knighton was also part speculator, one of the first of a new breed to see football as a business in which he could make money. Knighton says he did 'an academic study', foreseeing greater television money and the possibility of financially exploiting, through merchandising, the attachment of football fans to their clubs.

Sitting in the Isle of Man with time and money, Knighton drew up a list of football clubs he fancied. There were two kinds: 'Those everybody wanted and couldn't get, and those you could get very easily then struggle to know what to do with.'

One of Knighton's contacts in Manchester, textiles dealer Barry Chaytow, did some of the sniffing. They assessed Bolton Wanderers: in trouble, therefore possibly available cheap, big potential support. But they backed off. Then, in 1989, Chaytow, amazed, heard that Martin Edwards might sell the biggest prize of all. It was only eight years ago, but football was still only a game, seen as a hobby for rich men, not a means of making them more money. *The Financial Times* hardly glanced at the results. Manchester United, darling of the City now, one of England's fastest-growing 'leisure companies', was then available to a small-time businessman like Michael Knighton.

Knighton says he wanted 'to do something for the game I loved'. He was also convinced he would make a fortune. He remembers Martin Edwards as a heavy-smoking, charming, 'man's man', who wanted to get his cash: 'He was desperate to sell,' says Knighton. 'But he did feel responsible for United. I told him I would develop the Stretford End, complete his father's vision, and that is what clinched the deal for me.'

Martin finally gave him his price at Killochan Castle in Ayrshire, one of Knighton's pads. Martin was willing to sell his 500,000 shares, 50.6 per cent of United, for £20 a share. He wanted £10m and he'd leave Old Trafford forever.

The newspapers would allege later that Knighton never had the money. He claims he planned for twice that figure. He spreads his hands and smiles: it *was* the Eighties. 'I was doing it with a £24m overdraft, from the Bank of Scotland.'

Knighton finally sued in 1995 over the allegation that he never had the money, obtaining in March 1997 substantial damages and an apology from *The Sunday Times Illustrated History of Football*, which had recycled the newspaper reports of the time: 'Mr Knighton at all times had the necessary financial wherewithal to honour his obligations,' it said. 'However, his bid was subject to critical adverse media comment, which was, in the main, ill-informed and hostile. Mr Knighton quite simply withdrew his bid.'

This is true, but the pressure for him to withdraw had become tremendous. He accepts he lost United partly because of his display on the pitch, which he claims he hadn't planned: 'I just wanted to bridge the gap between fans and boardroom.'

But he also admits that, a footballer who never made it, and too old for *Jim'll Fix It*, he loved the whole thing. But it effectively lost him his backers, Robert Thornton, formerly Debenhams chief, who was taking 40 per cent off Knighton, splitting it with Stanley Cohen, of Parker pens. These sober financiers, who fancied football as a business, watched their man with sinking hearts, in moustache and shorts, juggling a football on the pitch. When the *Manchester Evening News* leaked Cohen's involvement, the media descended on Knighton and the two backers withdrew.

Martin Edwards came under pressure from people around him, including Bobby Charlton and director Amer Al Midani, not to sell to Knighton. Knighton could have forced it; he had a signed agreement, but under the extreme glare of all the publicity he was persuaded to withdraw, in return for 30,000 shares and being taken on as a United director. He stayed for three years. His bid was dead but the ideas, about 'exploiting United's captive market', 'maximising the value of the brand', stayed to characterise a new era at Manchester United. When United floated, in 1991, reborn as a moneymaking corporation, Michael Knighton was on the list of directors, described as 'company consultant and educationalist'.

A hundred years of relative innocence at Manchester United, of being purely a football club, of the chairman-as-overgrown-fan, effectively ended with Knighton's 1989 waddle on the pitch. Edwards, previously looking to get his money by selling out, was persuaded to stay on to get it by commercial exploitation of the club and its fans. They moved almost immediately to float Manchester United on the Stock Exchange.

The 1991 prospectus, the brochure which describes a company to potential investors in the City, set out four reasons for flotation: to raise £6.7m to redevelop the Stretford End, to 'widen the ownership' of Manchester United, to provide 'increased liquidity' to shareholders and, finally, to 'give employees and supporters a greater opportunity to invest in Manchester United'.

Maurice Watkins, talking about the flotation, stressed only the third: 'One of the principal advantages of the flotation,' he said, 'was that it released cash to shareholders.' Martin Edwards – and Watkins himself – were to get some cash out of their United shareholdings.

The club was faced with FA rule 34, still in existence, limiting dividends and clubs to only one paid director and, effectively, ensuring that clubs remain sporting institutions. They formed a new company, Manchester United plc, officially not a football club at all. It has three subsidiaries: Manchester United Merchandising, Manchester United Catering and Manchester United Football Club. Its duty, it says proudly, is 'to make money for its shareholders' among whom are Edwards, Watkins, Al Midani and assorted City institutions.

United plc floated with 10p shares, initially priced at £3.85, valuing it at £47m. Martin Edwards sold 1.7 million shares on flotation, immediately making £6m, while retaining 3.4m, 28 per cent of United. The City was not too impressed with football, but United promised future profits, openly boasting of 'introducing average admission price increases of over 30 per cent'.

It is a sign of the times that as recently as 1991, prices for Old Trafford seats ranged from only £5.75 to £7.50. There was still, six years ago, capacity for 20,000 people to stand for £4. The 90p terrace was still there, grown men with beards trying to blag their way in with their kids. But it was all to change very fast indeed.

The philosophy, Knightonian in origin, was to cash in on supporters' love for the club by exploiting it as 'brand loyalty'. At the same time, United would move the game upmarket, to attract richer 'customers', by offering a 'quality product'. Money from Sky TV, £305m coming into football in 1992, was washing through to make it all possible.

United brought in a dedicated finance director, Robin Launders, who came to the great football club from Reg Vardy, the new and secondhand car dealers. Edward Freedman, a retailer who had begun working for Spurs in 1987 after offering Irving Scholar a player for whom he was acting as a quasi-agent, was reborn at Old Trafford as 'Head of Merchandising'. United fostered a culture which sees profit as the company's primary object; in which the profit end seems to justify the means, however tacky. They have been single-minded and they have been successful, United the darling of the City, turnover, profits and share price meteorically up, all centred on the success of a mere football team, the creation of the real genius at Old Trafford, a middle manager who still has football coursing through his veins. Alex Ferguson, a misfit in a strange kind of way, a throwback, last in the line, perhaps, of the great Scottish working-class managers.

He arrived in 1986 from Aberdeen, immediately pledging, as he had done in Scotland, to attract the best kids to his club. In the short term, he boldly chucked out some old favourites, Whiteside and McGrath, and spent big. Ferguson has since proved beyond question that as a manager he ranks with the greats, but it is interesting that he still never took United to the First Division title. In its last season as the top division of a unified league, the title was won by Howard Wilkinson's Leeds, tearing past United at the finish. It was only after the top clubs broke away, no longer to share their television money with the rest of football, to form the FA Carling Premiership, that United finally won the League. It was as if, a floated corporation, they were bedded in, ready for football as a business, and the ring-fenced Premier League which would make it possible. Since it was formed in 1992, the Premiership has belonged to Manchester United plc.

They won it in '93, '94, '96 and '97, missing out only as runners-up to Jack Walker's Blackburn in 1995. The Double used to be a difficult, once-in-a-history achievement; United have done it twice, winning the FA Cup in '94 and '96.

Ferguson is an irony of this corporate age of football business. He has made outrageous fortunes for the men in grey suits, yet he is arguably at odds with their ethos, their treatment of football as leisure, as part of the entertainment business. Ferguson is a working man whose football is hammered into the soul. A Labour man at one of the greediest companies of these financial times, Ferguson began his working life as a toolmaker in the Glasgow docks, where he led a strike. As a footballer, his career was all grit and effort and elbows. In a plc obsessed with money, which pays its player-employees million-pound salaries, Ferguson's management is based on traditional virtues: graft, teamwork, skill. Not for him footballers as models, the game as showbiz. One of his star players might be going out with a Spice Girl, but there are no Spice Boys here.

Ferguson went about finding his boys with characteristic single-minded determination. Ryan Giggs, Nicky Butt and the emerging Ben Thornley were all attracted away from schoolboy associations with Manchester City. In 1996, United were fined £50,000, paying £75,000 compensation, for making an illegal approach to Oldham youngster David Brown, signing him on YTS while he was still an Oldham schoolboy. Jim Cassell, then Oldham youth development officer, now at Manchester City, brought the case: 'I lost friends at United doing it,' he says. 'But I had to, to stand up for the little clubs.'

Ferguson vehemently denies that he has ever paid money, to kids or their parents, before it is legal at 17. He says parents and children choose United because it is a great club and they know they will be looked after, that they'll get a career elsewhere if not at Old Trafford. But anyway, getting the young boys is one thing, bringing them through is another. The Nevilles, Scholes and Beckham, all now England regulars, have been there since they were nine. United's coaching operation is coherent and thorough, all the teams playing the same way, youngsters stepping up with alarming lack of nerve. Their coach, Brian Kidd, has followed his protégés up to the first team, his gleeful somersaults at Ferguson's side revealing his roots in Busby's era.

These well-brought-up young adults combine in Ferguson's team with temperamental snorters: Keane, Cantona, Ince, indulged by a manager with his own incandescently short fuse. He had to fight as a player himself, he understood teamwork and the priceless value of natural skill, learned the hardest way from not having quite enough of it himself. The whole United empire has this irony at its centre, Ferguson's team a classic blend, largely home-grown, recalling Busby more than faintly, while around him his employers have left their past behind.

Ticket prices rose more than threefold between 1988 and 1993. The end of the terraces was also the end of cheaply affordable entry, contrary to the recommendations of the Taylor Report. The Stretford End was absorbed into post-Taylor anonymity as the West Stand, ending the years of standing and chanting, of Glory, Glory, Man United. The new banks of seats were unveiled in 1994 with a further 60 per cent increase, bringing the average price of a ticket from £10 to £16. The 90 pence terrace is folk memory, Terry's nipper paying full whack or not getting in.

Corporate hospitality now has the stadium of 'Champagne Louis' surrounded. United fill all their boxes to capacity, six-seaters for £17,566 a season, eight-seaters for £25,556, the 20-seater North Stand Hospitality Suite £50,760.

The taming of Old Trafford has been a deliberate move, accommodating the perceived taste of these desirable new customers.

The Red Devil was deemed too scary a logo and has been replaced with 'Fred the Red', a cuddly, smiling, play devil, sporting unthreatening horns, carrying no trident. A cartoon version smiles from the front of the megastore, the devil of United replaced with a winking invitation to shop.

Inside this shop, blaring music dulls the ability to think, probably to discern, among the rails of cheap-looking clothes, made in Turkey, the mountains of baubles, the section churning out kits and replica shirts at £40 a time. Freedman described his work as 'building a brand'. This appeared not to involve building on supporters' feelings and emotions for United, but simply slapping the badge on anything which will wear it: paper cups, paper plates, keyrings, cuddly toys, flip-flops, United sweets, I ♥ MUFC keyrings for £3, pens for £1.50. The crowds rummage through towels, socks, flags, all kept, appropriately, in bins around the central counter.

Ryan is marketed as hearththrob to adolescent girls, who form a growing element of United's 'demographic'. Following on from a soft-soap Ryan autobiography, with its black and white shots of the boy wonder semi-naked, there is a bedspread, Ryan looking sexy-but-vulnerable, keeping your bed warm every night. No similar duvets appear to have been made featuring Gary Pallister.

One product above all seems to sum up the megastore's idea that football fans have no discernment, its lack of thought, of originality, of any design whatever. On a shelf near the mugs and mugshots is a pub kit. Pint pot, beermat, bartowel, all in a package for the home drinker, £4 with United's badge on.

In strips across the ceiling, overseeing the whole sorry pile, is the Umbro slogan, like a triumphant banner: 'THE HEART AND SOUL OF FOOTBALL.'

If dignity is in short supply, history has been almost obliterated. Manchester United, you would think, was invented in 1992. Favouring the flip-flops, there is not a book, a video, barely a memento of any kind to the Busby Babes, Best, Charlton or Law, to United's mythic past. Even Bryan Robson seems to be hurtling towards the bargain bins. Besides the garishly bad taste of the place, they seem to be failing to capitalise on a few brands here. It was always going to be interesting to see how the shop dealt with the memory of Cantona, the most idolised player of the Ferguson era and arguably the key to United's success. It took only a couple of months after the retirement of the man whom United fans regarded as 'Dieu' for Stalinism to do its work. After a commercial argument over royalties with the philosopher king, the club burnt its entire stock of Eric merchandise. In the megastore at least, by August 1997, it was as if Cantona had never existed.

The queue to enter the megastore is full of chatting, laughing people. The exit door releases silent beings, carrying shopping bags, wandering towards the match in a consumerist haze. There they will find a life-size Fred the Red, taking the field with the team to triumphal tannoy music. Muzak, faint, subliminal whispers of old United anthems, is piped through the concourses, even the urinals offering no escape.

A couple of years ago, United's glossy magazine featured some of the words to songs which supporters might care to sing. It included 'Follow, follow, we are United's boys,' but with the last line doctored: 'And if you are a City fan,' it read, 'surrender or you'll *cry.*'

I finally reach my seat in tamed, sedated Old Trafford for the game against Wimbledon with 25 minutes gone. Wimbledon are impressive, Gayle and Ekoku predatory, the defence resolute, even Vinnie looking classy in midfield. The spectators mainly sit on their hands, waiting for United to start beating them. In the East Stand, the diehards try to wake things up: 'Stand up for the Champions,' they sing, harking back to former, louder, days.

But their chants founder on passive sponges of indifference. All Premiership grounds have killed off the atmosphere – they admit it themselves, officially – but there is something disturbing, maddening, in the quiet at United. The spectators don't, most of them, seem to appreciate what they are getting. The club waited years for a single League win; now they are treated to some of the most thrilling sights in English football, ranking with the best ever: Giggs in full flow, the erect French philosopher and karate expert, Beckham's youthful arrogance. The Nevilles, never a foot wrong. Butt's elegant immaculacy. Yet there is an air of what-a-pleasant-evening about the ground. Keane, rare for him, mishits a pass, and the crowd actually criticises, collectively tuts.

Wimbledon score on 62 minutes, a Chris Perry volley. A couple of hundred Wimbledon fans, in the corner of the Main Stand, jump up and down delightedly in a stunned ground. There is a hint of affront in corporate Old Trafford, a we-paid-good-money-to-watch-a-winning-team annoyance about the quiet people in the Main Stand. God knows what they're saying in the North Stand Hospitality Suite.

United step up a gear, imperceptibly, easing the game and the three points away from Wimbledon. When they score, through Giggs and Cole, the noise momentarily shivers the hairs on the back of the spine, people piercing the night air with release.

But there is also calm applause, people vacantly clapping. And you think, if United want to tame football into the corset of a middle-class 'entertainment industry', why should the atmosphere be different from other places of entertainment, opera or theatre? Why should there be any noise at all during a performance? Didn't they used to applaud at the cinema?

Before the first match of the 1994-95 season, against QPR, the match programme contained a notice listing 'unacceptable behaviour'. Fans were told not to stand up or they'd be thrown out by United's very serious security men, run by SAS-trained Ned Kelly. Discontent rumbled all season among some of the pre-plc fans, who had felt United's personality change with a shocked affront of their own. In March 1995, during a home game against Arsenal, the tannoy told them to sit down. The whole East Stand stood up.

'After the game,' says Andy Walsh, one of those who did so, 'people were saying they had had enough of it, something had to be done. The feeling was that United were happy attracting corporate tickets and day-trippers, and were trying to get rid of the traditional working-class support.'

They called a meeting at the Free Trade Hall, an ornate slice of Manchester Victoriana which has, in its time, hosted political rallies by the suffragettes. There a very modern protest movement was born: the Independent Man. U. Supporters Association, IMUSA.

'We're not Luddites,' says Andy Walsh. 'We understand Manchester United has to make money, and we want it to be commercially successful, so it can pay players' wages. But there have to be some safeguards for poorer fans who have grown up supporting United, so that they do not get priced out, and so that they are treated with some respect when they do get in.'

IMUSA campaigns against price rises and wants a singing end, where people can support with some of the old passion. They have bought shares, to gain entry to the company's AGM, where Maurice Watkins regards them with a pitying amusement. In March 1996, Ferguson himself came to one of their social evenings, a tacit agreement, perhaps, with their call for a more heartfelt link between supporter and club. Ferguson bemoaned the lack of atmosphere himself in programme notes in November that year, citing the growing number of hospitality packages, 'people coming for a nice weekend', the move from standing to seating and, possibly, a contentment born of success: 'It doesn't seem as vibrant as the old days,' he said, 'when Liverpool found the atmosphere so frightening that more often than not they couldn't handle it.'

But this is all rough stuff and sentiment to the people who run Manchester United plc. Look at the figures: turnover £53m, profit £11m, the company valued at £460m. The team is winning, the ground is packed, new tier, boxes and all. Edward Freedman finally left the club in the summer of 1997. But Freedman was always supported by the club, his merchandise sold all over the world. The City fund managers are thrilled, and they are the people who matter now, not the ones hurrying along on a cold night in Stretford, with chips and gravy, a season ticket quadrupled in price and a copy of *United We Stand*.

The City has grown more interested in football as the years have passed. It woke up first in 1992, when the 22 top clubs voted themselves £305m by selling their captive markets to Sky TV. By December 1994, after Ferguson's United won the first Double, the plc's share price mushroomed so much they had to split the shares into tens. Three months later, Martin Edwards sold 1.2m shares, making £1.5m cash. In April 1996, just after United beat Chelsea 2-1 in the FA Cup semi-final, the Edwards family sold some more, making £4.4m. In June 1996, the Premier League announced its second Sky TV deal, £670m. United's shares puffed up to £4.50 and the Edwards family sold again, 3.7m shares, making £16.6m cash. In July 1997, the family sold again, making a further £5.57m.

This amounts to £28m cash made by the Edwards family, from selling a portion of the shares bought for around £800,000, in Manchester's terraced streets and a subsequent rights issue. Still, Edwards retains just under 15 per cent of Manchester United, worth, at the time of writing, £64m. His income from United, with dividends topping up his £321,000 salary, is around £1m per year. Maurice Watkins sold 176,000 shares on flotation, making £676,000. Still the company solicitor, still partner in James Chapman, Watkins' remaining shares, bought in his client, Manchester United Football Club, when he became a director in 1984, are now worth £11m.

One day, no doubt, they will sell their company. Some bids have already been made; in 1996 VCI, the media company, bid for a majority shareholding. Granada are strongly rumoured to have been interested in buying United as part of their media empire. Roland Smith, the man who masterminded the 1978 rights issue for Louis Edwards, now chairman of the plc, did not say no to VCI, but 'Not at that price'.

At the match, the lads in the East Stand, the likes of IMUSA, who stand, sing, feel football in the blood, avoid the tatty megastore like a septic tank, seem somehow like King Canutes, making a heroic, doomed attempt to stop an irresistible tide of consumerism and obsessive moneymaking. Every other football company in the country looks enviously at Manchester United, hankering for a trough of that size. There is no going back. Pay per view is next, probably the biggest exploitation yet of the captive market. The past, Duncan Edwards, Sir Matt Busby, Best, Law, Charlton, the legend of Manchester United Football Club, echoes only faintly now over these premises. Things were done differently then. This is the football business now; the future is profits. And the glory, glory is to Man United. Surrender or you'll cry.

3

THE BARCODE ARMY

You know your train is nearly at Newcastle when it emerges from a dense thicket of houses just past Durham and comes upon a square Sixties building bearing a clear plea: HAVE FAITH IN GOD, as the train swings leftwards on to the King Edward VI Bridge. Sitting on this approach, a train trundled slowly past, a jolt to the senses from the privatised swishness of the East Coast main line. A long snake of dirty wagons, piled to the brim with coal. A freight load of hard memories. On the side of the final wagon a piece of graffiti, very faint now: 'Coal not Dole,' it whispered, a reminder.

Quickly after came another train, a little sprinter, two nice neat passenger cars, bearing a lighter load, of Tyneside's new religion and industry. Geordies in black and white collarless shirts: the Toon Army, faithful followers of Newcastle United (plc).

It was 6 August 1996. The reborn football club was bringing the world to its doors once again, journalists pouring off the London train, summoned by press release, the Toon Army gathering outside St James' Park. Scottish and Newcastle Breweries, the club sponsor, had given 1,500 workers the afternoon off. This was a press conference to dwarf all the club's moments of rebirth, even the arrival of King Kevin, the Messiah from Marbella. This was Shearer, after his Euro '96 exploits, coming home to Newcastle.

Only the weather failed to do Sir John Hall's bidding. Newcastle was blanketed in grey, giving out steady drizzle, unfortunate for the 4,000-strong Toon Army, who were not to be allowed inside. Mostly men, many with kids, festooned in black and white stripes, they would be kept outside in the rain, given rudimentary amusement by Alan Robson, a local DJ and phone-in host. 'Say it with me,' he was urging. 'All bow together, and: WE ARE NOT WORTHY.' And they were doing it, standing outside the ground in the pissing rain, bowing and scraping.

Inside, away from the hordes, 12 men of various shades of grey were introduced: 'The chairman and directors of Newcastle United Football Club and Scottish and Newcastle Breweries.'

There was a patter of restrained applause, the type you get from workers invited to cheer their bosses. The middle-aged men took their places at a table in front of a board bearing huge Newcastle Brown Ale badges, and the ale's slogan: 'The One and Only.' 'WELCOME HOME,' said the backdrop, 'TO THE ONE AND ONLY ALAN SHEARER.'

Sir John himself was standing at the front with the microphone. He was, among the anonymous businessmen, instantly recognisable, the hard eyes and granite smile, from a thousand newspaper profiles.

Hushing the workers and journalists who had answered his call, Sir John summarised the club's progress in the five years since his takeover in 1992: the rebuilt ground, the cosmopolitan collection of players, now to be spearheaded by a shearer. 'We have found the right player,' he boomed. 'More especially, he's a Geordie. I take a great pride in bringing him back to the North-East. Because this region is a great region.'

The reception was restrained. Given Hall's national write-ups as man of the people, the crowd seemed to keep its emotional distance. The roar for Shearer was a heartfelt contrast, sheer release, the brewery workers letting rip in front of their bosses. Shearer trotted up from beneath the stand, a sporty young man in white polo shirt, pale face, pale hair, smiling his familiar smile. The hero of Euro '96. The One and Only. You could hear the Toon Army outside, ecstatic in the rain. The journalists were enjoying themselves, out of the office on expenses, a nice story, all laid on.

Keegan, in the middle of it all, looked uneasy. (I'm not being wise with hindsight; I made a note of it at the time – honest.) In a smart silk suit, he looked good for his age, like a successful, squash-playing accountant, among the grey, corporate company. His speech was strangely downbeat. He reminisced briefly about Alan having come to a Newcastle football day as a boy, having his picture taken with Keegan the Player, during Keegan's First Coming: 'It's too many years to mention,' Keegan said mournfully, 'and a lot of money.'

'It's your money,' he told the crowd. 'It's the money you've spent, on your replica shirts, home and away, on your season tickets and bonds, on the programmes and *Black and White* magazines.' He knew all the bits and bobs the Toon Army has to fork out for. 'I see it as my job to reinvest that money. You put it in, and I put it into the team.'

It was odd, Keegan earnestly reassuring the fans they were not being ripped off. Nobody had suggested they were. Certainly not the fans themselves, outside in the wet, intoning: 'We are not worthy.' Keegan, in his suit and bright silk tie, was like an executive with a nagging conscience, trying to persuade himself his job was worth while. That the money went on players, on the football itself, not into the pockets of these suits. But he sounded like he didn't believe it any more. Keegan looked that day like a commuter in mid-life crisis, outwardly successful but regretting, underneath, that he'd ever become an accountant in the first place. Who'd harboured, secretly, the wish to do something exciting, like be involved in football.

Shearer, of course, consummate professional, went out there and didn't put a foot wrong, well served by journalists who were there to enjoy, not poop, the party. 'How thrilled *are* you, Alan?' they asked; 'How much of a thrill *is* it?', giving Shearer plenty of openings to talk 'Mam and Dad', 'A dream come true', 'Always having wanted to play for N'castle' and all that it's-just-for-the-love business which makes football go round.

Nobody asked him how much his agent Tony Stephens had persuaded Newcastle to pay in signing-on fee or wages, or whether Newcastle had simply bettered the wages offer from Man United. Nobody asked whether this wasn't just handy flannel, the 'Coming Home' line. Why, nobody asked, had Shearer left Blackburn in the lurch only days before the start of the season?

The only man to approach mentioning the word which dared not speak its name was Paul Callan, of *The Daily Express*, who, with a bow tie, represents what passes for a character in Fleet Street these days. All red and smiley. 'Will the money change you?' Callan gently wondered, as if, until yesterday, Shearer had been on a hundred quid a week, working for a brewery maybe, or in a shop in the Gateshead Metro Centre. As if he wasn't several times a millionaire already. It was a perfect chance, and Shearer, clinical finisher that he is, did not spurn it.

'No it won't,' he smiled, before drilling home tomorrow's headlines. 'I'm still a sheet-metal worker's son from Newcastle.'

Did they love that or what! Inside and out, the brewery guys and the Toon Army, raising the roof. Forget the 15 million, they told each other, that's just our club thinking big. Shearer's one of us, he loves the club, he's a Geordie, he loves Newcastle.

Beaming widest at that lovely line was Sir John Hall. Throughout, he had smiled at Shearer with considered approval, pleased with his world-class control and delivery of all the right answers. It was another marvellous day for the club, the region, and Sir John Hall.

Ten years before, few people had ever heard of either of them. In 1986 Shearer was 16, preparing to uproot himself the length of the country for a Southampton apprenticeship under the strict care of Dave Merrington. Plain John Hall was 53, coming to the end of a longer, more grinding apprenticeship. A miner's son, he worked 20 years in the nationalised coal industry, being trained as a surveyor from the age of 16, then, from 1961, in the estates office in Ashington. There he learnt how property development worked, the grants available for development, the framework of necessary permissions, the money to be made by building on the land.

In 1965, he obtained £1,000 grants to make terraced houses habitable, making £2,000 profit on four houses in Sunderland. Hall finally left the National Coal Board in 1969, for estate agency and developing small retail and industrial units, searching around the North-East for land left derelict by heavy industry's slow local death. In 1976 he formed a company, Cameron Hall Developments, registering its office at the family home in Thornhill Terrace, Sunderland. Mae, his wife, was named the other director and shareholder. In 1979, following a move to Gateshead, Alison, his daughter, a secretary, and Douglas, his son, joined the business.

However much he was later to talk it up, when Hall bought an ash pit in Gateshead for around £100,000 in 1981, it was to be just another small-time development. Government help came in the form of Enterprise Zone status, a new Conservative Government scheme which gave tax allowances for building work and ten years occupation without having to pay rates. Hall lobbied Gateshead Council, to change its development plan to include the ash pit. The first plans went in: for a car showroom, a garden centre, a DIY store, a caravan centre. Out the back, 'leisure' – an artificial ski slope and a boating lake with some swings.

'That,' according to Ron Woodman, now marketing manager of the Gateshead Metro Centre, 'was the sum total of his ambition.'

The council helped Hall exhibit his ash pit at a hotel in 1984. They were absolutely stunned when more than a thousand people turned up, including some big names. The large chain stores were then first beginning to consider out-of-town malls, long integral to American shopping. Hall's ash pit offered ten years rate-free, and a position slap in the middle of Tyneside. Marks and Spencer, which had always done well in the area, taking smalls to Newcastle, showed genuine interest. Hall, 51, seeing the deal of a lifetime, worked like a man possessed to reel them in. Burtons, Boots and all the others fell in more easily after the idea had been blessed by St Michael.

John and Mae went to Canada to look at malls, returning with themed shopping, mother-and-baby rooms and 'leisure areas', stuff which passed for heroic vision in the thin Thatcherite horizons of the time, ditching or selling off industry, replacing it with 'enterprise'.

'It was serendipity for John Hall,' says Woodman, 'being in the right place at the right time. But then he brought it off very well.'

The Metro Centre opened in 1986, Britain's first and Europe's biggest shopping mall, 2,250,000 square feet including all the big stores and 'innovations', indoor theme areas like the Roman Forum: 'The Glory that Was Rome', and the Garden Court: 'An Oasis of Tranquillity'.

When journalists came up from London, invited for the day to see the new consumerist future in the post-miners'-strike North-East, they were given a giddy tour by a man with a stupendous line in rhetoric: 'I am a dreamer,' Hall told *The Independent*. 'A bit like Martin Luther King.'

'If you have a just cause,' *The Sunday Times* was informed, 'you fight for a lifetime, as I learned from Mao Tsetung.'

The main patter of this businessman, though, pushed constantly throughout his subsequently permanent command of newspaper space, has been to associate himself with regeneration of the North-East. In every interview, every opportunity, Hall has presented his own commercial developments in terms of their having some grand, wide benefit to the whole region. 'I represent the new North-East,' he proclaimed to *The Guardian*. 'I represent the rebirth of the North-East'.

He advanced the line that people like him were creating a new paradise in the ruins of manufacturing, which was being crushed, or left to die. He derided as 'stultifying' nationalised industry, which had given him a job as a teenager, trained and nurtured him for 20 years. He said the North-East could somehow be transformed by making it more attractive. And he called for more public money to be pumped into the region to make it happen. With Thatcherism triumphant about the land and full of evangelical zeal, John Hall appeared to believe what he was saying. But it was also a superb sales pitch from a property developer, linking his own business with wider regeneration, calling for millions of pounds of Government money.

When journalists failed to suppress reservations about the grand claims Hall was making for shopping, in a region where 18 per cent were unemployed, Hall said: 'Don't think about them. Think of the 82 per cent who are working.'

And he always took time out to stress his support for the Great Leader of the day: 'I owe my opportunity,' he told *The Daily Express*, 'to the Conservatives and Margaret Thatcher.'

In 1986, Cameron Hall earned £64m, making profits of £28m. They employed only 40 people. The Halls took the bulk of £719,000 in payments as directors. The Prime Minister herself, wanting monuments to her 'enterprise economy', short of friends in the North, embraced John Hall and his Metro Centre. Thatcher sent Environment Secretary Nicholas Ridley to the Metro Centre's opening, bearing a personal letter, which praised Hall's 'impossible dream'.

In October 1987, the Church Commissioners, who had funded half the £272m development costs, bought out Hall's share of the Metro Centre freehold. The amount fetched for the former £100,000 ash pit was never disclosed, but, looking at Cameron Hall's profits that year, it was probably close to £35m, although Hall would have had to pay back the bank and other funders.

He sunk part of the proceeds into another grand scheme, this one laden with symbolism. He bought Wynyard Hall, down the A19 towards Middlesbrough, the expansive country estate and stately home of the ninth Marquis of Londonderry. One era gave way to another as the broke descendant of mineowners handed the keys to a miner's son.

Again, Hall had to persuade the local council, Cleveland this time, to change its development plan to allow him to build. His planning application, for 1,968 of Wynyard's 5,400 green acres, promised job creation in a business park, golf courses, and a panoply of residential and leisure developments.

Planning permission was granted in August 1988.

'You will be sick of hearing about Wynyard,' Hall told *The Independent*, ploughing a familiar PR furrow. 'The North-East is rising from dereliction.' He said the housing, with upper-class amenities like golf, shooting and watersports, would be attractive to foreign businessmen. 'Inward investment' was becoming one of the main planks of the Thatcher project, attracting foreign companies with a low-paid, unemployed workforce and dollops of public money. Hall was talking Wynyard up as a potential site. The work was expensive, though, Hall having to build two roundabouts to link Wynyard with the A19, and pay to bring water, electricity and gas on to the site.

On Sunday, 10 April 1988, John Hall, out of the blue, suddenly announced his intention to 'rescue' Newcastle United Football Club. Appearing in an article by Bob Cass in *The Mail on Sunday*, Hall declared he would 'disturb the dynastic regime which has ruled St James' Park for decades'. The club, he said, was ruled by a discredited small board, and they should hold a rights issue to widen ownership and raise new money. He did not want control; Cameron Hall would lend £500,000 to the club to be a 'catalyst'. At this time, he does not appear to have seen the club as a means of making money for himself. It was four years before the Premier League breakaway, and the subsequent Sky Television deal which turned football clubs into lucrative businesses for their owners. Hall stressed he did not want control. He wanted the club to do well – for the benefit, he said, of the region: 'The North-East is coming out economically because the leadership and dynamism is starting to happen. That has to be reflected in the club.'

Hall had done quite well for newsprint out of shopping and buying a stately home, but football, on the back pages every day, written by mostly business-illiterate, servile sports journalists, was tremendous PR. 'The world will come to Newcastle United,' he promised *The Independent*. 'The club will be a major industry, marketing the North-East . . .'

But going to the papers first was guaranteed to alienate Newcastle United's stuffy, conservative board of directors. Led by solicitor and Football League bigwig Gordon McKeag, they would have liked a private, dignified approach, preferably putting in plenty of money and not asking for too much control. They were deeply unpopular with the supporters, presiding over a once-great club, centre of life for generations of Geordies, the ground decaying, the team becoming a seller, unable to keep its prodigious talent. Cries of 'Sack the Board' from the Gallowgate End were, in those days, no more than a sign that the season had started.

The directors, though, regarded themselves as 'custodians of the football club for the town'. This was the football director's traditional job description; he had been entrusted with the club, an institution which belonged to the people, and it was his duty to look after it and pass it on. In this fat-cat age it looks a worthy, selfless approach to running a football club and it certainly had many merits. The directors never looked to make money for themselves out of football; the position was seen as an honour and a service to the community. Too often, though, the directors' custodianship stagnated into a stuffy inertia, the pies passed around the boardroom with mutual congratulation while thousands stood outside on crumbling terraces in the rain. Nevertheless, club rules were based on safeguarding the club; no one man was to be allowed control. If anybody wanted to become involved in Newcastle United, he could talk to the sitting directors.

Hall, making his grand claims in the papers, soon backed by 'The Magpie Group', embarked on a long, bitter battle for the club. McKeag, remote from the fans, lost utterly in the PR stakes against Hall, who used his endless opportunities to present himself locally as the man for United, nationally as 'Mr North-East'.

Escalating the stakes, Hall began to buy Newcastle shares. There were 2,000 ten-shilling shares, descending from the club's original formation as a limited company in 1890 and its subsequent appeals for cash. At times in its history, the club's founders had hawked shares round pubs and clubs, looking for a few quid to bail the club out. The shareholders' register was a long, ragged, patchily updated list, including the living and the dead. Hall started offering traceable people £50 for their shares.

McKeag, believing Hall was indeed after control, umbraged by all the mouth in the papers, felt forced to fight. It sparked an unprecedented buying-up of shares in the club, their price rocketing as high as £6,000. McKeag, unpopular with the fans, derided by the Magpie Group, faced death threats, graffiti and shit through the letter box as passions were stirred over the fate of the club.

In 1989 Hall employed Paul Yeoman, a researcher and then Conservative European Candidate for Northumbria, whom he had first met at a Conservative Party Dinner. From an office in Wynyard Hall, Yeoman's job was to trace Newcastle United shares and buy them with John Hall's chequebook. The price went up to £500, then £1,000. Yeoman hired a genealogist to trace descendants of dead shareholders. He remembers finding one woman of Geordie ancestry living in the Australian outback, relieving her of six shares by fax.

Yeoman's fondest memory of what he describes as a 'fascinating time', John Hall 'an inspiration', was going one stormy night to a woman living in a small old house in the East Anglian fens. She had 15 shares.

'Her husband had gone to St James' Park every Saturday, and she regarded these shares as a memento of the passion he'd had for the club. When I offered her £1,000 each, it was like Santa Claus arriving.'

The share battle reached a stalemate, with Hall having accumulated 48 per cent of the club. The campaign is believed to have cost Hall and McKeag around £2m each.

With no rescue in sight, the club was relegated to the Second Division in 1989, laden with massive new debts from the building of the West Stand. Paul Gascoigne, tubby and brilliant, became next in a long line of gifted Geordies to depart, sold to Spurs.

In May 1990, peace was finally declared. McKeag had agreed to a deal with Hall, taking him in as director and agreeing to a public rights issue, providing that no single shareholder, including the two of them, would be left with more than 10 per cent. 'I do not want control,' Hall still insisted at that time. 'I want to return this club to its fans.'

In retrospect, the rights issue does not look such a bad idea. A minimum of £2.5m was to be raised. People would get an old-fashioned emotional stake in the club and a vote at general meetings, but the shares were emphatically not investments. The scheme was flawed, though; there was a £100 minimum purchase, a lot of money in an area of high unemployment, and no promise of democracy through, for example, electing a supporters' representative on the board. The club tried to muster some fanfare, McKeag and Hall posing for the papers with half-hearted smiles and outsized share certificates, but it flopped.

Hall walked away from the football club then, in December 1990, resigning as a director. He left in Cameron Hall's £500,000 loan, but instructed Douglas to sell the Hall shareholding in Newcastle United. He said he felt let down, particularly by the local business community's failure to support the rights issue, and now he wanted out. McKeag, his position also untenable, resigned, leaving George Forbes, a Northumberland cattle auctioneer, to take over as chairman. Grim, debt-ridden, second-rate years followed, manager Jim Smith having no chance of satisfying the yearnings of the Toon Army. Mick Quinn, a round man with an eye for goal, was the best they could do for a hero.

Hall concentrated on Wynyard, which, after the preparatory expense, was turning into a millstone. Property prices had slumped, there was no interest from housing developers. The sign to the business park off the second roundabout pointed only to a dead end.

Then, in December 1991, the news leaked that the Football Association was to back the breakaway of the First Division clubs from the Football League. The football world knew the top clubs were heading for a big television deal, which they would not have to share. Suddenly there was big money at the top of football. John Hall came roaring back: 'We must get into the Super League.'

This time there was no messing about. He wanted control. With the club crippled by debt, the directors sold one by one, including McKeag. Hall acquired 90 per cent of the club. He is believed to have paid no more than £3m in total. Scrap metal dealer Freddy Shepherd nearly sold, but didn't, retaining around 10 per cent, held by his trust fund, Shepherd Offshore.

Hall was not going to hang about in the Second Division, away from the money. Jim Smith left in 1991, citing stress; Ossie Ardiles arrived on a wave of optimism, but could not reverse the club's downward slide. In February 1992, after a 5-2 defeat at Oxford, Ossie famously received a vote of confidence from Douglas Hall, who told the papers Ossie's job was 'safe as houses'. He sacked him a couple of days later.

And so on 5 February 1992, the Second Coming. Kevin Keegan, who had vowed never to be a manager, the first English footballer to have made enough from playing to retire for life, was seduced off the Spanish golf course by the wake-up call from Newcastle. Nothing could have so pleased the Toon Army. They were ecstatic, down outside St James' Park, hailing the Saviour. They were to enjoy an extraordinary love-love relationship with Keegan, who appeared to love them back, or at least understand them.

More than the fans of any other football club, at Newcastle they have individual heroes, single talismen. Hall was feeding this tendency later, when he spent so much on Shearer, Les Ferdinand solemnly announcing he would 'give Shearer the number nine shirt'. It was always this way: Hughie Gallagher in the Twenties, Wor Jackie, 1946-57. Supermac. Mirandinha, flowering briefly. Keegan, incomparable. Gazza, the mad Geordie. Then Mick Quinn, the best they could do. Keegan's return tapped this well of adoration, of which he'd drunk as a player. He'd only played two years, 1982-84, yet the fans had loved him; promotion in '84, that twinkling triangle with Waddle and Beardsley. He was a legend, back to enjoy a special bond with the fans, a Shankly of the satellite age.

There was an early hiccough, Keegan walking out, complaining he had not been given money for players, returning to see Newcastle avoid relegation by a sliver, beating Leicester 2-1 in the last game of the season. He returned to 'Costa Ambience'. The Newcastle directors, Douglas Hall, Shepherd and Freddie Fletcher, beat an urgent path to the Spanish pile, begging him to stay, the man who could turn the company round. Keegan is believed to have secured a £120,000 annual salary, and been given assurances of money to spend on players.

'Kevin Keegan is delighted,' said a shameless press announcement, 'by the invitation to move into a house on the Wynyard estate.' It was pure Hall. At the time, Wynyard needed all the publicity it could get.

Keegan started buying heroes in. Beardsley's return, Andy Cole. A passionate, thrilling revival, promotion in 1993 and two-winger, cavalier football which foundered in 1996 only on the cold steel of Alex Ferguson.

Freddie Fletcher was Sir John's other shrewd signing. Fresh from his commercial transformation of Rangers, Fletcher, as chief executive, would spearhead the financial exploitation of the excitement generated by Keegan. From the start, the Toon Army accepted replica shirts as compulsory. £40 a time, plus name, plus number, home and away, for Dad and Mam and Kids. There are more replica shirts at St James' Park than anywhere else, established as uniforms of belonging, of Geordieness. When Newcastle score, tens of thousands of black and white stripes stand as one, a great human barcode.

Fletcher introduced all modern football's money-making elements, the shop, designed by George Davis of Next, an altogether classier place than Manchester United's megastore of baubles. The satellite money poured in, Sky attracted by the flair and spectacle of Keegan's side. Ticket prices were hiked immediately; from an average price of £5.26 in 1991, 1996-97's average was £16, sold mostly as season tickets.

Hall showed his ability to think big and bring schemes to fruition. Newcastle built new stands of some grandeur, St James' Park one of the more impressive post-Taylor grounds. Seventy executive boxes were incorporated at two prices, £1,400 and £2,100 per person per season. The 'Platinum Club' was introduced, giving the well-heeled a season ticket with food, and 'the right to buy such a ticket for the next 98 years'. It sold out, 1,389 season-ticket holders paying £3,000 each – total: £4,167,000, for the right to fork out the same year after year.

In 1994 they introduced a bond to get fans to pay for rebuilding, offering in return only 'the right to buy a season ticket for the next ten years'. The bond idea was greeted with suspicion at Arsenal, rejected outright at West Ham, but the Toon Army were told they might not otherwise get a season ticket, that they would be helping the club to be successful. Free cup-tie tickets were thrown in for three seasons, and the Toon Army forked out, 9,453 season-ticket holders somehow finding £500, some using hire purchase provided through the club itself – at 19 per cent APR. Total: £4,726,500.

Hall, in interviews, had called the Toon Army's passion unbelievable, 'frightening', and he has consistently said that the reborn club is 'vital to the region', approaching his business venture in the language of the general good. The fans seem to relish the description, proudly sacrificing themselves to make the football club successful. Turnover ballooned. In the year to July 1996, the club made nearly £29m.

Expenditure mushroomed as well, Keegan insisting on spending Toon Army money on players. Newcastle's squad began to gather: Warren Barton, £4m from Wimbledon, Robert Lee, star midfielder, the giant Peacock. Albert, big, strong, Belgian. The magnificent Ferdinand, a £6m touch. Ginola, tall, silky. In 1995, the reawakening had turned to boom. They had outspent everyone. They expected to win the League that year, playing celebratory football, led by the irrepressible, relaxed Keegan.

By the end of the season, freaked out in the run-in by Ferguson's ruthless psyching out, Keegan would implode, incoherent on Sky, losing his grip and the Premiership. Messianic, skipping joyfully towards the expected prize, he found that the little extra you needed was cold and hard. It wasn't Keegan at all, that deadly showdown. Something seemed to leave him that season; a spark went out.

The Halls, though, had finally had a result at Wynyard. Samsung, Koreans, had come over considering building a factory in the region. Sir John was in on the entertainment, inviting the helicopter to land at Wynyard, dining there, taking them to a box at St James' Park. They chose the green stuff of Wynyard over any of the brown sites they were shown. 'It was the football that won it,' a triumphant Hall told the papers, claiming the Newcastle match had swung the deal.

'With respect,' says a source very close to the negotiations, 'inward investment is a much harder business than that. Entertainment is lavish in every region. I know it wasn't the football, although Sir John contributed to the feelgood factor.' So did £58m of Government money, to ease Samsung into the North-East. They have said they will create 3,000 jobs in a decade; so far 800 have been employed. The Samsung deal, sweetened with public millions, turned Wynyard into a moneymaker. 'This is the tenant to transform Wynyard,' Hall gushed. 'Just as Marks and Spencer transformed the Metro Centre.'

Wynyard has boomed since, a Metro Centre of housing. The sign on the second roundabout, to the business park promised in 1988, still points only to a dead end. But housing developers have carved up the acreage, throwing up the kind of retro houses, Georgian style, which seem to reassure the *nouveaux riches*. Here there are golf courses and executive domiciles, trophy cars in the driveways, breathing artificial, fearful air, guarded by burglar alarms and a security man at the gates. Wynyard now is a monument to a backward-looking, unequal Britain, in which the haves look after themselves miles away from the nearest have-nots.

Keegan went into the 1996–97 season with Shearer signed, the magic gone and the Halls determined to float the club. The time was right, the City in love with football. They'd taken a big risk, especially with Shearer. They'd borrowed £21m to rebuild the ground, including £4.4m loaned in from Cameron Hall. They owed £12m in instalments on transfer fees. The debt was huge and by floating they could pay it all off and make a fortune for themselves. They reckoned it would fetch £180m, the old club of 2,000 shares. Cameron Hall Developments, still wholly owned by John, Mae, Douglas and Alison, would own 57 per cent of it, £102m. There was to be no hanging around.

Nat West Markets, organising the float, were practically living at St James' Park. In November Mark Corbridge, 33, came full time to Newcastle from Nat West Markets as joint chief executive with Fletcher, to see the company to the Stock Market. His package was £160,000 a year, plus an annual bonus guaranteed not to be less than 50 per cent. Plus company car, pension, and private and permanent health insurance. Fletcher was on the same deal. Fourteen days after the company hit the Stock Exchange, Corbridge was to get a lump sum, £300,000, 'in recognition of the part he has played in the recent development of Newcastle United'. Fletcher was to get £750,000. Plus options, each, on a million shares.

The prospectus issued by Newcastle United plc, like those of all the football companies, shows the City football's true face in the Nineties, all the passion of a banknote: 'Newcastle United is one of the UK's leading football businesses. It generates high-quality revenue streams by selling viewing rights to its football matches and by selling a range of branded products.'

It has a section of 'Key Strengths', noting 'The size and loyalty of its supporter base, which ensures large audiences'. The Toon Army in a clause, assurance of profits to the City of London.

Keegan had made good money himself out of football, but he did it playing the game. He did Brut and Pony adverts, the permed Seventies icon splashing it on all over with 'Enery Cooper, but he'd always given the fans 100 per cent, and, a working lad himself, he had always treated them with respect. Now, he was fronting the whole show, the shirts, the bonds, the *Black and White* magazines for a company about to make a fortune for the Halls, for Shepherd.

After the Ferguson head-to-head and with the club's moneymen, in the St James' Park corridors, preparing to float, Keegan tells the directors he's stopped enjoying it. He's thinking he might call it a day. On Boxing Day 1996, Brian McNally, an exceptional, investigative, impartial local football journalist, broke the story in *The Sunday Mirror*.

Corbridge, joint chief executive of the football company, sits down with Kevin Keegan, middle management. Keegan thinks he might stay till the end of the season, that'd be the best thing for the football team. No, says Corbridge, bad for the company. The football part of the prospectus is really quite important. They cannot describe Keegan as manager if they know he's planning to leave. That would be to mislead the City. Keegan has to decide, now: stay for two years, or leave. So King Kevin, the Messiah from Marbella, hero of the Toon Army, left the football club on Wednesday, 8 January 1997, in the middle of the season. In July, Corbridge himself would leave, his departure believed to be due to differences with the board over Sir John Hall's role in Newcastle United plc and the plans to build a new stadium on neighbouring Leazes Park and the Town Moor. Corbridge, after his eight lucrative months at the company, was reported to have been given a pay-off of £400,000.

In January, the directors were dashing for a replacement for Keegan with the Toon Army still weeping into the snow outside St James' Park. Sir John, a big fish, cruised regally to Spain, Bobby Robson the first call for all managerless English clubs. Hall, looking suddenly smaller, was given short shrift by the president of AFC Barcelona, an altogether more substantial figure in football's worldwide ocean. Robson said no anyway; he had a contract, he loves it out there and

Barcelona, with 120,000 members, is probably the grandest football club in the world. Even bigger than Newcastle United, vehicle of regeneration in the North-East of England.

The following Monday in *The Daily Telegraph*, journalist Henry Winter, who had recently collaborated with Kenny Dalglish on a dour autobiography, wrote a piece amounting practically to a Dalglish job application. 'The fire still burns,' Winter wrote. 'If the right offer was made for Dalglish . . . his response is likely to be yes.' Tony Blair, presenting at the time as a Newcastle fan, was never better served by his spin doctors.

Dalglish had won the League twice, and, although he'd left Liverpool citing stress caused by the trauma of Hillsborough, and walked out on Blackburn, he was credible enough for the City. So, just as he had replaced Keegan as a player at Anfield in 1977, 20 years on, Dalglish took his mantle at St James' Park, slipping calmly into the dug-out and page 26 of the prospectus.

The flotation went ahead, on time, on Wednesday, 2 April 1997. It was not one of the most solid companies ever to come to the Stock Market, floating to pay off debts, but it was another football business, bringing its loyal supporters as a captive market to the City, and the prospect of making them pay to view. The flotation valued the club at £180m.

The Halls' share was £102m.

Freddy Shepherd's share was £13m.

Somebody called Leonard Hatton had 3.7 per cent of the company: £6.5m.

From a couple of million spent fighting McKeag.

The flotation raised £47.4m of new money, wiping out the debts, and even promising to spend £10m on youth development. Sir John Hall talked a lot about this from the beginning, Newcastle fielding a team of Geordies, but he signally failed to do it. Geordies Lee Clark and Robbie Elliott have been pushed out by imports and Keegan scrapped the reserve side. Now, the money made, they're talking academies.

But none of the new money was to go towards the proposed new stadium – strange, as this is a very public, controversial next stage for Hall. His claims have become ever grander, talking about a whole sporting club, football together with ice hockey and rugby, which he has also bought, all booming from a brand new stadium he intends to build behind St James' Park. It will, of course, be a great asset to the City of Newcastle, the North-East as a region. Truly it is a dream of Martin Luther King, Mao Tsetung proportions.

Yet some individuals appear intent on opposing this great gift to the people. They are concerned that Hall wants to carve up a previous great gift to the people, Leazes Park, green land right in the centre of Newcastle, won in 1872 by the earnest hard work of a city Alderman, Fred Hamond. Like most parks in the ratecapping era, it has seen better days. But it has dedicated supporters, Friends of Leazes Park, led by Dolly Potter, a retired surveyor, who clean and tend the park. Recently their voluntary work has counted towards a £4m Lottery bid, by the council, to transform the park. Hall's plan for his stadium, a new, moneyspinning home for the plc he owns, involves building on the park and the Town Moor. Unique, the moor is a rambling green space in the centre of town, cows munching, oblivious to the post-industrial human plottings around them.

Following a meeting of Newcastle City Council's Labour Group on 9 July 1996, the council actually invited the football company to make an application to build the stadium on the park, contrary to the council's own development plan. This unprecedented decision is thought to have been taken because there was talk of moving the club out of Newcastle, probably to Gateshead, and building the stadium there. Newcastle's council had turned down a previous application to build an ice rink on Leazes Park; the Halls had licked their wounds, then come back with this massive plan. Trapped in parochial rivalry with Gateshead, and by the centrality of the club to the lives of the Toon Army, the council invited the planning application.

This is the Hall project reaching mammoth proportions. A grand piece of property development, on prime green land, by his own company, presented as some miraculous vision for the community: 'I am a dreamer,' he told *The Guardian.* 'Wherever athletes are competing throughout the world they'll have this little badge to carry the message of the North-East.'

For the first time, the rhetoric is being scrutinised by people other than servile journalists and football fans. Many thousands of local people, in an area blotched with available derelict land, are outraged by Hall's designs on the park and moor. A protest movement, No

Business on the Moor, collected 38,000 signatures against the plan. But its organisers have struggled to have their arguments calmly heard.

'If it was Tesco,' shrugs spokesman Mike Heckles, a deputy headmaster, 'people would see it for what it is: a plc hacking up the park to make money for itself. But because it's the football company, people are blinded. They think if you support the club you have to support the plan. And they think if you want to preserve the park and moor, you must be against the football club.'

Heckles' group has been denounced as middle-class people who don't understand football, ironic in the light of Newcastle United plc's executive boxes and Platinum Club.

The campaigners stress they like football, that it would be fine for the club to have a new stadium, just that it does not have to be built on the park. Heckles has carefully examined the council's report on alternative sites, which were all dismissed; he believes one, Newburn Haugh, near the river, a massive brownfield site, presents itself most obviously as a central Newcastle alternative.

Dolly Potter, of Friends of Leazes Park, herself a football supporter, is exasperated by the ignorance towards the park, which many fans have now convinced themselves 'nobody uses'. 'You cannot exaggerate the importance of green space to the environment, to health. Many people use the park: residents, workers eating their sandwiches at lunchtime, patients from the hospital, thousands of students. Yet here we have the council going cap in hand to the football company, inviting them to build on it. They are the villains of the piece; they should be protecting public health and amenities.'

A small patch of urban green in the centre of Newcastle, Leazes Park is a measure of English football's current omnipotence. Everybody, politicians, celebrities, proclaims support for the game. Football is booming, all-conquering, a world in itself, dismissive of context. In a North-East which is still wracked with structural decline, entrenched poverty and social problems, football claims to solve everything, to be good for the community, a 'great advert for the town'. And a football company can rely on the unquestioning support of its supporters. The black and white striped army want to believe it is all true. The Moor, not beautiful exactly, a walk-your-dog, go-for-a-jog space, with the surreal urban sight of munching cows, has fended off centuries of pressure on land. The freemen who control it steadfastly kept it green throughout the chaotic tumult of Industrial Revolution. Now, after all that, it could fall to football. 'The council just does not want to be painted as having driven Newcastle United out of Newcastle,' a source inside the Town Hall told me. 'People are feverish about the club at the moment.'

Newcastle was never a radical place; it suffered the cruelties of mining and shipbuilding mostly with an acceptance born of a constant aristocratic presence. There's a touch of cap-doffing feudalism about the city, which has the provincial air of a town. The Toon Army is ruled by a new aristocracy now, hard men who unearthed money, in property, in scrap metal, while industry collapsed around them.

'It is a widespread view among supporters not exactly to admire Sir John Hall,' says Kevin Miles of the Independent Newcastle United Supporters Association. 'Many struggle to afford to go to the match, and feel exploited. They know how much money has been made out of the club. But they're grateful for the recovery, for having a successful club.' I asked the club for an interview with Sir John Hall for this book. A spokesman said that he was now living in Spain. In September, he announced his retirement as a director of the football club.

Hall hadn't seen football as an investment at first, hadn't wanted control; the club was more a vehicle for his wider talk of regeneration, and he was in the papers every day. But when football became a business, Hall was perfectly placed to profit from it. His family now has £100m capital gain in five years. Personally. Out of football. Hall was a creation of the Thatcher era; he praised her, she praised him back, knighted him. As coal died, crushed in a cruel strike, Hall, trained by the Coal Board, made a fortune in the wreckage, in shopping, inward investment, executive housing, now football. Dole remains for many Geordies, making their way worshipfully to St James' Park on a working day, to stand in the drizzle, bow down, and say: 'We are not worthy.'

4

THE HOUSE THAT JACK BUILT

When the blue and white halved shirts of Blackburn Rovers lifted the FA Carling Premiership in 1995, few could resist the victory's wonderful romance. The bunting was out in the small old cotton town of East Lancashire; all the people rejoiced. Cloth caps, ferrets; simple folk, no Hovis-advert cliché was left unmoved. 'A great day for Blackburn,' cheered the papers, presuming there was nothing to the town but its football team.

The only niggle in this heartwarming story was that it didn't quite fit the David and Goliath tradition of football giant-killing. It wasn't a triumph of skill and hard work. It was no Cloughie job on Nottingham Forest; crafty, tyrannical management of a motley crew, coming from nowhere to conquer Europe.

Truth be told, it was precisely the opposite. It had been done by one rich man taking over the club, then pumping in as much money as it took. Throw out the old, import the new, bugger the cost.

So the world turned to that man, and found the romance there. Jack Walker never gave interviews, so the papers had to assume. They assumed he was a softie, throwing money at his football team without a care, wishing only for it to be successful. Bestowing a great gift to the townspeople, who loved him for it. Stuff like that. Benefactor, philanthropist: 'Uncle Jack'.

Jack Walker had made his fortune with his brother, Fred, building up the business, Walkersteel, inherited from father Charles in 1951. In 1954 they moved into steel stockholding, storing manufactured steel at a time of steel shortages. It was a good move, filling an emerging gap in the steel industry. After British Steel was nationalised in 1967, the industry looked increasingly for the efficiency savings of enormous, uniform steel runs. It relied on middle men prepared to buy in bulk, store the steel, then cut, parcel and distribute it to smaller industrial companies. Incentives to stockholders to take more tonnage were offered in the form of rebates.

Jack and Fred tracked British Steel's growth, becoming its biggest customer. Their 400,000 square foot 'steel service centre', the biggest in England, opened in 1970, a grey, brutal-looking monolith on the hill above Ewood Park. A former executive in a French steel company remembered doing business there. 'It was a showpiece inside. Well lit, palatial.'

The atmosphere, though, was 'feudal', he said, a complete gap between the directors and the workers, who knew their place. After a Rovers game in 1997 against West Ham, in 'Uncle Jack's', a pub named after the benefactor, I met a man who worked on the shop floor at Walkersteel. He said Fred Walker had been a workaholic, turning up in his Rolls-Royce at the crack of dawn and staying all hours. 'Fred was the kind of boss,' he said, 'where if there was something wrong with a machine, he'd roll his sleeves up, get on the floor and sort it out.'

So you liked him then?

'Oh no, we didn't like him. But,' he shrugged, 'at least he treated us all the same. We respected him for that.'

Jack they rarely saw. Since 1974 he had gone to be a tax exile in Jersey. Legend has it the brothers, planning to save on tax, tossed a coin to see who would go. Jack, says the legend, lost. To avoid paying tax, he can spend no more than 182 days in this country. While Fred worked on site in Blackburn, Jack directed operations from Jersey.

'We'd only ever see Jack on Walkersteel golf days for customers,' said the worker.

The brothers stayed determinedly open, flourished, during the steel strike, managing to maintain their stocks, and they drove to be the biggest operators in an industry where size is everything. In 1984 they bought GKN, a rival stockholding company, for £50m. By 1989, they were reckoned to be buying 7 per cent of freshly privatised British Steel's output. It was the best ever year for stockholding, with prices at an all-time high. The Walkers announced they wanted to sell up.

'They had British Steel over a barrel,' chuckles the former French executive. 'With the amount of steel they took, and their distribution network, British Steel couldn't afford to lose them, particularly to a foreign steel manufacturer.'

British Steel paid £330m for Walkersteel, the most ever paid for a family business, and, remarkably, the brothers sold only the business, keeping the land. Effectively British Steel paid the Walkers three times: building the empire with rebates, buying it for £330m, and still paying rent. It was the sellout prepared for when Jack had gone to Jersey 15 years before. His Jersey residence meant that the capital gain was not taxable. A capital gain is the difference, when an asset, like a company, is sold, between how much it originally cost to buy, and how much it is sold for. Walkersteel was started by Charles Walker in 1945 with £80. Therefore, the capital gain amounted to almost the whole £330m. In 1989, upper rate capital gains tax was 40 per cent. Jack's exile, away from Blackburn, his brother and his business, probably deprived Britain of around £132m. The whole £330m was paid into the Walkers' Jersey trusts, to accumulate interest luxuriously. Even at, say, only 8 per cent, the interest is an annual £26m.

In the summer of 1991, Blackburn councillor Maureen Bateson, canvassing in the terraced streets around Ewood Park, was told by worried residents that 'something was going on at Rovers'. Ewood was a tight-knit, white working-class community, originally of millworkers. Children tended to grow up and stay in the area, settling in neighbouring streets. People stayed 40, 50, 60 years. They lived with Rovers as a friendly neighbour; many were fans. They used to chat with the players, directors, as they met them in the streets.

In the last couple of months, Rovers directors Bob Coar and Terry Ibbotson had started knocking on doors. They were making offers, straight out, to buy people's houses. The streets, Nuttall Street, Kidder Street, were trembling with rumours. That Rovers had come into money, that they were going to buy the houses and demolish them, to build a bigger ground.

Bateson called for a meeting with Rovers on 17 July 1991. She remembers an 'unpleasant', brief audience with then chairman Bill Fox. Jack Walker was backing the club, Fox said tersely, the first official confirmation. Yes, he was looking to develop the ground. Yes, they did want some houses.

Jack Walker did have a history of involvement with Blackburn Rovers. He had supported them as a boy, and, while still UK tax-resident, watched the team of the Fifties, which boasted internationals Bryan Douglas and 580-game, one-club man Ronnie Clayton, England captain.

Although Jersey-based Jack did not go to many matches in the Seventies and Eighties, the skint, friendly Second Division club found Walkersteel a reliable business supporter, taking an advertising hoarding every season. Rovers were supported then by around 8,000 regulars, whose loyalty was faintly warmed by the dim hope that their decent team, Derek Fazackerley, 596 record-breaking games at the back, Howard Gayle and goalscoring Simon Garner, might one day get them up.

The directors were a well-meaning bunch of part-timers, doing their best and deriving enjoyment and local status from their involvement in the club. Conscious of Rovers' history, Football League founder members in 1888. And the club motto, coined by the public-school sons of millowners who had founded it in 1875: *Arte et Labore*: Through Skill and Hard Work.

'We saw ourselves as custodians of the club for the town,' says Robert Coar, vice-chairman then, chairman now. Dr Milton Jeffries, director since 1975, describes it as a kind of public service, keeping it going, a club strapped for cash, 'paying people on the drip', the ragged ground in need of repair. Rovers were too poor even to afford transport for the reserve team. 'We used to hire a mini-van. Coach Jim Furnell would drive that and I'd take the rest of the squad in my car.'

In 1988 Walkers donated the steel, £180,000-worth, for the roof of an all-seater stand on the river side of the ground. They called it the Walkersteel Stand in gratitude. Jack Walker liked that. He let the board know then that one day he'd like to help the club more substantially.

In May 1990, following the clearance of the £330m sale of Walkersteel by the Monopolies and Mergers Commission, he came back to Rovers. 'He said then,' recalls Dr Jeffries, 'that he wanted to put something back into the town. Those were his words.'

Custodians Coar and Fox interviewed Jack Walker. Jack said he wanted to set up a trust fund for the Rovers and fill it with £30m.

'We had always agreed that it was the town's club and if somebody came along who could do the job better than us, we would stand aside,' says Coar, shifting in his seat. 'After speaking to Jack Walker, we decided that would be the way forward.'

The whole of Blackburn Rovers FC is now owned by Rosedale (JW) Investments, one of Jack Walker's Jersey trusts. He is now the sole owner and custodian, ruling from Jersey, the former directors staying on to organise the awakening of Rovers. They were, Coar says, determined to do it properly. Jack insisted that the £30m was initial investment only; in a few years the club had to become self-financing.

'We were practically starting from scratch with the ground, with three sides needing doing. We got in a top firm of architects, Atherden Fuller. We were able to do it as we wanted. Get in as much hospitality as possible.'

That's what he said; chairman of Second Division Blackburn Rovers, historic club of a poor town, suddenly come into £30m. Get in as much hospitality as possible. They started looking to buy up the houses which neighboured close to the ground.

Some residents sold their houses willingly. Others, upset and bewildered, refused. Empty houses blighted their row. After six months' delay and some local distress, Rovers finally, on 29 January 1992, produced plans for a 25,000-seat stadium, within the then confines of Ewood Park. Atherden Fuller's model was displayed to residents at a meeting in a local club. Jack Walker came over from Jersey. There was a free bar. Jack told them softly it was his dream to make Blackburn Rovers great. Alternative sites, for a new stadium, had been proposed by the council, but Jack said he wanted the club to stay at Ewood Park. The houses would be demolished to build carparks. The club would employ surveyors to value the houses, and pay above market price, plus removal fees.

Resident Lynn Hindle remembers few people asking questions: 'It was friendly, and people were overawed, I think. Respectful to Jack Walker, with all his money, and sort of humble before people in suits.'

Gradually, a few more people sold. Those who remained found neighbouring houses left empty, to be vandalised and stripped, plummeting the value of theirs. And they were under pressure from the town. Football fever had broken out, with Walker preparing to wake up Rovers. The ordinary people of Ewood found themselves criticised for standing in Walker's way. One by one, many of them still unhappy, they sold, a domino effect.

The club formally applied in March 1992 for planning permission to build the 25,000-seater stadium. It was granted in April, with the condition that the club must offer to buy neighbouring houses on Nuttall and Kidder Streets, giving remaining residents the option of escaping building disruption and the future eyesore of a bigger ground.

Then, in October 1992, the club put in a second application, this time for a 30,000-seater stadium. They said they had made 'unexpected progress' in buying up the houses, everybody had sold, so they could stretch the stands out further, 'executive carparking' at each end. It would save them the expense of moving the pitch. As if expense was a problem now for the football company, owned offshore.

'They had made offers for houses on the basis they didn't really need them,' says one resident, who has become something of an expert on planning law. 'Then, as soon as they had bought them, they put in another planning application.'

Robert Coar confirmed to me in an interview for this book that the club did have in mind right at the beginning of the process the possibility of building a bigger stadium. But he argued there was nothing underhand about their tactics, that the club had paid a market price. It was, he admitted, the market price based on an ordinary terraced house in Ewood, averaging £35,000, not the market price for land wanted for development by a multi-millionaire company, planning to get in as much hospitality as possible. He maintains the price was fair.

Rovers completed their new ground in 1994. Ticket prices were then averaging £10.15. The 5,000 extra capacity guaranteed Rovers £50,000 extra, whenever they filled the ground. And prices have gone up since. With corporate boxes at £24,000 a season, the increased capacity guarantees Blackburn many millions of pounds of extra revenue, forever.

In 1994, Maureen Bateson was on a Business in the Community tour round Bangor Street, Blackburn. Jack Walker was there. Bateson had a go at Jack about Rovers' dealings with the Ewood residents. 'We paid a fair price,' he told her. 'We paid over the odds for some. In fact, there was one woman I'd felt sorry for, I offered her a few thousand extra. She never realised she was sitting on a gold mine.' It was a strangely cold strain of philanthropy, this. 'Uncle Jack', wanting to 'put something back into the town', immediately buying up people's homes to demolish them.

Says Lynn Hindle, 'They didn't seem to have respect for us. We'd been neighbours for years. Suddenly Jack Walker appeared and the local people were just in the way then.'

The council has been criticised for not standing up to the club, not insisting Rovers move to a new site. Maureen Bateson feels some guilt. But the council believed the revolution at Rovers would be good news for the town. Blackburn is a poor town, its heyday in the cotton cradle of the Industrial Revolution long gone. Unemployment is high in the population of around 140,000, particularly among adult males. The town has a large Asian community, who came from Pakistan, Bangladesh and India to work on cotton mill nightshifts just as the industry was entering terminal collapse. In the recession of the late Seventies, Blackburn, like many Lancashire cotton towns, was bruised by a growing National Front. Most of the Asian population still lives in poorer, inner parts of the town, in some of the worst housing in Britain.

'We struggle for inward investment,' says councillor Peter Greenwood, former leader of the council. 'For companies relocating or setting up in the North, Blackburn is always losing out to Manchester.'

The council believed the club might provide an economic as well as moral boost to the town. The directors consistently said it would: 'The success of Blackburn Rovers is the town's best possible advertisement,' wrote Terry Ibbotson, justifying the second planning application. 'The club, with the unique opportunity afforded by Mr Walker's financial backing, has become a major influence for the future development and progress of our town.'

And, to be truthful, in a historic football town, with not too much else going for it, many of the councillors are fans, and could not but be thrilled.

Permission was granted and work began in 1993, demolishing the terraced houses which the club had bought, and completely rebuilding three sides of Ewood Park, with as much corporate hospitality as possible.

On the field, they rushed for immediate success. Manager Don

McKay, who had led the club to three successive promotion play-offs, was sacked in September 1991 because, even with the money, big stars wouldn't come to Blackburn. 'Don had done very well,' Coar says. 'He'd brought Steve Archibald here on loan, and Ossie Ardiles.'

Gary Lineker, though, had laughed. Jack Walker had not liked that. In October, following a brief, successful caretaker spell by Tony Parkes, Kenny Dalglish came out of his post-Liverpool sabbatical. He is said to have asked for a £400,000 salary, and assurances that big money would be available to pay for and to players. Blackburn, the football world was served notice, were serious.

Dalglish's time at Rovers was, for the fans, a thrilling rollercoaster. New players were signed, good promotion players: Alan Wright, £400,000 from Blackpool, Colin Hendry, returned from Manchester City, £700,000, Gordon Cowans, £200,000 from Villa, Mike Newell, £1,100,000 from Everton, all within a month. Tim Sherwood, £500,000 from Norwich, came in February 1992. They finished sixth, but went up via the play-offs, 1-0 against Leicester, a penalty. The fans could hardly believe what was happening. It was, they felt, pure romance, paid for by a favourite uncle.

They truly arrived in summer 1992 when they bought a player for £3,600,000. Every club in the land was after him. Explaining his move, he smiled: 'To win trophies.' Twenty-one years old, the estimated £500,000-a-year salary may just have been a factor. He was, still, only a sheet-metal worker's son from Newcastle. Shearer. The player's player in the Premiership age. England, England's number nine.

Four days before, Dalglish had signed Stuart Ripley, £1,300,000 from Middlesbrough, to supply the crosses. Shearer was clinical immediately, thriving with Newell. Sherwood crafted alongside Mark Atkins, one of McKay's humble signings, living with the new company. Hendry, at the back, was committed to the point of self-endangerment. Jason Wilcox was praised to the sky, being the only home-grown player in Dalglish's team, the exception that proved the rule, of money.

That season, Manchester United, whom Shearer had turned down in his hunt for trophies, won the Premiership. Blackburn finished fourth. In 1993, Dalglish spent again. Blackburn, pumped up from Walker's steel-lined pockets, still had more money than other clubs.

This was still before the big city clubs, with their bigger crowds, more Sky money, gate money, corporate boxes and merchandising, caught them up.

The fans were disbelieving. They had never even dreamt of this during those long, cold, windy seasons in the Second Division. 'We were very grateful to Jack Walker,' said the steelworker in 'Uncle Jack's'. 'We knew he'd do it properly, stay for the duration. Don't get me wrong, though, I thought he was doing it for himself, for his ego, as well as for us.'

A few minor grumbles were heard in the cavernous new stands of Ewood Park. 'Uncle Jack's' charity was applied with a sharp commercial edge. It was costing the fans. The price of tickets was going up, from an average £3.83 in 1990–91 to £10.15 in 1994–95. The atmosphere was . . . organised. Loud tannoy announcements to cheer the players, to greet goals. Exhortations from 'Radio Rovers' for the fans to spend money in the 'Roverstore'. Very many new fans, who seemed to be rich and mostly without too much knowledge about the game: 'snotters', as one fan contemptuously called them. The fanzine bore a sheepish title: *Loadsamoney*.

Atherden Fuller built corporate scoffing into the heart of the new Ewood Park. People availing themselves of the 'Red Rose' or 'Centenary' hospitality suites, or executive box holders, would get carparking included. These carparks, where houses used to stand on Kidder and Nuttall Streets, are full on matchdays of BMWs, Range Rovers, Jags.

So there were grumbles, but it felt grudging to express them in the midst of such transformation. Dalglish bought Kevin Gallagher for £1,500,000 in March 1993, Graeme Le Saux for £700,000 three days later. In the summer, Paul Warhurst came for £2,700,000. In October, Dalglish bought David Batty, £2,750,000. In November, Tim Flowers from Southampton for £2,400,000.

They finished second, eight points behind Manchester United, who won the Double.

It is a true irony of the current, money–ruled era of English football that the hyper–inflation of transfer fees, the outrageous players' wages, were spiralled by the signing of an old–fashioned English target man. Dalglish, shopping, along with all managers, at a particularly well–stocked Carrow Road, plumped for Chris Sutton out of the Norwich side which had finished third in 1993, then destroyed Bayern Munich in the UEFA Cup. He looked a perfect foil for Shearer, even though Blackburn had Newell. They paid £5m. Again, Manchester United were said to be after him, as were Spurs. His package from Rovers was said to be £500,000 a year, £10,000 a week and rising. He was 21 years old, and had played 89 full league games for Norwich.

'It was an absolutely unbelievable deal,' recalls Mick McGuire, licensed football agent and executive head of the PFA's player representatives. 'Shearer may have been on the same, but he was the outstanding young player of his time. This, for Sutton, 21, uncapped, was incredible money. The deal was in the press; all the players and agents saw it. It was the quantum leap in footballers' wages.'

No footballer has ever, yet, admitted that, as a professional, he has gone to a club because they offered him more money than any other. They always have to be 'coming home', or 'wanting a new challenge'. Sutton's justification for going to Blackburn was a classic. He went, he said, 'Because Blackburn's a nice town, a similar size to Norwich.' It was reckoned to be the first time anyone chose to work in Blackburn because it is a nice town.

By 1994–95 Blackburn weren't the little club any more. They were the biggest moneybags in a millionaires' league, and they'd won nothing yet. Their play developed a hard edge, Batty flying in, Shearer all elbows and nudges, Sutton prepared to mix it. Dalglish's team, given his playing style and Liverpool tradition, was surprisingly joyless. It was a grim, professional march on the title, to justify the money.

They wobbled badly in the run-in. Expecting to cruise it, it went to the last game of the season, with Man United closing. Blackburn lost 2–1 at Anfield. United, at West Ham, could have pipped them, but could only draw 1–1.

Rovers had done it. They carried the Premiership trophy with its schlock golden crown back to a delirious Ewood Park. Uncle Jack was given a cut glass bowl by the Borough Council in an official presentation on the pitch, Maureen Bateson forced to let the man kiss her. Cue the bunting, the cloth caps. All the people were happy and truly they gave their thanks.

Immediately Dalglish stepped down. 'Stepped up' was the official line, but on £300,000 a year, the 'Director of Football' did not want 'day-to-day involvement'.

'People found it odd that I rejected the chance to manage a team in the European Cup,' says Dalglish in his autobiography, written in collaboration with Henry Winter. 'Europe wasn't an attraction for me at that time. I had had enough of the daily grind. I didn't want that any more. I just couldn't be bothered.'

People might find this odd. These are not off-the-cuff remarks at one of Dalglish's famously minimalist press conferences. This is his autobiography; presumably they took some time to think about it. And the best he can do is: 'I just couldn't be bothered.'

By his own admission, in 1995-96, Dalglish did not do much directing. Ray Harford, more coach than manager, struggled in the anti-climax. Blackburn, despite goals from the sheet-metal worker's son, made an awful start. Their performance in the European Champions League was embarrassing, finishing bottom in a group with Spartak Moscow, Legia Warsaw and Rosenborg. In the Premiership, though, they climbed steadily, reaching seventh in April 1996 with a 3-2 victory over Wimbledon, Shearer scoring twice.

With Euro '96 close, Shearer was allowed to miss the last two games of the season to have a minor groin operation. Had Rovers won the first, instead of drawing 1-1 at home with Arsenal, they would have made it into Europe. They finished seventh. At this stage, there was no talk of Shearer leaving.

Football was coming home that summer. Three lions on the chest and all that. Shearer was sensational, brilliant, in Euro '96. He made his name, Rovers' man, scoring twice against the Dutch, poaching one against the Germans. There really was, ITV stressed that summer, only one Alan Shearer.

Throughout, there were rumours he was going to leave. The tabloids said he was booked on Man United's pre-season tour to Japan, that Bryan Robson had sorted the move during the tournament. Shearer denied it. Robert Coar, the tabloids descending on him, denied it too, angrily.

After the tournament, Shearer went to Jersey with Tony Stephens, his agent. Sharp new agent for the new age, former commercial manager at Aston Villa where he picked up David Platt. Who roomed with Shearer on England duty. Jack Walker talked through a new package, massive money. When they left, he thought Shearer had agreed to stay.

The next day, Shearer announced he was going to Newcastle.

Jack had got his return for him, £15m, make no mistake about that. Newcastle were making their own statement of seriousness to League and Stock Market. They had the number one striker in Europe. The One and Only. They'd pay the fee off with the forthcoming flotation. It was football transfer as corporate acquisition.

The bubble burst at Blackburn that day, 31 July 1996. Before that, it was a rollercoaster ride, from amiable obscurity to the very top. The fans could believe in Walker as sentimental, philanthropic 'Uncle Jack', if they took it with a pinch of sugar. They could ignore the sharp edge, even welcome it, the commercialism, the prices, the invasion of suits. Persuade themselves solemnly it had to be that way, so the club could compete. Dismiss the nagging doubt that this generation of players were mercenary, just here for the money. With Hendry, a fantastically committed, pre-Walker Blackburn player, and Shearer, consummate professional, giving it 100 per cent, they could believe footballers had some loyalty, felt something for the fans.

When Dalglish had gone, that was just Kenny, funny like that. But now Shearer was gone. He'd had his little operation, fine tuning, then waited till after the tournament. Then he'd gone, up to Newcastle, talking 'Mam and Dad', and 'dream come true'. For £15m and a salary package rumoured to be £2m a year, plus a Jag.

They'd begged and borrowed for their season tickets, up to £320, and Shearer had quit, a fortnight to go. Replica shirts with SHEARER on at £40 a time and now he was gone. Left them dangling.

Blackburn should have been excused the start of the 1996–97 season on the grounds of ill-health. It was painful to watch. Harford, gutted as anyone, couldn't lift them. They were rooted to the bottom. Rock bottom. It was as if a great party had suddenly ended, the ecstatic fug clearing to reveal the grey reality of headache and a mess to clear up. That ground. Whose idea was that? Three yawning, functional stands. All that steel cladding on the roofs, presumably to give them that Walker feel. Very clever. The exteriors: featureless. Red brick and blue glass. Headquarters of an alien corporation.

At each end, those carparks. Long, wide spaces of tarmac where people used to live. Sharp steel railings. The police at the entrance to Top O'th Croft, waving through the Mercs, to join their Jaguar and

Bentley friends. 'Uncle Jack' and Robert Coar say they paid a fair price for the houses, and all's fair, after all, in property and war. But it seems a soulless reason for wanting someone's house, so that BMW owners do not have too far to walk to their corporate entertainment.

Inside, surprise surprise, the ground is dead. Silent. A few half-hearted shouts of 'Barmy Army' at the Blackburn End. Louder shouts from the away fans: 'Where Were You When You Were Shit?' In between, in the Jack Walker Stand, rows of suits.

When Shearer came back with Newcastle on Boxing Day, the crowd gave it to him. Real hatred. 'Judas,' they booed. Usually the iceman, it unsettled him. Newcastle substituted him. 'There's no loyalty in football,' he moaned, unbelievably.

Robert Coar, minding the place in Blackburn, taking his orders on the phone from Jersey, gets all the stick. From what you hear, you'd expect some heartless under-sheriff, cold puppet of an absentee landlord. But, in his air-conditioned office, the tabloids constantly circling, he seems like a bloke in a small town, who was a custodian of the local, dignified football club, who has found himself haplessly at the centre of a great commercial beast.

'It's a business now,' he says, with an uncomfortable looking shrug. He's a builder in Blackburn, employing joiners, carpenters, electricians. He knows how hard life is. He accepts that many ordinary working people, loyal supporters, are now being priced out. 'It's unfortunate,' he admits, blinking hard.

And there's him, signing direct debits of £500,000 a year for 21-year-old footballers.

'Market forces. What can you do about it?' But you can tell he thinks the players are greedy. He says managers complain that players cannot be motivated any more because they're paid too much, that they don't try. He cannot think of an alternative, does not appear to have regrets about his custodianship, but you can tell he's not at peace with it, that he feels something major has gone wrong.

It was all romance at first. 'Uncle Jack', just a sentimental kind of tax exile, 'wanting to put something back into the town'. Giving the small town its football glory again, 'putting Rovers back where they should be'. Professional football started in these damp Lancashire hills, illegally, neighbouring Darwen caught paying two Scots, Fergie Suter and Jimmy Love, in 1879, six years before the FA legitimised professionalism. Suter had moved to the Blackburn Rovers team when it reached the FA Cup final in 1882.

The parallels with today are remarkable. Rovers stole a march on everybody else through money, paying players when it was forbidden. They won the cup three times running, 1884–86, Suter playing in all three. Rovers were the club from the working-class North, paying players, defeating the dribbling game of the ex-public schoolboy amateurs, Royal Engineers and Old Etonians. But when professionalism was legalised, the big city clubs began to pay players as well, and they caught Rovers up. Rovers won the cup again, in 1890 and 1891. But this very beginning of the Football League was their best ever time. Catchment area became the decisive factor then; the more fans, the bigger the gate, the more you could pay players. The big city clubs moved through to dominate. Rovers, from a small town with a big tradition, slipped back to respectable secondary status.

Jack Walker said he wanted to put Rovers where they should be, but that's where they should be, true to their identity, a Blackburn club. History has repeated itself, Blackburn outspending everyone at the birth of the Premier League, then being caught by the big city clubs, making more money, from bigger crowds and Sky and all the other coinery. Newcastle gazump them and Rovers look suddenly small again.

Jack Walker may well have genuinely believed, having amassed his pile of tax-free money, that what he was doing with it was genuinely philanthropic. As an obsessive businessman, maybe he knew nothing else, did not have any other way of thinking about his intentions for the football club, other than to turn it into a business: 'Everything's commercial with Jack,' says Peter Greenwood, former leader of the council. 'Everything at Ewood Park has to wipe its face.'

Maybe it was the job of the custodians, if their roles meant anything, to ensure that the rebuilding was done with benevolence, with care. To look after the club for the town. They may have needed the money, but they were still the club's custodians. Charity is giving, selflessly, to a good cause, not buying the cause. The custodians didn't have to sell lock, stock and barrel to the man. They were there, they knew the club, it was up to them to give sincere thanks for the offer of help, and the money, then to ensure it was spent wisely, for the long term, a bit at a time maybe, where and how it was needed. Taking care, obviously, not to destroy what was good: the traditions, the friendliness, the loyalty. Thank you very much, Mr Walker, they could have said. We'll even name a stand after you.

Instead it has all been done with the hard touch of acquisition. Some reckon, with pay per view coming, Jack might even start making money out of Rovers. 'Nothing wrong with that,' says Dr Jeffries. 'Many people's hobbies turn into profitable businesses.'

But it was not supposed to be Jack Walker's hobby. He was supposed to be 'putting something back into the town'. To some extent, of course, he has. The fans are still grateful to him, for the transformation, for the breathtaking good years. They wouldn't be where they are, they say, without Jack. They'd be down with the Prestons. The club hurtled to the title in the hands of Kenny; it was great, with Shearer, breathtaking. But the football club has become a business. This has undoubted gains: safety, big stadium, glamour. But it has downsides too: high prices, lifelong loyal fans priced out, players paid silly wages, too much money and corporate chat in the air, not enough atmosphere in the ground. Damaged relations with the formerly friendly neighbouring community.

There is an awareness that football has changed, from something which belonged to its people, to a business. And the Blackburn fans are aware that their club has helped to create that change, has embodied it, the excesses of the Premiership, the rising prices, inflated transfer fees, spiralling wages, the unbridgeable inequality opened up between the top clubs and the rest of football. Rovers, pre-Walker, had always been dead against the idea of the Premier League: 'The big clubs want all the money,' chairman Bill Fox had said. 'What's going to happen to the 72 clubs left behind? We've heard stories about clubs going to the wall, but this is reality.'

Peter Greenwood says the change has not brought any wider benefits to the town: 'In a way it has put Blackburn on the map because everybody has heard of Blackburn Rovers,' he says. 'When I go and see the Housing Minister there might be a bit of banter about Shearer or something. But that doesn't influence a decision one jot; how can it? People don't invest in a town because of its football team. It might have cheered local people up when Rovers won the Premiership, but the number of jobs created is nil – except for those at Ewood Park itself, Jack's new business. I think the club should be doing a lot more for the town.'

Making claims that it stands for the town, Blackburn Rovers is Jack Walker's new business. Ewood Park is its monument: large, clinical, the blue glass of countless business parks. A football business. Built in the name of sentiment and philanthropy in the poor town where he was born and made his fortune.

With all its problems, at least it was a club before. The fans who went felt it belonged to them, it was part of their town, hard and honest. It had a soul. The players tried hard, stayed many years, developed an emotional bond with supporters. The ground may have desperately needed rebuilding, the club might have been short of cash. But it was a club with many good things, worth custodian-ing. Now Blackburn Rovers is another Walker business, near his others, the old beast of a steelworks and, on the land he retained, the Walker Industrial Estate. The soul of a football club, communal, loyal, ragged, has been bought now, propelling Rovers to the top of the Premier League, watched from the subdued stands of the House that Jack Built.

5

BLUE AND WHITE AND RED ALL OVER

One of the strange things about Everton Football Club is that, even in the current period of Sky's-the-limit football hype, the eruption of newspaper space and new magazines on the game, you have actually to go there to gain any understanding of the club. Everton, acknowledged, certainly until recently, to be one of the Big Five, has never received the attention routinely dished out to the other major football clubs. Even in 1970, when the Everton 'School of Science' – Ball, Kendall, Harvey – won the League, Bill Shankly stole much of the thunder.

Go to Goodison Park, then, and Everton is a stately surprise, a club of long tradition, a grand dignity seeped into its walls and the narrow streets around the ground. The last 30 years may have been all Liverpool in the publicity stakes, but at Goodison, they know their history. They know they came first. The club was formed at the start of football's spread from the middle class – the public schools and universities – into the urban working classes. The Church, along with schools and some employers, was a major promoter of football, seeing in 'muscular Christianity' the opportunity to encourage physical health and outdoor exercise into the crowded, drink-soaked culture of the inner cities. The football club was formed in 1878 as St Domingo Church Sunday School, changing its name to Everton the following year, after the area of Liverpool in which it played.

In Liverpool, as in all the chaotic, harsh new industrial cities of late

Victorian Britain, football was catching on at phenomenal speed. Richard Holt, history lecturer at the University of Stirling, writing in his book *Sport and the British*, found football attracted the skilled working class, who had more money than the unskilled, and, eventually, a little leisure time. They were drawn to the new game on the Saturday afternoons off, given by factories as the Industrial Revolution matured and treated its workers a little more like human beings, not mere drones. The growth of these cities – Manchester, Birmingham, Liverpool and, later, Newcastle – involved huge traumas. People were uprooted after centuries of relatively peaceful, if hard, rural lives, surrounded by family, church, community. Holt sees the urban attachment to football, erupting in mass, passionate support for the clubs, as an expression of community, by men adrift in these fractured cities:'In a world where industrial production and urban life had cut loose from the more intimate and human scale of the past – where factories employed thousands of men and cities housed hundreds of thousands – supporting a football club offered a reassuring feeling of being part of something . . . Supporters achieved symbolic citizenship.'

In Liverpool, where the work for the masses was in the docks, the dislocation was even more acute. The quaysides offered almost no full-time jobs. Men had to turn up early in the morning hoping to be taken on for the day. The Scousers became a cynical, bolshie lot, starved of even the small securities: the apprenticeships, the regular wages, the potential for promotion, which work in Lancashire cotton mills or Brummie metal-bashers could provide. From the beginning, they loved their football clubs, symbols of Scouse pride and defiance.

In 1884, attendances rising dramatically, Everton Football Club moved on to a field on Anfield Road big enough to enclose, installing turnstiles for a paying gate. The following year, 1885, professionalism was legalised by the Football Association. Three years later, with the clubs finding it difficult to arrange enough fixtures to pay the players' wages, William McGregor, of the Birmingham club Aston Villa, thought up and organised a league, ensuring professional clubs regular fixtures, and therefore regular gate money.

The Football League began on 8 September 1888, one division of 12 professional clubs, all from the North or Midlands. In the order in which they finished after the 22 games of the first season, the 12 were:

Preston North End, Aston Villa, Wolverhampton Wanderers, Blackburn Rovers, Bolton Wanderers, West Bromwich Albion, Accrington Stanley, Everton, Burnley, Derby County, Notts County and Stoke City.

In 1891 Everton won the Football League, pipping Preston, who had won it both previous years. The following year the club's landlord, brewer John Houlding, one of the first football entrepreneurs, wanted to increase the rent. This demand was the last straw for the club, on top of interest payments to Houlding and his monopoly of the Anfield refreshment stands. George Mahon, the organist at St Domingo's Church, found the club a field on Goodison Road, on the north side of Stanley Park from Anfield. It was now, in 1892, that Everton formed a limited company; they retained the church, community ethic, but needed to protect the founding members from the expense of buying and building a brand new ground.

Everton moved to its fresh site at a time when football was taking off. Simon Inglis, in his authoritative book *Football Grounds of Britain*, describes Goodison Park as 'the first purpose-built football ground in England'. Houlding, left at a deserted Anfield, hired a whole new team. Before Jack Walker was so much as a twinkle in a tax haven's airport lounge, Houlding waved his cheque-book to bring a squadful of Scots down to Anfield, the 'team of Macs'. He called this new club Liverpool.

So, however many European Cups and League Championships Liverpool have gone on to win, to Evertonians they will always be upstarts: shallow, commercial pretenders. No amount of Emlyn Hugheses, Kenny Dalglishes or Spice Boys can change that.

'My grandad used to take me to Goodison when I was a young lad,' says Everton supporter Tony Tighe. 'He used to say to me: "Whatever you do, son, don't ever go over to the red shite over there".' Tighe, a grown-up man and successful public relations professional, can still barely understand how Evertonians Steve MacManaman and Robbie Fowler can play for Liverpool.

Phil Redmond, editor of *When Skies Are Grey*, the Everton fanzine, one of the most substantial and wittiest of the breed, is keen to scotch the notion that the Liverpool v. Everton derby is the friendly affair of *Football Focus*, look-at-the-blue-scarves-in-the-Kop legend. Redmond, fourth generation Evertonian, his family's support stretching back to his step-grandfather's father, grew up in Liverpool at a bad time. 'I was at school in the Seventies and early Eighties; Liverpool were winning everything and Everton winning nothing.'

It was hard. Shankly passed on his Championship-winning Liverpool to Bob Paisley, his inscrutable protégé, in 1974. Paisley, a Geordie of few words and quiet certainty, became the most successful manager in English football history. It was a smooth, continuous march, successive teams playing the same passing game, players bought two years early, learning the Liverpool way in the reserves, before stepping up to replace old legs. They hoovered everything: seven League Championships in nine years, four times European Cup winners, the last under Joe Fagan, the next manager to emerge from the Anfield boot room.

'The Liverpool fans thought football was all about winning,' says Redmond, who had it tough at school. 'They were so arrogant. Even the teachers. Everyone knew I was an Evertonian, and there weren't that many of us at that time. We got constant stick. Don't believe all that stuff about the friendly derby. We hate them.'

And all this time, throughout the Shankly and Paisley years of European domination, for 25 years in total, Peter Johnson had a season ticket at Anfield. You imagine Johnson applauding, not cheering exactly, the Liverpool team as they ran round Anfield with their constant stream of trophies. Taking it all in, the fulfilled happiness of the Anfield crowd, without quite being taken in by it himself. 'Oh, I did used to enjoy it,' he demurs. 'We had some very good nights out afterwards.'

Johnson seems to have partaken of his football with a sense of detachment. When he was a kid, he says, he went to Tranmere, the local club, and he remembers 'looking up to the players like gods as they came out on to the cinder track'. When he grew up, he went to Tranmere for a while, then 'a pal' had a spare season ticket for Anfield and he started to go there, in the Fifties, the Billy Liddell era.

Johnson, like many provincial people who make a lot of money, has never lived outside his place of birth. He missed out on National Service, which he still says he regrets, losing out on the chance to get away, enjoy himself with his 'pals'. Instead, he stayed in Birkenhead. He wished he could have stayed on at school, but he wasn't bright enough. So, at 16, he went into his father's butcher's business, being put to making sausages, carving raw meat. He was miserable at times, had fights with his Dad. 'But I loved him, respected him,' he says.

The Johnsons had several shops in Liverpool and Birkenhead, good business in the era of rationing. Peter, a somewhat trapped lad in the Merseyside midle class, knuckled down and looked to make money out of it.

One day when he had been there ten years, a local salesman came in. Over a cup of tea, he told Johnson about food hampers, which were being sold in Liverpool. For a small payment every week, subscribers were given a package of food, some drink and mince pies at Christmas. It was a way for the poor families in economically troubled Merseyside to be sure there'd be food on the table at Christmas. 'Well, I thought that was a good idea,' says Johnson. 'I thought we could do that.'

They put fliers on the shop counters, which were snapped up by Birkenhead's housewives. Then they began to put adverts in the local press. It was excellent business. Presented as a 'savings club', the money came in steadily all year, but Johnson did not have to organise the work, buy the hamper contents or employ anyone until a couple of months before Christmas, when it would all be quickly packed up and sent off to the families. The business grew; they advertised further afield, into Wales, they used an agency system, people selling hamper subscriptions to their friends for small commissions. Soon it was the dominant family business, and Johnson was making a fortune. He floated Park Foods on the Stock Market in 1983, and moved on to a huge site a mile from the end of the motorway, one of the few big companies in the economic wasteland of Birkenhead.

In the early Eighties, after his quarter century of watching Liverpool ('We offered a woman a turkey at Christmas to park in her drive'), Peter Johnson was asked to bail out the local club, Tranmere Rovers, which was crumbling close to insolvency. He enjoyed the involvement of running a football club, the local prestige, the association of himself with the object of supporters' hopes. He built up the ground and financed a team-building which took the club from the Fourth Division to the brink of the First. But not quite. 'I realised that with Everton and Liverpool close by, Tranmere were never going to be in that league.'

In 1993, Sir John Moores died. He was another Liverpool

businessman who had built an empire on small weekly payments, having copied the idea for the pools from the early attempts of a man called John Jervis Barnard in Birmingham. Moores started it as a sideline with two friends in February 1924, calling the scheme Littlewoods after one of the chaps' surname. After early losses, halfway through the 1924-25 season, the other two dropped out. John pressed on. Over the decades, he transformed the weekly subscriptions into a three-cornered empire: pools, retailing and mail order. During the Fifties and Sixties, with the incipient collapse of the docks, the people of Liverpool clung fervently to their football. Sir John, a local emperor, becoming one of Merseyside's most important employers, understood the importance of football to the city. He bought a controlling share of Everton Football Club. He also bought some shares in Liverpool, which is now majority-owned by David Moores, his grand-nephew, inheritor of a slice of the Littlewoods family fortune.

John Moores was intent on making Everton a top footballing power again. At the time a football club was not a way of making money, it was a way of spending money made in real life. Gates were high, but turnstiles charged only shillings, and commercial activities were minimal. Merchandising was not a word heard above the clatter of club rattles. Everton opinions vary about the true quality of Sir John's rule in retrospect, but he did underwrite Harry Catterick's big-name signings for the championship-winning side, including the then record-breaking £110,000 for Alan Ball in 1966, earning the club the nickname 'The millionaires'.

By the time he died Sir John had been ill a long time. He had never believed in flotation for Littlewoods, because it involves handing control of a company to the faceless institutions and money men of the City of London. Littlewoods had become the largest family-owned company in England, left to his children, John junior, Peter, Janatha and Betty, Lady Grantchester.

His instructions for Everton, which his children did not want to finance, was that the Moores legacy be succeeded by 'a safe pair of hands', who would 'have Everton's best interests at heart', and not 'use the club for a speculative purpose'.

The family asked the board of directors for its ideas for the future of the club. At the time, the best word to describe Everton, chaired by

David Marsh, a Liverpool GP, and with ex-Littlewoods, future North-West Water executive Desmond Pitcher among the directors, was stagnation. Howard Kendall's very good, potentially great 1985 Championship-winning team, Reid, Bracewell, Sharp, Andy Gray, Ratcliffe and the rest, had been, much to Evertonians' eternal disgust, banned from Europe as a result of the Heysel disaster, caused by fighting Liverpool fans. They won the League again in 1987 with mostly the same talented team, but after Kendall's departure and the appointment of Colin Harvey that year, Everton slumped badly, replacing excellent footballers with only decent players, all at once. In Merseyside's continuing economic depression, gates slumped to the lows of the pre-Kendall era. On 4 December 1993, a home game against Southampton was watched by 13,667 people at an echoing Goodison.

Peter Johnson stepped into the vacuum, offering to invest in Everton, take it over. At the same time a consortium had formed with the same idea: Tony Tighe, Mike Dyble and Tom Cannon, Manchester-based Scousers and lifelong Evertonians, the money coming in from builder Arthur Abercromby and theatre impresario Bill Kenwright. The consortium stressed the broad nature of their combined skills and made proposals for investment, commercial development and a future flotation, in a manifesto entitled *Nil Satis Nisi Optimum*, after the club motto: 'Only the best is good enough.'

They pitted their impeccable Evertonian credentials against Johnson, season-ticket holder at Anfield throughout the years of Red supremacy. Johnson, with bags of money, played the media better; he was local, a big cheese. The *Liverpool Echo* ran a piece on his opposition, dismissing them as 'The Manchester Consortium'.

The fight was bitter at times, Johnson waging a single-minded battle to win individual control of the club. The various eras since the men of St Domingo's had formed their company in 1892 had produced 2,498 shares, 1,000 of them owned by the Moores family, 400 on the 'dead register', the remaining 1,000 owned by a shoal of others, sentimental holders of Everton birth certificates.

Both Johnson's and the consortium's proposals were to put money into the club by way of a rights issue. This meant that each shareholder would be entitled to buy one extra share for each one currently owned. The capital of the company – the number of shares

– would therefore double, to 5,000. The family would choose its own investor, on the advice of the board. The consortium's September 1993 plan was for £2,000 to be paid for each new share. The family would take up their rights to 1,000 new shares, putting in £2m. Allowing for some smaller shareholders to take up some rights, the consortium would take up the rest, bringing another £3m into the club.

Bid and counter-bid in a furious war saw the price pushed up, Johnson going up to £3,000 per share. The family nevertheless decided to back the consortium, believing the five's lifelong support for Everton was more important than an extra couple of million pounds here or there. Lady Grantchester, on behalf of the family, signed an agreement to vote for the consortium's proposals.

Johnson upped his offer to £4,000 per share, a total of £10m hamper money for Everton. He was, he said, determined to get the club. If the price went up again, he'd put in another £10m, then another, if necessary.

'That blew us out of the water,' says Tighe sadly. Kenwright, a director, could have swung it their way in one board meeting, but he had not wanted to. 'Bill didn't want a public row – that's why we didn't go to the press much. He wanted the board to be unanimous. As he saw it, he didn't want Everton's name to be dragged through controversy.'

The consortium had lost its unity by February 1994. Kenwright did not want to fight, Abercromby had been courted. Johnson took them all to Prenton Park, to see the fine job he'd done at Tranmere. That evening, Tighe, Dyble and Cannon went back to Tighe's house and signed away their rights to the family's agreement. The signatures were witnessed at 11.45 p.m. by a taxi-driver, who had come to take Cannon home.

Even the accountant who advised the board to vote for Johnson, Peter Shennan of Coopers & Lybrand in Liverpool, said this process, a rights issue, major shareholders being advised by a board of directors, is not appropriate to a football club: 'People buy and hold shares in football clubs because they are fans. Football clubs were never intended to be anything other than clubs. It is something of an anomaly that they are limited companies, and that the shares are tradeable. This means that company law applies, imposing on the directors the duty to act in the club's best interests as if it were an ordinary commercial company. And so they cannot really base their decision, in law, on anything other than how much money is on offer from the two different parties.'

And so five people with a range of relevant and useful skills – public relations, advertising, management, building and entertainment promotion, over a century of Everton support between them, blue-blooded – lost out to a Liverpool supporter who had more money, a fortune built on hampers for the families of Merseyside.

I interviewed Johnson at Park Foods in the summer of 1994, just after his triumph. Driving in off the decay of Birkenhead, I was guided to his office. He was sitting behind his desk, wearing a black pinstripe suit. 'Everton is an absolute giant of a club,' he said. 'When the opportunity came up to buy it, I wasn't going to miss it. I would've bought it whatever the price.'

I asked him why, after going to Anfield all those years, he'd wanted to buy Everton. 'You should not confuse being a fan with ownership of a club,' he said. 'My loyalty is to wherever I happen to be at the time. You can move your passions.'

A new one, this, to football supporters. Johnson denied he was in it just for the money. It was obvious, and he did not try to deny, that the breakaway of the big clubs to form the Premier League, which meant they had to divvy up Sky's £305m only amongst themselves, had transformed underfinanced football clubs into potentially very profitable companies. His £10m, big in the short term, could be worth much more if he built up the club, then took it on to the Stock Exchange.

But talking to him, it emerged that he was in it for more than money alone. 'It's a rich man's hobby,' he said. He became animated for the first time. He said he liked the 'clamour' of the crowd going to the game, the noise. His eyes flashed a little, he clenched his fists. He cited an L.S. Lowry painting, *Going to the Match*, which captured the pre-match tension and jangling nerves. 'Football can make or break the dreams of 40,000 people,' he said.

And so Johnson revealed his motives to be as much in keeping with the Sir John Moores local-emperor tradition of football-club owner-ship as the get-rich-quick motives of some more recent arrivals. Hampers were all very well, good business, good money. And money brought you power, status. But if you wanted the Scousers' hearts, you needed to own their football club.

A coach cruised slowly beneath his window. 'That'll be Tranmere's reserve side,' he mused, peering out, the man who bought his football club as a training ground at the bottom of his road.

As I was leaving, he called me back. 'You know about Nightfreight, do you?' Nightfreight turned out to be an overnight delivery company in which he'd taken a 33 per cent stake for £500,000 in 1987. The company had just floated on the Stock Exchange, in May 1994, valued at £50m. He'd made a capital gain of around £16m.

'You're going to float Everton, aren't you?' I asked.

'It's nowhere near ready for a float,' he said, not dismissing the possibility.

I remember finding something chilling about Johnson, although he is personally pleasant, charming. Birkenhead is one of the most depressed places in Britain, a dry dock, shipbuilding port which has built no ships for years. The Cammell Laird yard is a mere wafer compared to the massive employment cake it used to provide. Birkenhead is pockmarked with dereliction; industry has gone and not cleaned up after itself; great hulking container tanks stand rusting by the harbour. Scrap land scars the place; many houses are boarded up. It has long been an unemployment disaster; adult men and women are around on the streets at all times during the day. In the Eighties, Birkenhead had the worst heroin addiction problem in the country.

And there was Johnson in the middle of it, in his pinstripe suit, on the phone to his City brokers, wanting to own the dreams of the local people.

I went back to see him for an interview for this book. This time I had a tour of the hamper works. A very nice woman took me round. She liked Johnson. 'He's a friend as well as a boss,' she said.

She left me waiting by a sparse-looking canteen, near the clocking-in cards, while she fetched a white coat for me to put on. Young girls in hairnets, some lads in hats, were sitting in there eating their sandwiches. 'Are you an inspector?' they wondered.

'No, I'm a journalist. I've come to interview Mr Johnson.'

'Well, tell him the pay's crap,' said one, and they all laughed.

Inside, a hundred people were packing Harley Davidson deodorant and L'Oréal two-for-the-price-of-one shampoo bottles into boxes. It wasn't the Christmas season, but Park Foods now does contract-packing during the rest of the year. At Christmas they need up to 300 workers, whom they get through the Job Centre. Barely a single job offered is full time. They get inundated with applications.

'We get 500 to 600 boys, looking for three months' work,' said my guide. 'We can't even see all of them. Mostly they are young, 16–17, but we get grown men who've worked for years and been made redundant. It's very menial work. It's very sad really.' She told me that Johnson pays packers £2.75 per hour. Supervisors get £3.25 per hour. One of the lads had an Everton shirt on. Average ticket price in 1996–97 was £13.

The reception to the Park Foods offices, through the automatic doors and on to the settee by the pot plant, offers a small selection of magazines to Mr Johnson's visitors. One is *Queste: The Official Magazine for Rolls-Royce and Bentley Owners* (Summer 1996 edition). Then there is the *Veuve Clicquot Magazine*, with a cover picture of two white women on camels at the Egyptian pyramids, drinking champagne. Nigel Burgess' *Yacht Charter 1997* and *ET* – the Executive Travel Magazine, February 1997, complete the broad-based reading matter at the corporate headquarters of the chairman of Everton Football Club.

Johnson took me into a boardroom this time, five chairs along each side of a long, curved table, one at each end. He turned the spotlights on with remote control. On the walls of this Birkenhead power centre were classic English pastoral watercolours: sheep grazing in gentle valleys, babbling brooks. Johnson poured the coffee and sat down. There was an air of world-weariness since I saw him last. He looked a lot older.

For the first time in years, Park Foods' profits dropped in 1996, falling 30 per cent to £9.5m. Its share price had fallen, the value of the company dropping from £194m to around £80m. Johnson blames the introduction of the National Lottery, which has seen his poor customers put their one pounds on the it-could-be-you, one-in-14,000,000 chance of a completely new life, rather than on the mundane certainty of a turkey at Christmas. 'It's the something-for-nothing society,' sneered Johnson, sitting in his spotlit boardroom. No, he says, impatiently, to my question, it isn't that the Lottery appeals to the desperation of poor people in a world of dole and low pay. 'No, I know my customers. They want something for nothing.'

The Lottery, unsurprisingly, has also laid waste Sir John Moores' old empire, Littlewoods having laid off 3,000 of its 4,000 pools workers in Liverpool, which, with unemployment of 12 per cent, can ill-afford it. Camelot, apparently, employs 400 people nationwide.

Johnson, £216,000 salary, including pension, in 1996, will be affected by a minimum wage, which will mean his company, turnover £160m, will have to pay its packers a few more pennies. For the moment, he is looking to revive Park Foods with frozen chips, which will be flavoured, heated up as fast food in pubs. Cheese and onion, scampi and lemon, garlic and herb flavour infused chips: his Big Idea – DJ Spuddles Original Gourmet Fries. The project, though, has so far not lit up the eyes of drinkers with the munchies quite in the way predicted by Johnson and Cliff Finch, his marketing director. They hired a building firm, Tysons, which was known around Merseyside to be on the brink of going bust, and it duly went into receivership in May 1995, halfway through the work. It took nine months to find another builder. Johnson then insisted the factory would be churning out the washed, sliced, microwaved, mashed, extruded, baked and frozen chips by Christmas 1995. In the event, the first fragrant spuddles did not emerge until January 1997. At the time of writing, besides a test marketing exercise in some Scottish pubs, Park Foods have sold only 350 cases of these microwaveables, representing just over a quarter of a single day's production. You can smell them being infused as you walk round Park Foods.

Last year Johnson negotiated seriously to sell Park Foods, but the talks foundered, said to be because the proposed buyer, former director Stuart Marks, offered only the cost of the chip-making equipment, not the value of the next great fast food craze. Johnson stayed on and Marks left.

Had Johnson sold, he would have concentrated on Everton, such has been the Stock Exchange's interest in football in the three years since Johnson won the club. Last year he bought John Moores junior's shares for around £1.25m, upping his stake to 66 per cent. The club then had a second rights issue, entitling each shareholder to buy six shares, for £500 each, for every one held. This meant Everton's capital increased from 5,000 shares, to 35,000 shares. Johnson took up all his rights, paying another £10m. He says, still, that he is not ready yet to float the club, but, given the salivations of the moneymen for pay per view, Everton shares are trading, at the time of writing, at £3,000 each. With 35,000 shares, this values Everton at £105m. Johnson's 66 per cent, for which he has paid around £20m, is now worth £70m, a gain of £50m, personally, in three years.

Football was a ready-made business, the supporters having proved their loyalty over more than a century. The City analyses football fans' support as 'brand loyalty', their demand as 'inelastic'. This means that clubs can raise ticket prices dramatically but the supporters need their football, are loyal to it, they still come. Supporters are prepared to buy stuff with the club badge on it, and the City is really rubbing its hands at the promise that the fans can be made to pay per view. That, they believe, will bring real, digital fortunes for the owners of the clubs. That is why the City is prepared to pay £3,000 for a single share in Everton, which has not been particularly successful under Johnson. Joe Royle took them to the FA Cup in 1995, surprisingly beating Man United, but he has departed now, in a puff of slump around Goodison. Johnson has, though, appointed Cliff Finch as commercial director, and opened a shop.

I asked Johnson about brand. The football world is always talking about it. What did it mean?

'We have a brand Marks and Spencer and Burton's would die for,' he said. 'People will buy things with the club's badge on. When we have an Everton fan young, we have him for life.'

So how come that didn't happen to him? How come he, of all Merseysiders, could watch the great Liverpool sides of the Sixties, Seventies and Eighties, then 'move his passions'?

'I don't know,' he smiled.

Is it that football fans are actually mad, I asked, that it's a stupid thing, supporting the same football club all your life, regardless of how well it's doing? Is it that the fans are stupid and you're sensible?

'You said that,' he smiled, 'not me.'

How can you justify making so much money out of Everton?

'I never knew I would,' he said. 'Who could have known the City would fall so in love with football?'

'You knew,' I said. 'When I was here in 1994 you knew what you'd got. You'd got a sleeping giant. You were going to wake it up and float it.'

'No, I didn't know. Someone like Alan Sugar, he's shrewd, he knew from the beginning what was going to happen. I didn't.'

Johnson said he was 'pals' with Doug Ellis, chairman of Aston Villa; they meet when they go sailing on their yachts. 'I met Jack Walker last year, on holiday in Barbados.'

I'm just asking, I said, just for the book, how people like you justify making so much money out of football, when supporters regard Everton as their club, not as some business for an individual to make money out of.

'I didn't know I would make money,' he repeated softly. 'It was an accident.'

'Why do you keep trying to tell me that?' I asked.

'Because if I keep selling you the idea,' he said, 'you might buy it.'

I don't buy it at all. Football has brought fortunes to these businessmen. They saw it as underexploited. They knew it was immensely popular, even in the dark days of hooliganism and after the disaster of Hillsborough. There was phenomenal 'brand loyalty'. When Sky put £305m into only 22 clubs, who had created the conditions for not having to share it round at all, businessmen woke up to football as an emerging industry. The same money would have come pouring in if there had been a similar satellite television interest in overnight freight companies. The City's interest has exceeded expectations, because football has entered a period of boom and middle-class acceptability, but it was easy, basic business. Takeovers of sleeping giants, to be woken up by dollops of cash from the outside. Helped immeasurably by a worshipful press, whose back pages know nothing about what moves businessmen, who have welcomed them uncritically, and who give their product, football, endless pages of gushing, hyping free space.

But in fact it has not been all plain sailing for Peter Johnson, hence the weariness. The football business is not now merely a matter of sitting back and collecting the money. After Joe Royle left, Johnson's search for a manager made the farce sections of the sports pages. Johnson went on the Bobby Robson run, coming back empty-handed, another local chieftain surprised Robson could be happy at a foreign club like Barcelona. Thought he'd be dying to come home. Johnson then hit on the idea of Andy Gray, who has talked a good game for years now in Sky's tabloidised football coverage. Johnson appeared to agree with the English chairman's traditionally low opinion of the football manager's art, believing training to be unnecessary, just a former career as a player and an apparent capacity to bollock people. Luckily, Gray himself had second thoughts, and stayed to up his share of the Murdoch shilling. Johnson went back to the man he had turned down, the thrice-returning Howard Kendall, hoping for the triumphs of his wonderful first spell, not the imploding mess of his second.

Despite having no manager, a threadbare squad, no reserve-team manager, Johnson presented the fans in 1996-97 with a proposal to leave Goodison and purpose-build a brand new 60,000-seat 'superstadium' for the club. He did not yet have a site, but he produced a sketch. It looked like one of those grounds you'd get in *Roy of the Rovers*, packed with people wearing scarves, dotted with speech bubbles saying things like: 'Roy's going to get his third and put Melchester through!'

I asked Johnson why he wanted to move the club. He said: 'Because at Goodison we cannot incorporate the revenue streams needed to compete.'

Revenue streams. One of the buzz phrases of football in the Nineties, ranking just behind 'brand loyalty', just ahead of 'quality product', and well ahead of 'we are custodians of the football club for the town', which you never hear any more in the Premier League. Johnson has already built a big shop, so he can only mean revenue from catering and executive boxes. Historic Goodison is tightly embraced by pubs, rich with decades of fans' custom. Moving to a site in the middle of nowhere, the club would get all this food and drink money. And boxes, silly money from the corporations. Even though the Goodison capacity is 40,000, it is hard to develop it, he says, to incorporate the glass boxes in which suits like to entertain.

A campaign, 'Goodison for Everton', was set up by some fans to fight the move. They hung banners with the slogan: 'A hamper is for Christmas, Goodison is for life.'

Johnson dismissed them as 'sentimentalists'. Following a vote, with brochures, including the sketch of Melchester Rovers' old ground and a voting form, issued at the turnstiles at the Chelsea home match on 11 May 1997, 22,600 people voted, a stunning 84 per cent of them supporting the move. Phil Redmond, whose postbag at *When Skies Are Grey* registered a similar majority, believes Everton fans, aware of their traditions and many disappointments, scared of being left behind, have voted for the dream, of a new stadium and a fresh start. As in 1892. A move for the millennium. Head off for *Roy of the Rovers* land.

'Personally, I voted against,' says Redmond. 'I believe in Goodison as a place of tradition, very many people over the years having lived for the place, had their ashes scattered there. I think Goodison is a very important part of being an Everton supporter. Johnson hadn't convinced me that Goodison couldn't have been developed.

'But I do believe in progress. If I really thought Everton were going to get a fantastic new stadium, I would have voted for the move. I think he's genuine, wants Everton to be successful, but is he going to bring off this stadium?'

Johnson is not a property developer. He has not accumulated the nous and nose and political contacts garnered over the years by professional developers. His last building project was the DJ Spuddles Original Gourmet Fries factory, and there is not too much revenue streaming out of that so far. Surprisingly, Redmond does not hold Johnson's Red past against him, or the moneymaking. 'Our attitude at the magazine when we met Johnson was, fine, he's loaded. He can make loads of money out of Everton. If it makes Everton successful, then we're all happy. But I just don't think he understands Everton, as a club. Or Everton fans.

'It's like the merchandise. We pride ourselves on having a bit of style. Everton fans have never sung much at matches. We used to wear little badges. We're not against commercialism, merchandise, you have to have it. But in our shop there's just a load of generic crap you get everywhere. You go to away matches and you see the same minging stuff with other clubs' badges on. I don't want to see the Everton crest on a piece of chocolate. I want something a little bit of thought has gone into, in keeping with the tradition of Everton.'

An emerging pattern of England's top football clubs is that they are coming to reflect the styles and personalities of the thrusting, acquisitive businessmen who have taken them over and turned them into their own businesses. Everton fans are not protesting about Johnson's takeover at just the right time, tripling his millions in three years. They are more concerned about his personality, his style. Having shown himself strangely unmoved in the heart by years of watching football, developing no passionate attachment to Liverpool, now here he is with a grand scheme, talking about a superstadium for Everton Football Club. Some supporters are questioning his capacity to do it, to produce something up to the grandeur of the Everton tradition. Steeped in generations of support at the dignified, historic club, *Nil Satis Nisi Optimum*, the supporters worry now for Everton's future, cut adrift from Goodison Park, sailing off to new revenue streams, steered by the skipper from Birkenhead.

6

THE DOUG ELLIS CHAPTER

When you meet the man, you need no reminding of his name. He's a familiar face, glowing, paunchy, a bespectacled picture of good feeding and wealthy living. On a chilly Birmingham morning, a permanent-looking tan overlays his face. He is a smooth, soft talker. His office is a cosy den: nice big desk, pictures of the family and of him fishing. A large selection of spirits for evening snifters. If you were in any doubt as to his identity, he provides a helpful reminder. There, on the pocket of his yellow striped shirt, sits a discreet, curly-scripted monogram: HDE. This is, of course, none other than Herbert Douglas Ellis, the chairman of Aston Villa Football Club.

Ellis, who apparently prefers to be known by his middle name, made his money in package holidays in the Fifties, at the beginning of that industry's boom. He first bought into Birmingham City in the Sixties, and was a director at St Andrews for three years. In 1968, the opportunity arose to get into Aston Villa. As always with football clubs, it came about because the club was in trouble. Ellis loaned Villa £100,000, with the option of converting the money into shares. He also became a director.

Aston Villa did, therefore, exist for a little time before Doug Ellis became its chairman. The club was originally founded in 1874 by members of the Villa Cross Wesleyan Chapel. In the early 1880s, William McGregor, a Methodist who ran a small draper's shop in the grim, rough area of Newtown, became interested in the emerging game of football. By the late 1870s, McGregor was firmly involved with Villa, a local team. As football grew in popularity, McGregor was an early supporter of the need for working men to be paid for the time devoted to playing the game in front of rapidly multiplying crowds.

In 1888, with friendlies awkward to arrange and subject to cancellation, McGregor invited other professional clubs to join Villa in forming the professional Football League. It is thought to have been the very first league in the world, although some believe McGregor borrowed the idea from American baseball. During the first season, on 31 January 1889, Aston Villa formed a limited liability company, to manage and protect members against the expenses incurred developing their grounds at Perry Barr. Under the committed, Christian direction of McGregor, Villa were phenomenally successful. They won the League five times between 1894 and 1900. Since then, they have only won it twice, in 1910 and 1981, just before the club was taken over by Ellis.

He says that he did not in 1968 become involved in Aston Villa with any thought that he would personally make money out of it: 'No, I had enough money. The motivation was to be involved in football, in some way. I hadn't been good enough as a player. I'm a frustrated player, really.'

Before the Sky TV money turned football from a poorly run game to an industry in which entrepreneurs could make fortunes, there was a mixture of motivations leading people to become directors or shareholders of clubs. Few made money out of it; you couldn't legitimately, because of FA rules and because the clubs were not run to make profits. The shares would maintain their value, because the clubs were cherished institutions, but they weren't traded in rapid style. Football was a rich man's hobby, a way to 'put something back' into the community, be of public service. Some found football an excellent means of social climbing. The fame, for rich but obscure men, was a boost to the ego. It was a kind of power, particularly in the provinces, where football was the urban lifeblood, and a means of reflected glory. The chairman as frustrated footballer is a recognisable sub-breed; people who played the game as kids but were not good enough to make it. Knowing its magic, they looked to be involved in another way. Some such people become referees or run Sunday teams; others get rich and buy clubs. Ron Noades of Crystal Palace admits to this motivation. Irving Scholar had something of that in him.

Few of them, though, go to the lengths of Doug. Noades' office at Palace is a portakabin, a stern working-place, the only books on the shelves a series of *Rothmans Football Yearbooks* in date order. Ornaments consist of two flat footballs on a shelf. Ellis has positively hoarded stuff to swell a huge trophy cabinet in his warm room. Among the cut glass, the gleaming silver, the pennants from Juventus and AC Milan, are trophies from some of Villa's finest hours, Coca-Cola and FA Cup replicas.

In 1972 Ellis had a row with another director, who accused him of taking too much personal glory. Although this is difficult to imagine, he was nearly forced to resign. In 1975, he did resign as chairman, saying then he needed to spend more time with his businesses. In 1979 he had a fight with the then major shareholders, Ron and Donald Bendall, arguing they had too much of a share in Villa, which made the club less democratic. The issue went to a vote, in which, bizarrely, the winner would buy the loser's shares. Ellis lost.

He sold the option on his shares to Bendall and left the club. For a brief spell he was involved at Wolves, another great footballing institution in the West Midlands. While Ellis was away, Aston Villa, with a perfectly balanced team, monumental at the back, workaholics Mortimer and Bremner in the engine room, the striking partnership of Withe and Shaw fed by a dancing Tony Morley on the wing, swept to the League Championship. The following year, Ron Saunders' successor, the unassuming Tony Barton, led Villa to the greatest triumph in their history, the European Cup.

Back home, Villa were involved in a financial scandal, the police investigating contracts for building work at Villa Park. Doug Ellis came riding back in. He bought out the Bendalls, capturing 42 per cent of Villa for himself. He still refuses to disclose what he paid, but he hints that the commonly quoted figure, £500,000, is not far from correct.

Since he has been there, Ellis is generally thought to have done a reasonable job of running Villa, which he has done full time since 1982. Although many fans talk grudgingly about him, at least, they admit, they enjoy a good team, managed by Brian Little, whom they adore, in a Villa Park which has been rebuilt, in a mishmash maybe, but with at least some nod to history.

William McGregor does not lack for a memorial. The restaurant at Villa Park, reopened recently, is named after him: McGregor's. A fine gesture. It offers, according to its flyer, 'The perfect venue to the local business community to wine and dine clients or key personnel. Book your table at McGregor's – it makes perfect business sense.'

Above the fireplace in the restaurant is a large oil painting of McGregor, gilt-framed. He looks a gentle, worldly Victorian, with pale green eyes, full white beard. A watch chain nestles beneath his greatcoat. From that little corner, McGregor watches benignly over a new generation of Brummies, ordering from the menu (businessman's special £7.50) over fags and pints of lager.

Larger parts of the ground are dedicated to another great figure in Aston Villa's and English football's history. A whole stand, a somewhat nondescript post-Taylor effort which replaced the old Witton Lane Stand, has been named after this man. It is the first stand you see from the road, his name the first sight of Villa Park. A monument to a man during his own lifetime, the stand was unveiled in 1993 with huge purple letters on the side. THE DOUG ELLIS STAND, it proclaims proudly, to all who come to Villa.

The monuments to him do not stop there. Villa Park contains 71 executive boxes, ranging in price from £12,000 for the season to £26,000. In the North Stand, local companies may pay for the privilege of doing their corporate entertaining in any of the glass boxes, with armchairs, christened 'The Doug Ellis Executive Boxes'. Pictures of the great man decorate the famous ground. Here's Doug in the directors' guest lounge, depicted in a watercolour by someone called Keith T. Smith. Here in the boardroom is a photograph of the fellow, H.D. Ellis, large, smiling, framed, alongside huge pictures of his fellow directors.

So Doug Ellis got plenty of fulfilment and profile and enjoyment from being involved with Villa. He is on all sorts of committees at the FA, including the 'Instructional' committee, responsible for youth development, and the international committee, whose members take turns to go away with England. The intention, he repeated, was never to make money for himself.

Late in 1996, he decided that Aston Villa should float on the Stock Exchange. The reason for this, said the prospectus, was to raise £5.5m to complete the Holte Suite – a new conference and banqueting area under the Holte End – and to install giant video screens. A further £10m of new money would be spent on players. The total value of the club would be £126m, including the shares issued for the £15.5m new money.

Aston Villa plc eased on to the Stock Market on 7 May 1997, elegant as Dwight Yorke in full flow, smooth as the head waiter in McGregor's. Ellis put 363,636 of his shares on to the market at the flotation price of £11, making himself an immediate £4m. This left him with 3,828,064 shares at £11 each, 33.4 per cent of the company. Ellis' personal holding, bought from Ron Bendall after the 1982 European Cup victory for £500,000, was now worth £42m.

On the way to Villa Park, I got slightly lost, ending up in the middle of an industrial estate, beneath a motorway flyover. It was just what you'd expect in Birmingham: heavy industry, engineering works, an unlovely, hard-working crush, no frills. There was a workman's cafe, Sophie's, so I went in to ask for directions. A few blokes in oil-grimed overalls were drinking 40p mugs of tea, eating breakfasts, reading the papers, taking hard-earned breaks, talking in a desultory, knackered kind of way, smoking.

'Why yer going there, mate?' asked one of the blokes. 'Is there a match on?'

No, I said, I had an appointment with Doug Ellis.

'Ask him about his bleedin' shares,' he muttered.

So the first thing I did was ask him about his shares: 'How can you justify making so much money out of owning Aston Villa?'

He was seamlessly smooth and unflapped: 'It's just paper money. I only sold the £4m worth because the brokers said they needed it to make a market. Anyway, all 300 shareholders at the EGM agreed.' He went on to tell a story, spread widely at the time, of 'a little old lady' going into the brokers, asking if her 15 shares, bought for £5 in the Sixties, were worth anything. It turned out to make her, too, a paper millionaire.

Yes, I said, but of course all 300 shareholders agreed, because they stood to make money as well. What about your average fan, the bloke in the cafe, how can you reconcile his conception of what Villa is, a football club, belonging to its fans, with you making £46m out of it?

'It is not real money,' he smiled. 'It's just a row of noughts. I will never forget that football is the working man's game.'

Besides the new valuation of his ownership of Villa, Doug Ellis, in 1996, paid himself a salary of £128,000. In 1997, he is to get a 17 per cent pay rise, to £150,000. It is a two-year fixed contract which can then be terminated on a year's notice. He also gets, from the club, 'a fully expensed car', health insurance and home telephone expenses.

When I walked in, Ellis was looking at a glossy brochure from some estate agents called Saville's. A huge Tudor farmhouse pile was pictured, in acres of lush ground. It was a property called the Carrington Hall Estate. 'I'm thinking of buying it,' he was musing. 'Only thing is, I'll need a helicopter to get me to Villa Park.'

He was unbudging on the question of whether it was right that he should make so much out of the working man's game – particularly when the working man, often now on poorly paid, short-term contracts, is having to pay continually increased prices for football match tickets. He had never, he repeated, gone into football to make money. 'Anyway,' he said, 'at the time I did invest, there was a wealth tax. So I couldn't have got my money out.'

'Don't you think,' I asked, 'that perhaps there should be a wealth tax now, given how much you and your fellow bosses are making out of football?'

It was the only question which made Douglas Ellis pause, all warm, cosy, in his trophy-laden lair. He stuttered, speechless for a second, before dismissing taxation as not a question for him. I thought I saw his suntan blanch, just for a moment.

7

HILLSBOROUGH

Philip Hammond was only 13 in 1988, still probably too young to be allowed to go to the FA Cup semi-final that year between Nottingham Forest and his beloved Liverpool. As it turned out, the semi-deatched house in Aigburth, Liverpool, where Philip lived with his parents, Phil and Hilda, and brother Graham, ten, never rang with the peals of teenage disappointment, the firm beat of parents putting their feet down. Philip was a drummer in the Liverpool Boys Brigade band; the band had reached their own finals in Blackpool, to be held on the same day. Philip had to go to play in the band, and that was that.

The following year, 1989, the band reached Blackpool again, and Liverpool the semi-final, but this time there was no clash. Liverpool, with the Barnes, Beardsley, Aldridge team performing to its scintillating peak, would meet Forest again, at Hillsborough, on 15 April. The Boys Brigade band finals were not till the week after.

Philip was 14, old enough to go. He was excited, scrubbing his golf clubs the day before, knowing he'd be too tired after the match to clean them ready for a round on the Sunday.

'He loved all sports,' Phil Hammond senior says of his son, 'but he lived for football. He was a very good player himself, a striker, and he lived for Liverpool Football Club.'

Phil, manager of a district post office, used to take his son to Anfield as a child, but for a couple of years the youngster had stood on the Kop with his friends. Phil, knowing the boys' favoured spot, used to look over to them from his seat in the Kemlyn Road Stand. Philip and his friend from the Boys Brigade, Ian Southgate, and two other lads, had queued up for their £6 Leppings Lane terrace tickets for the semi-final, and saved £8 for the coach over to Sheffield. It was his first ever away match.

Many Liverpool fans had complained about Hillsborough as the choice of ground again. Sheffield was a lot further for them to travel to than for the Nottingham people, who had only to pop up the M1. Those who had been the previous year knew that 24,000 Liverpool fans had to fill the whole of the north and west ends of the ground through only 23 turnstiles. They complained that Forest had been given the Spion Kop again, with more turnstiles and room for 21,000 to stand, but that the Leppings Lane terrace was small and nasty, with room for only 10,000, forcing many more Liverpool fans to pay for seats. Liverpool Football Club itself had put these points to the FA, arguing that Old Trafford, more central and much neater a ground, would have been fairer. But the phone call protesting the decision, from Liverpool's chief executive Peter Robinson to Graham Kelly, chief executive of the FA, had never been put to the relevant FA committee.

Hillsborough was retained, according to Kelly, because 'the 1988 match had been considered a successfully managed event'. The Liverpool supporters would have disputed that assessment, but none could possibly have imagined that they were heading, in their cars and coaches, to a deathtrap.

Philip, like the rest of the Liverpool supporters making their way excitedly across the Pennines that fine spring morning, was looking forward only to the match. He, like most supporters, would never have heard even of the existence of the Home Office Guide to Safety at Sports Grounds – the 'Green Guide' – introduced in 1973 to prevent a recurrence of the Ibrox disaster in which 66 supporters died in a crush or that the Green Guide forced football clubs, for the first time, to have Safety Certificates, itemising the layout of their grounds, their capacities, crush barriers, entrances and exits, methods of counting fans in via turnstiles to monitor when the various parts of the ground were full. Nor could they have known that Sheffield Wednesday Football Club had failed to comply with it; that Dalglish's team was to be playing in a ground which was in vital respects in breach of the framework governing safety at football grounds.

Some may have faintly recalled that in 1981, at the FA Cup semi-final at Hillsborough between Spurs and Wolves, there had been a near-fatal crush, caused as a result of fans arriving late on to the Leppings Lane terrace. That 38 people were treated, either by St John's Ambulance or in hospital, for broken arms, legs and ribs.

They were not to know that since then, in 1981 and 1985, the Leppings Lane terrace had been divided into seven separate 'pens', at the insistence of police, looking to have better 'control' of supporters, and to be able to segregate them. Fences were built to create these pens, straight up the terrace from the perimeter fence at the front. These changes made the capacity of Leppings Lane significantly lower than the 10,100 stated on the Safety Certificate, and in any case made the total capacity less important for safety purposes than accurate capacity figures for the individual pens. None of the people fidgeting excitedly, singing, joking, on their way across the Pennines, could have known that all these changes had been made without incorporating any way of counting how many supporters had entered the individual pens and therefore whether they were full.

The supporters who'd gone in 1988 would have remembered the ground's narrow entrance gates outside on Leppings Lane itself, and the too few turnstiles. Some may have been involved in the crush which had happened there, outside the ground, that year. Many will have recalled the tunnel leading from the turnstiles on to the Leppings Lane terrace, 23 metres of darkness with a one in six downhill slope. They may even have felt the two low brick walls on each side of the end of the tunnel, which acted as rails, pushing them naturally straight ahead rather than to the sides. But they could not have known that the crush barriers preventing a headlong fall forward from the back had been removed in 1985 and 1986.

Young Philip Hammond, 14, good footballer, good pupil, Boys Brigade drummer, a lad with a brimming personality and keen sense of right and wrong, excited, going to his first away match, was not to know that no changes had been made at all to Sheffield Wednesday's Safety Certificate since 1979, not even to amend the capacity figures. Or that for the last three years, the Safety Certificate had been buried in the understaffed bureaucracy of Sheffield City Council.

Given the treatment of football fans at the time, the Liverpool supporters would not have expected to be greeted by the local police force with welcoming arms and friendly smiles. But they would not have imagined that the officer from the South Yorkshire Police, in charge of ensuring the safety of the 54,000 people at the semi-final, had been appointed on 27 March, only 19 days before. Chief Superintendent David Duchenfield had not policed at Hillsborough at all for ten years before the semi-final. Now he was in command of the whole operation, of officers seasoned in policing football at Hillsborough.

In 1988, South Yorkshire Police, preparing for the match, had learned that Liverpool fans tended not to arrive early at games. At home at Anfield, it was easy and quick to get into the Kop, and as alcohol had been banned from football grounds, the Liverpool crowd tended to eat, drink, or chat outside the ground, and cut it fine getting in for kick-off. At the 1988 semi-final, this had resulted in a crush outside the ground, a build-up of Liverpool supporters serviced impossibly slowly by the bare minimum of turnstiles.

As long before as 1924, police were officially advised to monitor a crowd 'some considerable distance from the entrance to the ground'. This would enable them to filter out people without tickets, or those misbehaving, before they actually reached the turnstiles. This, the police learnt 65 years before, enabled them to prevent delay at the turnstiles, and prevented congestion.

But the English police had long since unlearned much of the wisdom accumulated over the early decades of supervising the huge crowds attracted to football. In the Sixties and Seventies small groups of young people had gradually begun to extend support for their football teams into kicking the heads in of the opposition supporters. The football authorities tried for a long time not to acknowledge this emerging problem. The scrapping grew, hardening into nastier, more organised violence, 'football hooliganism', as it was dubbed, erupting at many games all over the country. Still, though, no official analysis of any depth took place as to why it was happening and what could be done to prevent it. It was for a long time simply dismissed, as the work of a 'tiny minority'. Football argued it was becoming the focus for social problems beyond its control, which it could not possibly solve on its own. In a famous phrase, Alan Hardaker, secretary of the Football League, had told Prime Minister Margaret Thatcher: 'Get your hooligans out of my game.'

But however true, it was not an approach likely to win the favour of that Prime Minister. In the Thatcherite lists of 'them and us', football was firmly 'them'. It was not one of the activities, like building shopping centres, which had much of a place in her vision for the enterprise future of Britain. As her minister Kenneth Clarke said, 'Margaret Thatcher did not understand why anybody would want to go to a football match.'

In the age in which all institutions were to be bulldozed by the searing injunction to market forces, football had no place. There was no economically productive purpose to it; people gathering, week after week, to watch teams of men kicking a ball about. Football was ragged, passionate, communal, mostly working-class in support. In the early Eighties, the most confrontational of times, an era of the British Government 'taking on' sections of the population, Thatcher sensed in football, with its eruptions of trouble, something dangerous, to be stamped on, contained. She insisted the clubs themselves sort out the hooligans. Nobody then talked about how decaying and crumbling the football grounds were, the ordinary supporters neglected by the custodians in the boardroom. Any suggestion that hooliganism was a symptom of wider social problems, or that football should modernise itself, was dismissed as 'wet' or 'bleeding heart'. The response of Government, football and the police was collectively aggressive, to segregate and control the supporters. The 'mindless yobs' of football were to be crushed, ruthlessly policed, punished.

Away supporters began to be met off trains to be marched straight to grounds by police with dogs. There they would stand on badly maintained terraces, with barely a toilet or any decent food or drink, in front of fences erected to prevent pitch invasions. Famously, Ken Bates introduced a 12-volt electrified fence at Stamford Bridge, although the local council did not, in the end, believe the Chelsea chairman's custodian duties extended to electrocuting his customers, and they refused to let him turn it on. None of this worked; hooliganism seeped further into the heart of football, all incidents given massive media coverage. As the fighting deepened and spread, nothing except increasingly punitive controls was ever suggested to combat it. Barely a politician spoke up for the beautiful game. Football and its supporters were collectively stigmatised, as some underclass. Unlike today, few celebrities, authors, comedians or actors ever confessed to supporting the game. 'A slum sport played by slum people,' said Murdoch's *Sunday Times*.

Meanwhile, the grounds were decaying. On 11 May 1985, a cigarette dropped into a pile of litter beneath the wooden floor of Bradford City's main stand, which was due after that day to be rebuilt, igniting a fireball which consumed the stand, killing 56 people. The disaster would result in an official report into football by Lord Justice Popplewell, a wise assessment of the game, in which hooliganism would be attributed to the work of a small hard core of criminals, and the conditions of grounds, the running of football by the then 'custodians' of the clubs, would be severely criticised. But only three weeks after the Bradford fire, years of bad behaviour and the failure to control it resulted in the hooliganism disaster waiting to happen: Heysel. An old stadium in Brussels insufficiently segregated, ill-equipped to deal with the violent, tribal rituals of English football supporters, crumbled under the weight of a rush by Liverpool fans on Juventus fans. Thirty-nine people were killed, most of them Italians, and 454 people injured, before the European Cup final, watched live on television by a massive, horrified audience all over Europe.

This time hooliganism could not be ignored or dismissed. Thatcher was determined to act. She dismissed even the suggestion that increasing unemployment, or inequality, or poor education might at least be contributing factors to young men fighting at football. The clubs were not called to account for their facilities, told to treat people decently. It was treachery, a failure to take responsibility, to argue that toilets, roofs, seats, might at least help to civilise behaviour at football. The blame was to be heaped on all supporters. The sale of alcohol at grounds was immediately banned. The clubs protested they would lose money, so this was changed to allow drinking, but not 'in sight of the pitch'. This is in force to this day. It is the law which forces the suits in corporate entertainment boxes to draw blinds across the glass screens before raiding the mini-bar.

But Margaret Thatcher was going much further than this. Thatcher was to force people who wanted to go to a football match to carry an identity card, which they would have to show at the turnstiles. Those who misbehaved would have their cards confiscated, and so be unable to get in. In a decade in which 'individual liberty' and 'rolling back the state' were proclaimed as ideals, football supporters were to be identified by the state as a shameful group. Football argued this would kill the game, make it too hard for people to go, drive crowds down. But the Prime Minister was not too concerned about preserving football. The scheme, she said, would stamp out hooliganism.

In April 1989, as young Philip Hammond was chatting excitedly with his mates on their coach to Sheffield, The Football Spectators Bill, which would force him to carry an identity card in future, was at an advanced stage in Parliament, close to becoming law. A Football Licensing Authority was already established to implement the scheme, headed by chief executive John de Quidt, a civil servant who had spent the Eighties dealing with prison riots, another aspect of the civil unrest which characterised the Thatcher years.

The policing at Hillsborough for the 1989 semi-final ran along standard lines of the time: the supporters were invading hordes, hooligans to be controlled. The 1988 match had been policed the same way: streets blocked off, police patrolling with a stern, hostile attitude, looking to spot trouble. The supporters were not considered as people, whose safety was to be ensured; they were considered potential threats to public order. No attempt was made to filter the supporters at a distance away from the ground, despite the insufficient turnstiles and the Liverpool supporters' known habit of cutting it fine. Instead, they were allowed to make their way straight to the ground. Even when they reached the turnstiles, there was a delay while they were searched for weapons. The seven pens, cages in effect, had been built after police requests, to contain hooliganism. The emphasis in the police control room, with its five video cameras, the whole strategy of the day, as at every match, was to control the hooligan scum. In the gymnasium at Hillsborough, which was serving as a police canteen, boards were in use to pin up pictures of known touts, hooligans and pickpockets.

In 1988, the crush outside the Leppings Lane turnstiles had not been too bad. This year, though, a sunny, warm day, more Liverpool supporters chose to take their time outside, then go down to the ground for around 2.30. By then, there was already quite a build-up outside the turnstiles, which were too few, working one supporter at a time, to let people through quickly enough. More people came in behind between 2.30 and 2.40. This squeezed everybody, in the middle and at the front, into a tight crush. At one point, a police horse was lifted clean off its feet by the force of the crowd.

In the control room, the police had cameras watching this developing chaos outside the Leppings Lane end. Yet Superintendent Bernard Murray, Chief Superintendent Duckenfield's assistant, told him at 2.30: 'We'll get them all in by three o'clock.'

A police constable outside, Michael Buxton, trying to police the crush from his Land Rover, saw it was hopeless, the crowd too big, the turnstiles too few, and radioed Duckenfield to ask him to delay kick-off. Duckenfield refused. His pre-match plan had been that kick-off would be put off only if fans had been delayed by motorway congestion or fog. The build-up continued. The crush at the front was compacted by more people arriving at the back. People's relaxed, high spirits on Cup semi-final day were turning sour by then; the fans' discomfort and potential danger increasing as nothing was done to ease the pressure, and, as the minutes ground on, the likelihood of missing the kick-off.

Those who did get in were not then directed by any signs or stewards. The tunnel was right in front of them, with a large sign above it, and supporters were naturally drawn down it, rather than around it to the side pens where there was lots of room. The central pens, 3 and 4, directly behind the goal, had filled up, and by 2.50 they were seriously overcrowded, causing bad crushing inside.

Outside the ground, at the entrance to the turnstiles, the pressure had become potentially lethal. The policeman in charge, Superintendent Marshall, knowing it was dangerous and not done except in extreme circumstances, reluctantly asked Chief Superintendent Duckenfield if he could relieve the pressure by allowing supporters in *en masse*, by opening two large exit gates, Gates A and C, rather than insist that the supporters continue to file one by one through the turnstiles. Duckenfield ignored him. Marshall asked again, and was again ignored. The third time, he shouted that someone was going to be killed out there, in a crush outside the football ground. There was still a pause. Superintendent Murray, sitting beside Duckenfield in the control box, said: 'Are you going to open the gates?'

Duckenfield, his control box directly overlooking the Leppings Lane terrace, its central pens overcrowded, with five cameras showing what was happening, gave the order at 2.52 for the gates to be opened, to let people come streaming through.

Duckenfield ordered some policemen to go to Gate A, to stop supporters with terrace tickets coming through it and trying to get into the seats. There was no fence in front of the seats, so he was guarding against hooligans getting into the seated area from where they could launch a pitch invasion. But no officers were sent to Gate C, to direct supporters away round the sides of the tunnel. The supporters, naturally, saw the tunnel and the sign, and headed down towards pens 3 and 4.

Under the section of the Taylor Report entitled 'The Blunder on Opening the Gates', Lord Justice Taylor says of Duckenfield's decision: 'This illustrates again the preoccupation with avoiding pitch invasion as against safety and the risks of overcrowding . . . The possibility of overcrowding was simply not considered.'

The Liverpool supporters released through Gate C proceeded down that dark chute, hundreds of them, kept straight by the low brick walls at the end, to arrive in pens 3 and 4, right behind people already packed in too tight.

The match kicked off at three o'clock, dead on time. Four minutes into the game, Peter Beardsley hit the Forest bar. Hearing the noise but unable to see, fans at the back of the Leppings Lane terrace struggled to get a better look. The pressure was so unimaginably great by now that two metal spans of a crush barrier were twisted and broken in pen 3. The people standing behind it were flung forward, plunging to the ground, pressed right down immediately by people falling on top of them. At the front of the pens, people were hemmed right up to the low wall and the terrible wire mesh fence above it, built to prevent people going on the pitch. An emergency gate at the front of the pen sprang open due to the weight of human pressure, and a policeman, with people beginning to die in front of him but trained only to look for pitch invasions, pushed it shut again. People were screaming, feeling tremendous pressure on their chests and the light, airy sense of dying.

The police had been instructed not to open the gates at the front, giving access to the track and the pitch, except with the consent of a senior officer. This was to prevent a pitch invasion. In 1988 there had been a minor pitch invasion at the end of the game, so this instruction to the policemen was hammered home, put into capital letters in their orders. Even as people died in front of them, the policemen on the perimeter stood and watched. In pen 4, a policeman finally plucked up the courage to defy instructions and open the gate at the front, allowing people to come through it, by the side of the pitch and round to the side pen where there was room. The Taylor Report quotes his evidence: 'I thought, if I'm wrong, I'm going to get a right bollocking for this.'

When he had let a few people out, he closed the gate again. Seeing the crush again, he reopened it. The policeman at gate 3, in front of pen 3, radioed for permission before opening the gate, but, faced with dying, screaming, desperate people and no answer from the radio, he opened it before getting an answer.

People struggled to spill out, gasping for air. In the control room, the nature of what was happening was still not recognised by the commanding officers, who were fixated on football supporters as a mob. The appearance of human beings on the pitch signalled to the police that there must be trouble, even though there had never, in all the sorry history of football hooliganism, been a pitch invasion before a game. Duckenfield, with his video screens showing people dying, a sight which was, anyway, visible from his control box position right above the Leppings Lane terrace, nevertheless responded by alerting dog handlers, to contain what he believed was a pitch invasion.

When the surge had come, people were pushed down and forward in an agonising, mortal crush. It was a primaeval place of disaster, a football match, covered by the BBC, in 1989. A horrific blockage developed at the front of the terrace, near the narrow opened gates. Some people had died by then, their chests and lungs crushed, a terrible, helpless, forsaken death at one of England's most prestigious sports grounds. Bodies lay on top of each other and entangled in a dreadful pile of the living and dead. People clambered desperately to try to get out or on to the fence and into some air.

On the ground, in the face of this scene, Superintendent Greenwood, Ground Commander, still thought it was 'retrievable'. He climbed on to the fence with some other officers, trying to wave fans to move back. Those trying to scale the fence were pushed back. It was impossible to move at all, let alone back. In the meantime, the game was still going on.

'The football contined to joyous shouting and singing around the rest of the ground,' Lord Taylor noted, 'while those crushed and trapped slowly expired.'

The police officers, called by Duckenfield to fight a pitch invasion, arrived upon a scene from hell: 'They had been summoned in response to what was thought to be a threat to public order. What they found was a horrific scene of carnage and some young officers were shocked into impotence by what they saw.

'It was truly gruesome. The victims were blue, cyanotic, incontinent; their mouths open, vomiting; their eyes staring. A pile of dead bodies lay and grew outside gate 3.'

Still, from the control room, there was no activating of an emergency plan, no calling for ambulances, no calling over the tannoy, even, for doctors or nurses. Advertising hoardings were ripped up to serve as makeshift stretchers for the dead and the chronically ill. Supporters and policemen tried desperately to give mouth-to-mouth resucitation to dying fans on the turf. The players were taken off at five past three.

Duckenfield, even at 3.06, still believed he was facing an outbreak of hooliganism, and called for all available police resources to come to the ground to help him fight it. His assistant, Murray, though, had gone down to ground level, seen the dead and dying, and radioed for ambulances. Another policeman, Chief Superintendent Nesbit, arrived to take charge of the cadaverous hell at Gate 3, where people were getting in each other's way trying to pull bodies out. Nesbit organised a chain of policemen to pass bodies back. Police and fans, with no bolt cutters, pulled with their bare hands at the wire mesh, managing to make holes and get people out.

There was no call for doctors or nurses until 3.30, and nothing else was broadcast on the tannoy. Most people in the ground could not clearly see the terror at the Leppings Lane end. The Forest fans, at the other end of the ground in the Spion Kop, were too far away. There was some booing from their end, because, in the absence of information, they assumed Liverpool fans were invading the pitch. Some Liverpool fans, emerging from the scenes of death, went running towards the Spion Kop end, some hysterical with grief and outrage. This brought about that eternal, shameful image of Hillsborough, of football at the time, the line of police officers pushing the Liverpool fans back, then standing on the halfway line doing nothing, as people died in front of them.

At 3.15 Graham Kelly went into the control room with Glen Kirton of the FA and Graham Mackrell, secretary of Sheffield Wednesday and 'safety officer' at the ground. Duckenfield told them the Liverpool supporters had forced open the exit gate. 'That's the gate that's been forced,' he said, pointing to the TV screen. 'There's been an inrush.'

With people still dying visibly to the naked eye, and on his screens, David Duckenfield, the policeman in charge of the ground, lied about his order to open the gate.

Ninety-five people died that day. Another, Tony Bland, had his higher brain functions destroyed, leaving him in a coma for four years, until his doctors were allowed to stop feeding him and giving him medication. He died on 3 March 1993, and was buried to the strains of *You'll Never Walk Alone*. Ninety-six. Trapped to death, in a vice, between the decaying negligence of football, the oppressive, official demonising of football supporters, and the shocking incompetence of the police in charge on the day. A disaster waiting to happen, circumstances finally conspiring for it to befall those 96 innocents.

Phil Hammond senior was at home in Aigburth that day, watching the snooker on telly. At about five past three, the BBC cut in to show the unfolding disaster at Hillsborough. 'I just had a feeling that Philip was in trouble,' he says now about his reaction at the time. 'It was a gut feeling. I can't explain it. I just knew.'

He telephoned his wife Hilda, sister in charge of intensive care at Walton Hospital in Liverpool, and told her to come home. Wringing their hands, they rang the coach company, Abbeyline, which had taken Philip and his mates to the match. Abbeyline told them the coaches coming back were full. Two friends, Sonia and Alan Williams, went down to pick Philip up. They came back without him. They were told the police had been shoving Liverpool supporters indiscriminately on to all available coaches, to get them away from the area. The Abbeyline coaches were indeed full, but Philip wasn't on them.

Brian, Phil's brother, decided to go over to Sheffield, and to phone from every service station on the way to see whether Philip had somehow found his way home. Ian Southgate, one of the friends

Philip had gone to the match with, turned up at the house with his Mum and Dad. He told the Hammonds he had looked and looked for Philip in the Hillsborough chaos and hadn't been able to find him.

Later that evening, the doorbell rang. Phil Hammond opened the door, saw a policeman. His heart sank. He said: 'Don't tell me he's dead.'

And the policeman said: 'No, he isn't. He's alive. You've got to phone this number in Sheffield.'

At that minute, Brian returned. Phil said he had this phone number and they ought to set off back for Sheffield to find Philip. But Brian said: 'No. He's dead. I've had to identify him.'

Phil and Hilda barely remember the next few days. It was a parent's worst nightmare, a blur of uncontrollable grief. Phil has a vague recollection of the doctor coming round to give them something to help them sleep.

'We just didn't know where we were,' he says. 'We couldn't get over it. Our family, especially Brian, and friends, they kept us going, really.'

The Hammonds' home, like so many in Liverpool, became a house of mourning, grieving for mostly young lives. Philip's cleaned golf clubs were still in the hall, ready for the game he was never to play, the day after the semi-final.

Brian, Phil's brother, never talks much about what happened. But the family knows he had to go to the infamous gymnasium at Hillsborough, where the corpses were laid out on the coroner's instructions and the boards, ready for pictures of hooligans, had instead been covered with polaroids of dead supporters. The photographs were slapped on with no thought to separate them into adults, young people, male, female. Relatives had to look through every one, all 95 who died. Brian Hammond found his young nephew there, on that board, right at the end.

On the Monday, 17 April, Lord Justice Peter Taylor was appointed by Home Secretary Douglas Hurd to inquire into the specific circumstances of what had gone wrong at Hillsborough, and to look generally into safety at sports grounds. Taylor was to be assisted in his invetigations, as the coroner would be, and the Director of Public Prosecutions, by the West Midland Police, headed by Assistant Chief Constable Mervyn Jones.

On the Wednesday, 19 April 1989, with the whole of Liverpool still in grief and all football supporters in a mournful shock of solidarity, *The Sun* produced a front page. 'THE TRUTH,' it said, spewing forth allegations that the disaster had been caused by a foaming mob of drunk Liverpool hooligans. There were allegations, said to have come from senior police sources, of 'mass drunkenness', of supporters urinating on the police and on the dead bodies on the pitch, and of theft.

The Hammonds, consumed in their own private catastrophe, never saw it, but many on Merseyside did. It prompted burnings of Rupert Murdoch's tabloid rag, and a boycott which lasts to this day among many Liverpool people. But it succeeded in producing a lasting myth, an easy answer to the awful, complex, calamitous web of stigma, negligence and blunder. Four days after the disaster, with Taylor barely appointed, there was a simplistic, false image for the unknowing wider public, ready-made scapegoats. It was all the supporters' fault. Scouse football hooligans. It was them wot done it.

'It was all set up, wasn't it?' says Phil Hammond. 'From the moment Duckenfield lied, a whole story was brought out to support that lie. This story, put out by the police, that Liverpool fans were drunk, they forced down the gate, they were hooligans. The police have still, to this day, never said sorry. Everything the police have done and said, at the Taylor Report, at the inquest and since, has been to support those lies.'

Taylor reported first on 1 August 1989, his Interim Report, dealing with the events at Hillsborough. He itemised in clinical detail the tawdry, disgraceful list of failures by Sheffield Wednesday, Eastwood & Partners, the club's engineers, Sheffield City Council, and the South Yorkshire Police. Taylor said of Chief Superintendent Duckenfield: 'He could not face the enormity of the decision to open the gates and all that flowed therefrom. That would explain what he said to Mr Kelly . . . his aversion to addressing the crowd and his failure to take effective control of the disaster situation. He froze.'

Taylor dismissed the stories of drunkenness, although he said 'an unruly minority who had drunk too much aggravated the problem' outside the Leppings Lane terrace. He specifically criticised the police for coming to his inquiry refusing to take responsibility, ready to blame the whole tragedy on a story of drunkenness and late arrival. And he took time out to say that not a shred of evidence had been produced to support *The Sun* and other British so-called newspapers which colluded in that line. He found that 21 of the dead had themselves arrived late at the match, being let through Gate C after 2.52 and propelled, off their feet, with no crush barriers to break their progress, flowing 'like molten lava' down that terrace to terrible deaths. Almost none of the dead had significant levels of alcohol in their blood. 'Those who made the [allegations], and those who disseminated them,' said Taylor, 'would have done better to hold their peace.'

Most of the families had not come to know each other yet. Many, like the Hammonds, were too raw to share their grief. They now looked towards the coroner's inquest, in which the truth would formally be established, by a jury, as to how their loved ones had died.

'We thought that the Taylor Report was reasonable,' says Hilda Hammond. 'It laid to rest the lies about drunkenness and misbehaviour which had been put about. It showed how dangerous that ground was and how negligent the police had been. We thought that at the inquest we would find out how our son died. And we assumed that if anybody was found to have been directly to blame for his death, they would be identified and punished.'

Lord Justice Taylor moved on to produce his second, final report, into football grounds generally, in January 1990. Somehow, the story has since gone into myth that Taylor was a football fan, a Newcastle supporter. This appears to be another example of the back pages' fixation that anybody remotely involved in football must be a fan. It is the same simplistic pap which produces glowing portraits of businessmen coming into football, painting them as football-loving philanthropists. Peter Taylor may have gone to St James' Park sometimes when he was young. But when he was called upon to inquire into the Hillsborough disaster he was not standing in the rain on the Gallowgate End, watching Mick Quinn and shouting 'Sack the board'. He had, in truth, taken little notice of the game in the decades he had spent working his way up Bar and Bench.

If he had, he would not have produced the report he did. It is written in calm, clear language, but between the lines it is wide-eyed with shock. Had he been a fan, Taylor might have been outraged by the decay which had eaten into many of the grounds of England's historic football clubs, but he would not have been surprised. He would not have expected to find anything better than an inert Football Association and boards of club directors whose custodianship had turned into the stale stuff of provincial ego-boost. Taylor emerged from the fusty cocoon of the House of Lords to pick his way gingerly, hands behind his back, through the abysmal crumbling and detritus of English football. He was absolutely appalled. The game was in an awful state. He could not believe that in the age of the yuppie, the mobile phone, the big bang trappings of unleashed corporate wealth, people were expected to watch the national game in conditions largely unchanged since the Thirties, standing in the rain in gloomy grounds, fed with soggy chips, forced to use the back of the stands as urinals.

'The picture revealed is of a general malaise or blight over the game due to a number of factors. Principally these are: old grounds, poor facilities, hooliganism, excessive drinking and poor leadership.'

His final report is the one now commonly referred to as the Taylor Report. It has gone down in football history as a call for stadia to become all-seater. In fact it was much more than that. The all-seater requirement was only the bare minimum, intended to be a guarantee, at least, that nobody would ever be killed again at a football match. But his recommendations were for a much more fundamental change to take place in football.

His analysis of hooliganism was very different from the Prime Minister's. He specifically rejected the identity card plan, calling it a 'sledgehammer to crack a nut'. Taylor agreed with Lord Justice Popplewell's account in the report into the Bradford fire. There was a hard core of criminals who liked to fight and hurt people, and they found football a 'convenient theatre' for their violence. The wider problem, Taylor said, was that this violence had become fashionable amongst a larger group of football fans, accepted as the norm.

Taylor said that the clubs' and police's treatment helped to create the conditions for the bad behaviour to spread and continue. Taylor listed football's squalid conditions, edging into degradation: the absence of toilets, the prevalence of rubbish because of the lack of dustbins, people getting wet on uncovered terraces, the awful food, the 'stench of stewed onions', all producing a dismal scene in which bad behaviour did not seem as unacceptable or out of place as it should have been.

His call was for the opposite of what Thatcher had wanted. He wanted football to treat supporters as human beings. 'The vast majority of supporters abhor violence,' he concluded, quoting the Popplewell Report, 'and wish only for an afternoon of pleasure at a football match.'

The call for all-seater stadia was just a starting point in Taylor's call for a complete change in the way football supporters were treated, in the way the game was run, right from the top. The Football Supporters Bill would be hi-jacked just as it was reaching the end of its journey, amended to require the seating of the game, not the branding of its supporters, much to the disappointment of Thatcher. The Football Licensing Authority was kept on, but its duties were changed; it became responsible for licensing the rebuilt grounds, for supervising a strenghthened Green Guide on safety.

Taylor saw the danger that clubs would try to pass on the costs of this rebuilding in increased ticket prices. He specifically asked that they should not: 'Clubs may well wish to charge more for seats than for standing, but it should be possible to plan a price structure which suits the cheapest seats to the pockets of those presently paying to stand. At Ibrox, for example, seating is £6, standing £4.'

This was January 1990.

Taylor also acknowledged the worry that seating would diminish the tremendous atmosphere of football grounds on a good day. But he believed the atmosphere could be maintained: 'I am not convinced that the cherished culture of the terraces is wholly lost when fans are seated. Watching the more boisterous and demonstrative sections at all-seater grounds, I have noted no absence of concerted singing, clapping or gesticulating in unison. The communal spirit is still there and finds ready expression.'

Taylor recommended that the clubs be given public money, from a reduction in the tax on the pools, to help them pay for the rebuilding of their grounds. In return, he called for a change in attitude.

The Football Association and the Football League were both criticised for failing to give a lead to their member clubs to ensure reasonable standards of safety and comfort for spectators. These two governing bodies had both made written submissions that safety was not their responsibility. It was the clubs who had to be responsible for the supporters, said the guardians of the beautiful game.

Lord Taylor had a look at the club directors, the custodians of the football clubs for the towns, sitting in their wood-pannelled boardrooms as their customers were put at risk of their very lives on crumbling terraces. Taylor did not like what he peered into: 'As for the clubs,' he reported, 'in some instances it is legitimate to wonder whether the directors are genuinely interested in the welfare of their grass-roots supporters.

'Boardroom struggles for power, wheeler-dealing in the buying and selling of shares, and indeed of whole clubs, sometimes suggest that those involved are more interested in the personal financial benefits or social status of being a director, than of directing the club in the interests of its supporter customers.'

From the very beginning, the 1880s, the comfort of fans was given scant regard by professional football clubs. The early founders, seeing the popularity of their new game, had simply seen the opportunity to charge for entry, enclosed their grounds and introduced turnstiles. These were the first days of leisure, emerging out of early industrial mayhem. It was not the style of the time to think too much about creature comforts for the masses. Somehow, in football, run amateurishly, this culture had remained, hardened even, into a division between board members, comfortable in directors' boxes, and fans standing in the rain. Still, pre-war and post-war, football crowds expected little better than to be given an uncovered square foot on the terraces and a glimpse of Stanley Matthews. Supporters' fierce loyalty meant they came to watch their teams regardless of the conditions. Periodically, there were disasters, as at Burnden Park in 1946 when 33 people were killed in a crush. But, as Taylor gloomily noted, nothing ever changed as a result.

The wheeler-dealing was not usually done by directors looking to get rich themselves. The chairmen were more concerned with their positions, and so when their clubs were in financial trouble they would often try to get more money in without giving too much control away. A common tactic was to create several different classes of shares, including 'non-voting shares', which could be issued to a new investor without diluting the control of the sitting directors. There were some good chairmen, who felt a sense of duty to their clubs, supporters and community, but competence was in short supply. All directors spoke of their job as 'custodians of the club for the people', and almost none saw football as a means of making money. But too often they were small-minded, the clubs their personal fiefdoms, a thrill coursing through their veins at every mention of the words 'Mr Chairman'.

'To these butchers, bakers and candlestick makers', the financial benefits Taylor talked about were mostly small-time; perks and meals and tickets in the cushioned directors box. The Eighties had seen the emergence of the new-style chairman, such as Martin Edwards, Irving Scholar, David Dein, who had begun to fight to be allowed to make money, but generally the clubs remained in the hands of the old-style custodians. There was still the remains of an ethic about running a football club, of providing a service to the community, of 'putting something back'. But by the end of the Eighties it was largely exhausted by the inadequacies of the people in charge, by the infighting and meanness of spirit of the football administrators, by the inability of football to modernise itself. The clubs had a sort of curdled Victorian character, small-time Dickensian burghers, hanging on, inadequate and outdated, in a different age. It was the supporters who had paid the ultimate, terrible price.

The Hillsborough disaster was the watershed for this way of running football. It could not carry on like this. As an industry it had to bring itself up to scratch and up to date. The English had, as Taylor noted, given the beautiful game to the world, and he completed his look at the dank decrepitude into which it had sunk by recognising that the game still had its kernel of beauty, which had kept it alive throughout all the trauma and stigma of the Thatcher years: 'Despite [those features which disfigure football today] and despite the decline in attendances from the peak years, the game still commands massive public support and interest. Indeed, in the last couple of years there has been some increase in attendances . . .

'After the horror of Hillsborough . . . the lesson is surely that now is the moment for the fullest reassessment of policy for the game.'

Lord Justice Peter Taylor died on Tuesday, 29 April 1997, aged 66. He had lived to see the football grounds of Britain rebuilt, sat down. But much of the spirit of his report had been left to gather dust in Her Majesty's Stationery Offices. After Hillsborough, despite the terrible waste of young life, the suffering inflicted upon innocent people, the revelation of moral bankruptcy in the running of football, Lord Taylor died with his most fundamental recommendations ignored. Ticket prices rose, the atmosphere was destroyed, there never was the fullest reassessment of policy for the game. To this day, there never has been. The response to his report sank to yet another depressing episode, revealing football's administrators in all their smallness. There was to be no repentance to the families of those killed at one of football's showpiece events, no following of the spirit of the Taylor Report. With the critical eyes of the nation on the football authorities, the governing forces of the game proceeded only to demonstrate why they had been unfit to run the game in the first place, let alone be responsible for the safety of its supporters, who had gone along in high spirits to be sacrificed on the terrible landscape of football's neglect.

8

THE GAMES PEOPLE PLAY

Professional football was forced to make its stadia all-seater via the revised Football Spectators Act, but the spirit of the Taylor Report was not similarly passed into law. While they were at it, perhaps the Government should have forced further reform on the running of the game. As it was they attacked the symptom, the crumbling grounds, not the cause, the decaying quality of the people in charge. Like some black joke, the order to sit down, and the Taylor Report's damning criticisms of the inadequate, divided, selfish administration of English football, came to be considered by just those inadequate administrators. Lord Taylor's call for the fullest reassessment of policy for the game, made after 95 people had been killed at an FA Cup semi-final, dropped like a headache into the comfortable committee rooms of the two main ruling bodies, the Football Association and the Football League.

The existence and survival of these separate governing bodies, which often find it difficult to work together, is a frustrating by-product of the rich history of English football. The game evolved out of the social and economic circumstances of its Victorian time, and so it bequeathed several features which no sport would choose if it were starting from scratch.

The Football Association came first, before any other football body not just in England but the world. It in fact has a glorious history; it was responsible for developing the game, for creating the first ever set of rules. The current senior people at the FA look even less substantial in the light of the knowledge that their organisation really was the one which gave the great game of football to the world.

A masterful, fascinating account of the birth and development of football is given by two sociologists, Eric Dunning of Leicester University and Kenneth Sheard, then of Cambridgeshire College, in their book *Barbarians, Gentlemen and Players*. They acknowledge the theory that some form of football originated in ancient Greece or Rome, but find no written account of the game until the fourteenth century in England. There the game has its roots: a rough, no-holds-barred battle over an inflated bladder; people kicking, maiming, wrecking property as they rampaged through the streets. It was just one of the many wild, bloody pastimes through which people used to let off steam in medieval times and it was officially banned on more than 30 occasions between 1314 and 1667.

Such bans, though, in the absence of a police force, were difficult to enforce. The games continued until the nineteenth century, developing rudimentary sets of rules based on taking and defending territory. Armies of people from opposing villages, including men, women and children, rich and poor together, joined in the battle to maraud with the ball into the heart of the opposition territory. That was the 'goal', the aim. These folk games were a part of rural society, along with cock-fighting, hunting and bull-baiting, in an age when violence was a more accepted part of everyday life, less rare and shocking, than it is now.

'These folk games were rough and wild, closer to "real" fighting than modern sports,' says *Barbarians*. 'They were more symbolic struggles for territory than ball games as we know them today. The whole identity of the contending groups was at stake and not simply their ability as players.'

By the middle of the nineteenth century, rapid industrialisation had laid waste many of the rural communities, sending their people into the cities as factory or mill fodder. Some folk pastimes, like cock-fighting or badger-baiting, carried on underground, illegally, in the cities. But apart from historical oddities like the Shrove Tuesday football match at Ashbourne, which survives to this day, folk games like football were destroyed by urbanisation's ruthless sweep. The cities offered neither the time nor the space for the game, and gradually the population was too crushed, physically and in spirit, to have much desire for it anyway. The establishment of a national police force helped to enforce prohibition. And a new industrial class system was forged to keep working people in their place, putting a stop to pastimes in which whole communities used to join together.

In this social and industrial revolution, the public schools were a cocooned world. The sons of rich men – landed aristocrats or, increasingly, industrial magnates – went to Eton, Harrow, Rugby, Charterhouse, for an education which was itself gradually changing. Until the early nineteenth century, Dunning and Sheard note, the schools were chaotic warehouses for the wild lads of the rich. There was little control from the teachers, on whom the boys looked down as lower-class. The schools were playgrounds for hunting, fighting with the locals, rebellion against the teachers, bullying and, for fun, rough folk games like rudimentary football.

Football was regulated, toned down and given a respectable role in school as a result of the wider 'civilising' changes introduced by the reforms of a new kind of headmaster. Matthew Arnold, head of Rugby School in 1828-42, was a noted, although not unique, influence in seeking to give the boys a more structured, formal education. His reforms, introducing order, enhancing the status of teachers, banning hunting and other bloody games, were gradually copied at other schools. But Arnold saw in football an opportunity to allow boys to 'let off steam' within safe, controlled circumstances, and, later, an arena in which to develop character and teamwork. It was the start of the belief in 'games' as part of a school curriculum.

The boys, in competition with other schools, began to develop rules for football. Rugby School, retaining handling, developed different rules from Eton, which did not allow it. When these upper-class chaps went to university, they were all playing different versions of the same game. At Cambridge, committees were formed to try to develop a common set of rules, with more or less success. Eventually, when these gentlemen left their formal education for work and adulthood, they formed independent clubs to carry on playing football. The point was purely to play the game for its enjoyment: 'It was one of the earliest leisure activities not to be organised commercially,' says *Barbarians*, '. . . but largely for the pleasure it afforded and because it was a vehicle for expressing currently important values.'

But because the rules were all different, the early clubs, like Old

Harrovians, had difficulty finding opposition. A call went out to thrash out a common set of rules. On Monday, 26 October 1863, delegates of 11 clubs met to do just that at the Freemason's Tavern in Lincoln's Inn Fields in London. It was the inaugural meeting of what would become the Football Association.

It took six stormy meetings to agree and finalise the definitive set of rules for the game of football. At the fourth, Blackheath, a London team of largely Rugby School old boys, stormed out after being out-voted on the issue of 'hacking'. This was basically the right to stop an opposing player's dribbling by booting him in the shins. Blackheath insisted hacking was 'manly' and should be allowed. But the others were determined their game was to be more civilised, a game of skill and artistry, not brute force. The rules which did emerge were almost exactly the same as today: teams of 11, a round ball, kicking, no handling, no hacking or pushing; a game in which the ball had to be worked into the 'goal' with dribbling and passing on the deck. Blackheath went off to form a cruder, more physically confrontational game, which became known as rugby.

Football remained an entirely upper-class game for some years afterwards. The concept of sport as character building had taken hold, and a firm 'amateur ethos' developed, in which there was a purity, amid the mean commercial strivings of life, about the competition between two teams playing football. The early FA officials developed the game: Charles William Alcock, an old boy of Harrow, and, later, Francis Marindin and Arthur Kinnaird, both old Etonians. The game grew in popularity, particularly after Alcock, in 1871, adapted an old 'sudden death' inter-house competition from his schooldays and called it the FA Cup. Early entrants in the FA Cup's history were the likes of Harrow Chequers and Old Etonians. Royal Engineers, Wanderers and Oxford University were the three first winners of the Cup.

The new game was first taken into the tougher north by sons of rich provincial men, returning from public schools or university where they had played the enjoyable new game. Blackburn Rovers was formed by Lewis and Constantine, formerly of Shrewsbury School. One of the club's first players was A.N. Hornby, who had played at Harrow. Gradually the game came to be watched and played by the skilled working classes, who had by then been given a little leisure time. By the 1870s and 1880s the Church had developed 'muscular Christianity', a kind of games ethic with Jesus thrown in, for the pale, undernourished inner cities. They began to promote teams like those which would become Everton and Aston Villa. Wolverhampton Wanderers was originally St Luke's, Blakenhall, formed in 1877. Christ Church FC, Bolton, also took the name Wanderers for itself later. Blackpool, Barnsley, Fulham, Swindon and Southampton, formerly Southampton St Mary's, 'The Saints', all started life as church teams before changing their names around the onset of professionalism in the 1880s.

By then the game had spread rapidly, formed by men in works teams, old school teams, some just backed by the local pub, which might have a field they could play on, and the only changing facilities in a pre-sports centre landscape. People grasped the new game as something wonderful, urgent. City men found a sense of community, a place to let off steam, a sense of belonging, something to support, on the early enclosed grounds of the North and Midlands. In Yorkshire and parts of the North-West, rugby league had taken off amongst the working class, but not on the same scale. There was something unique about football. Nobody has ever really been able to explain its appeal and attractiveness; it has a higher quality which is indefinable, escapes description. Professor Eric Dunning has a go: 'At its best,' he says, 'football is incomparable, isn't it? It is balletic.'

Even Pele, the greatest player the Old Harrovians' game was ever to produce, the man who won three World Cups and scored over a thousand goals, could only shrug his shoulders. 'It's the beautiful game,' he said, memorably.

Football emerged from decades of civilising, nurturing, regulating in the public schools; men thinking, arguing, refining the style of the new game, at a time of social cataclysm in the wider world. They had started from the wild abandon and rough stuff of less controlled times and produced this simple game, with a round ball, two goals, clear rules. Football had defined its space and its conduct, intent on fostering skill, competition, enjoyment. Over time and fierce debate, they had somehow managed to reduce, retain and distil the essence of wildness of the old folk games. Only a game, simple to play, football was unleashed among a new, harassed working class, bringing within it the very soul of freedom, the breath of a less restricted life. It had skill and cunning and strength, a flow which was exciting and easy on the eye, like a chase; it was intensely competitive, it required sustained effort, stamina, determination, and then there was the intense, uproarious release of the 'goals'. The game was magic. In the 1880s and 1890s it spread amongst the working classes like a life-enhancing drug.

It was consumed to slake the thirst for excitement, beauty, spectacle, by people whose hearts were parched by the grim demands of the new urban life. But, from the start, football came to fulfil even more profound human need. The crowds found a sense of belonging at the ground, at the game, standing together in communal support of these clubs. In a world which had undermined the old certainties, of community, religion, ritual, football provided all three, around its central, indefinable magic. The clubs developed their own characters according to where they were, their own styles of play. The crowd grew attached to its own local club, to seeing the same team and players every week, supporting through thick and thin, urging the team to greater heights. Support was as much worship as spectating. It was fervent, loyal, unquestioning. The grounds became precious places, places to send the heart beating just to pass, just to get inside. Football clubs filled all these needs, becoming for many people one of the prime, deeper experiences of modern life, an escape from work and street and the poverty of home. As the next generations were born, football support came to be family and local tradition, handed down, articles of faith people were born to, and would feel 'in the blood', all their lives.

As the game spread, the FA developed a regional structure to administer it, establishing semi-autonomous County Football Associations around the country. They registered all teams and competitions in their areas and provided one delegate each to sit on the central policy-making body in London, the FA Council. Beginning in this distinguished fashion, literally the inventors and early developers of the great game, the FA is still even now run in the same way, by the FA Council, which has grown to 93 representatives. Men who give years, decades, of honest toil to the form-processing, registrations and disciplinary hearings of 43 amateur County Football Associations finally get elected to the FA Council as a treat in their anecdotage.

Because reform can only come from within, the council has never been modernised. To this day, the representatives at Lancaster Gate are relics of the FA's evolving, amateur history; the Army, Air Force and Navy have a seat each, as do Oxford and Cambridge University, the latter represented by the delightfully named D.J. Insole. Even Australia and New Zealand sit at English football's top table, as 'Representatives of British Commonwealth Associations'.

The real holders of power now, though, as they have been for some time, are the representatives of the professional football clubs. Professionalism, paying to get the best players, came about as the inevitable result of fierce competition between the new football clubs in a North forged in hard work, not in the wealth and luxury which produced the amateur ethos. Rumours that players were being paid were rife in the late 1870s and early 1880s. Scotsmen had suddenly appeared from nowhere, filling well-paid jobs in Lancashire cotton mills and crucial positions in the Darwen, then Blackburn Rovers football teams.

The Football Association, determined to preserve amateurism, passed a rule in 1882 to throw out any club found paying a player. But the payments continued. Accrington were banned in 1883 for making payments. Then, in 1884, Upton Park accused Preston North End of paying players, after an FA Cup match in London. Major Suddell, the manager of Preston, drew the FA's fire by admitting it. He explained that anyone wanting to keep up with Blackburn Rovers had to pay their players, because money ruled at that club. And he explained to the upper-class legislators that the game would cause hardship to a working-class man if he had to give up time to play, yet was not paid for his efforts.

Many in the FA argued that professionalism was completely against the spirit, of enjoyment and sportsmanship, of the game. The professional clubs threatened to break away in 1884, which brought the FA to a compromise. In 1885, at Andertons Hotel on Fleet Street, professionalism was legalised. The FA decided it was more prudent to allow payments to players rather than forbid it and drive the cash underground. It was more practical to seek to regulate its excesses, to stop, as they saw it at that time, the influence of money ruining the underlying ethic of football. The FA, as the governing body, saw it as its duty to protect the great game from the damaging effects of professionalism or, more particularly, commercialism.

In 1888, William McGregor, who was not a rich man, made his invitation to the 11 other clubs to join his Aston Villa in the professional Football League. It was not intended at all to be a rival of the FA. The two were different: the FA was the governing body, responsible for all of football. The league was to be a competition, registered with the FA, to ensure the professional clubs regular fixtures. The FA allowed it as inevitable, but were wary, conscious always of its regulatory role. The League became exceptionally popular with spectators, who flooded through the new turnstiles, and it quickly expanded, forming a Second Division in 1892.

The Football League was concerned from the start to ensure a degree of equality between its member clubs. After the First World War this would be done by sharing gate receipts equally between home and away teams. A small town team playing away at a big city club would get half the gate, and therefore be able to compete financially. There was also a 4 per cent levy on the total gate receipts of all League clubs for the season, which were then distributed equally to every club in the League. The principle was that all the teams needed each other, to ensure competition and the wider health of football. The big city clubs could not hog all the money, just because they happened to be in the centre of bigger populations. Clubs also, less admirably, looked to control their collective costs by doing the players down, paying the emerging stars a small maximum wage and retaining their registrations, not allowing them to move at the end of a season.

Professionalism and the expense of building grounds were the main reasons for clubs becoming limited companies in the 1880s and 1890s. This was a defensive measure, protecting the founder of the football clubs from personal liability for the clubs' debts, not a springboard for making speculative money out of the game. As football grew in popularity, the FA moved around 1912, make sure this remained the case. It imposed upon clubs' articles of association – the constitutions of these companies – rules to prevent profiteering. The rule is still in force today, somewhat laughably, because the FA now allows it openly to be bypassed. Rule 34 prevented money leaking out of a football club by imposing a maximum on dividends and outlawing payment to club directors. It also provided that if a club-company was wound up, its property would have to go to other local sporting institutions. These rules provided a neat bulwark against people coming into football looking just to make money for themselves. An entrepreneur putting his money into football could not make a profit, either from annual dividends on his shares or by paying himself a salary. Nor could he wind up the club and sell the ground for profit. People backing clubs had to be doing it for football and the clubs' sake, not their own.

The FA was robust at that time, protecting football clubs as sporting institutions. Pre-war, the old class certainties remained, ensuring a confidence among the upper class, in their amateur ethos, their need to control the rough, commercial men of the North, for the good of football. Gradually, representatives from the Football League were brought on to the FA Council. Players were increasingly unhappy at their oppressive treatment. But the two administrative bodies were in good health before the Second World War: 'The power of the League strengthens the Association and the authority of the Association safeguards the League,' wrote William Pickford, FA President 1937-38.

After the war, though, the old class system began to break down, and the FA's certainty, its Oxbridge-bred, haughty confidence in its right to control the upstart professionals, wavered. Stanley Rous, who had been a one-man FA during the war, still kept a firm hand on the game, but the Football League, entering its heyday, the golden age of enormous crowds and the Finney, Matthews era of all-time great players (on £20 a week maximum), grew in influence. The League and its clubs began to make big money, and the FA increasingly wrestled with its dignity, like a man of breeding suddenly finding himself strapped for cash. Relations between the two bodies began to grow tense, with the club v. country issue often the catalyst for arguments.

Most other countries in the world, starting from scratch to organise football, avoided this separation of governing body and League. Just about every country, from the beginning, established a single football federation governing the lot: the professional and amateur games, youth development, a pyramid of leagues.

'Other countries have learned from our problems, learned not to reproduce them,' was a recent grumble of Howard Wilkinson, whose newly created job of FA technical director largely involves banging all the different heads together.

The divisions in English football do not stop there. History has also given the game a separate English Schools Football Association, the Professional Football Association, officially the players' union but, in the vacuum of leadership in the game, increasingly pushed by chief executive Gordon Taylor as an administrative force in the game. Even the supporters cannot speak with a joint voice, the National Federation of Official Supporters Clubs being considered far too subservient to the clubs by the independent Football Supporters Association.

In the absence of reform, the FA Council, incredibly, remains English Football's premier governing body . They have been shown in recent years to be out of their depth in the satellite age, but they cling on, unwieldly and outdated. The unkind jibe about the councillors is that 93 is the average age as well as their total number. In 1995 the FA's then commercial director Trevor Philips made a presentation to a conference. 'I must say,' he began, 'after spending so much time talking to the FA Council, it is a real pleasure to be speaking to a live audience.' Philips left in 1996, over some allegations about ticket sales for Euro '96, when Football Came Home.

The FA has developed some 22 committees to keep all these councillors busy. All policy, developed by the FA's staff, has to go through these committees, which then put proposals through for stamping by the council. So, for example, Howard Wilkinson's 'Charter for Quality', his 'radical, even revolutionary' proposals to 'lift standards throughout the game', announced in May 1997 with a chorus of trumpets and a blanket of secrecy, must now go plunging into the committee stage. 'It will have to go into a number of committees,' according to FA spokesman Steve Double. 'The instructional committee, the international, the executive – any number of them, to be honest. Then, as the points go through, they will be ratified by the council.'

The tortuousness of the procedure and the large number of people involved has for a long time now undermined the FA's ability to be an effective governing body. Anybody working there, wanting to get anything done, needs to find allies at every stage. Wilkinson, for example, is now going to need supporters in each committee for each proposal, then support for each one by a majority of the council. The effect of this has been that for decades now the FA has turned in on itself, becoming obsessed not with football but its own internal politics.

Allen Wade, Head of Coaching and Education at the FA from 1963 to 1982, recalls that politics were integral to the job. Formerly a student and PE teacher at Loughborough University and semi-pro player for Notts County, Wade was given the new post to arrest a potential decline in the skills base of the game. As society changed, boys were no longer spending every waking minute playing football in the street, which had produced England's flow of 'natural' footballers. 'Remember, Pele never had a moment's schooling in his life,' says Wade. 'He had just played football. Our players had been similar, but it was changing. I used to tell the FA, you're not just going to get another Bobby Charlton or Jimmy Greaves coming through. You have to coach them now, as they're doing on the continent.'

The West German Football Federation, rebuilding after the war, had organised a sophisticated coaching system based at the Sports High School in Cologne. Coaches had to take courses in movement, nutrition, physiology and psychology, as well as football skills and tactics. This structured, cerebral approach, reaping reward in the 1954 World Cup, was reproduced in Holland and Scandinavia. In Italy, land of technical football skill, the course was a year long. Still, in Germany, no player can become a manager without doing two preliminary month-long courses, followed by six months at the Sports High School. Tony Woodcock, ex-Nottingham Forest and England, had to do this before being allowed to coach in the German Third Division. His old club in England, in trouble in 1996-97, did the standard English thing. Promoted a player, their left-back, with no preparation or training whatever for the very different job of management. A great player, Stuart Pearce, complained – 'My head's full of it' – that he couldn't sleep. Forest went down and Pearce resigned at the end of the season.

Thirty-four years on, Wilkinson's brief is wearily similar to that of Wade: to reproduce what the continentals have done in the way of coaching. Wade tried his best; in fact, Wilkinson was one of the first to come through Wade's new system of national coaches, and eight regional coaches who coached football in local schools. The likes of Bobby Robson, Dave Sexton, later Jack Charlton and Terry Venables were among the first to come through.

But the job was all politics, playing the committees, playing the council. 'It's about making sure you've got people on your side. If someone is leaving, you need to get someone in you can work with. That's the vital thing, the succession. The FA was all politics. I never enjoyed it but you had to do it.'

After a while, Wade realised the FA was not interested in his constant push for change, for a quality structure to rival that of the continentals. 'I was banging my head against a brick wall. They didn't want to be bothered with me banging on about revolutionising the system. They were 70 years old, the councillors. I'm 70 now, I know what it's like. You want an easy life, you don't want to have to think about changing everything.

'I could see us slipping behind in the skills league, and that the FA didn't care about it. After 20 years, I became weary. I didn't protect myself politically as much as I should have done.'

In 1982 Allen Wade was sacked by the Football Association, whose politics had developed an insular, mean kind of ruthlessness. They told him his position was redundant due to a reorganisation. But soon they appointed another Head of Coaching and Education, Wade's protégé, whom he had taught at Loughborough and first brought on to the FA in 1964: Charles Hughes.

Hughes, also a former PE teacher, stayed at the Football Association for 33 years, blooming in the politics-infested stagnant atmosphere, extending his own influence. He popped his head over the parapet only once, triumphantly calling a press conference in 1990 to launch his book, *The Winning Formula*. This book contained the results of 'analysis' of goals stored on film in the FA library. Twenty-five years of sitting in darkened rooms at the FA with a notebook had produced statistics, on how many passes had led to each goal. He noted, for example, that of 109 games played by Liverpool and various international sides, 87 per cent of the goals were scored from five passes or fewer. Of the six World Cup finals between 1966 and 1986, 92.5 per cent of the 27 goals were scored from five passes or fewer.

Hughes, not getting out enough, had developed this into a theory of 'direct play', which urged players, among some more subtle technical advice, to use 'long forward passes to the back of the defence'. He argued that Brazil could have been more successful if they had followed his theories: 'The facts are irrefutable and the evidence overwhelming.'

There is something almost terrible in the memory of Hughes, after years working quietly away in the bunker at Lancaster Gate, emerging blinking into the world armed, proudly, with just this flimsy book. The assembled ranks of national media, summoned for his finest hour, were astounded. They casually strafed him with machine-gun fire, lambasting him as a guru of the long ball. Hughes retreated immediately back to the security of Lancaster Gate, where the sandbags of political protection were thick, packed hard over time.

Hughes, unlike Wade, his mentor, was a consummate politician in Lancaster Gate, playing the arcane committee structure, winning over the FA Council. Under Hughes the coaching department changed from one which spent money on coaching to one which made money for the FA. By then the FA had developed a keen liking for anything which made it a bit of money.

Hughes retained a powerful distrust of journalists which verged on the paranoid. He openly said he hated and didn't trust them, they lied, failed to research anything. He would not talk even to the FA's own press office. And yet, really, Hughes had an easy ride. The media roundly rubbished his life's work when he invited them to view it, but they left him alone after that. He continued to be a very powerful figure at the FA, responsible for all youth development. Safe, powerful, in the bunker. Hughes was to play a pivotal role in the response of the Football Association, the game's historic governing body, to the Taylor Report. And despite media criticism, *The Winning Formula* continued to be a set text on all FA coaching courses, retailing at £9.99, on which Hughes himself was on a personal royalty deal.

In the meantime, in the Eighties, the Football League was imploding into an infighting political mess. The issue, pure and simple, was money. The big club chairmen wanted more of it, not to have to share it with the other clubs. Television and sponsorship, new sources of money, first arrived in the Sixties, small beer at first but becoming more substantial, despite ITV and the BBC acting together to keep the price down. All this money was distributed equally to the 92 clubs in the League.

A new breed of executive emerged, like Martin Edwards, paid for the first time, who did not share the ethos of equality in the Football League. They wanted more of the money for themselves. They were also frustrated by needing a two-thirds majority of all clubs for any decision, which meant the First Division continually being frustrated by the tiddlers. Decision-making was difficult and the Football League was in need of reform, but the big clubs just wanted away. The first heretic whispers around the 'Big Five' – Spurs, Arsenal, Manchester United, Everton, Liverpool – about breaking away to form a 'Superleague' came in 1981. They were bought off by an agreement that in future home clubs could keep all gate receipts, not have to share with the away club. This was the first step towards the bigger clubs' total financial dominance over the smaller clubs.

In 1985 the Big Five made a more serious, concerted effort to break away. This was only averted after crisis meetings mediated by Gordon Taylor, chief executive of the PFA, awarding the First Division 50 per cent of all TV and sponsorship money, greater voting rights in League decisions, and a reduction in the end-of-season gate levy to 3 per cent. This was the winter following 56 deaths in the Bradford City inferno and 39 in the shame of Heysel, and the big clubs were squabbling for more cash, giving their petty scrap an overblown title 'The Heathrow Agreement'.

The Big Five convinced themselves that their motives were honourable, that football was in crisis and that they wanted to 'be in control of their own destiny', as David Dein put it. But they were also after the cash. Martin Edwards betrayed the underlying feeling. 'The smaller clubs are bleeding the game dry,' he said. 'For the sake of the game they should be put to sleep.'

The centenary of the Football League, in 1988, was marked by breakaway talk again, headed off this time by the Big Five doing their own television deal with ITV's Greg Dyke. Dyke had moved quickly to face down the emerging satellite threat from BSB, paying £44m to show the chortling Saint, the grinning Greavesie, and live Sunday matches, mostly of the big clubs. The Big Five therefore got most of the money. But some still had to be shared: 50 per cent to the First Division, 25 per cent to the Second, 25 per cent split between Third and Fourth. The 3 per cent gate levy remained in force.

As the Eighties drew to what would be their terrible close, the Big Five began to get used to the idea of having the bulk of the cash. Irving Scholar, then chairman of Spurs, denies that the motivating factor was greed: 'We wanted to be able to compete in Europe and build our clubs up without being constantly held back by the rest of the Football League.'

But by then Spurs had floated and there was money in it for him as well. The businessmen owners have tended to intertwine their own interests with the wider good of football, as if the whole of football would somehow benefit if they did not have to share any more. They still do that now, wallowing in Premiership riches, talking about the good of the game, while the rest of football struggles for the most basic amenities. Smaller clubs relied on the historic sharing principle to maintain themselves and the 92-club structure.

In his Final Report, Lord Justice Taylor had criticised the lack of leadership given by either body, the FA or the League, and identified that as one of the many causes of Football's Decline. With logic blindingly obvious to anyone with so much as a glimpse of the real world, the football world was told that its divisions were now counter-productive. The Government agreed to reduce the pools tax and give the saving to the Football Trust, a huge figure, to donate as grants to help the rebuilding of the grounds. In the aftermath of Hillsborough, with public money coming in, the different organisations bequeathed by history were asked to recognise that times had changed. They should, it was argued, be smelted to produce one body to govern for the good of the whole of football.

In October 1990 the Football League produced a document, *One Game One Team One Voice*, bearing the badges of the Football Association and Football League side by side. It proposed an end to football's historic divisions and the establishment of one joint board, six members from the FA, six from the League, to run football.

The League was careful to pay its respects to the FA's wider role, its responsibility for all of football, from the grass-roots to the international team, and the entirely unpaid, voluntary efforts put in by dedicated people in the counties, which makes football go round. Stressing the obvious common interests of the FA and League in every area of the game, then League president Bill Fox, chairman of Blackburn Rovers, concluded: 'We are not projecting the advantages of the Football League . . . neither are we projecting the case for the Football Association. What we are doing is projecting the way forward for FOOTBALL!'

But the document, with its basic, obvious common sense, did not fall to be considered by people who had had a glimpse of the real world, but by the FA Council, guided by Charles Hughes and Graham Kelly. With major tragedies having killed supporters, the stench of death hanging over the game the FA had nurtured and given to the world, the governing body's response to the call for unity was almost unbelievably small-minded. It is a truly sad reflection on the inward-looking, self-perpetuating, curdled politics of Lancaster Gate. They simply looked upon it as a threat to their own administrative power: 'The Football League were wanting to play a bigger role in the overall administration of the game. They wanted equal shares at the FA,' says Kelly. 'We couldn't countenance that.'

The FA councillors felt threatened, because, under the League's plan, they would be replaced by a professional board of 12. The worthies would be banished, back to the counties where, underneath it all, they know they belong. Graham Kelly, 20 years behind him previously as an administrator at the Football League, simply saw *One Game One Team One Voice* as a strategic move by the League for power, which needed to be countered. He turned to the best politician and administrator at Lancaster Gate to formulate the governing body's own response to the Hillsborough disaster: Charles Hughes. Hughes set to work on *The Blueprint for the Future of Football*. When it appeared, it would make apparently grand proposals, but the *Blueprint's* aim from the outset, rather than to determine a healthy future for football, was to show the League who was boss.

In November 1990, only a month after the Football League had made its plea for unity, its Big Five clubs went to talk breakaway over dinner with Greg Dyke at London Weekend Television. Overlooking the Thames, amongst the clinking glasses and gentle napkins, in the wake of Hillsborough and the call for a total reassessment of policy for the game, the men had two aims: money and power. Money was first. They wanted more, and they didn't want to share it.

And hang the rest, they thought. They should be put to sleep.

Dyke had his own agenda: heading off the satellite threat, which would surely come from the just-merged BSkyB amalgam, when football came up for negotiation in 1992. Dyke believes football is 'the key television product in England', bringing its guarantee of loyal supporters who can barely survive without football on telly. At the dinner, he told the chairmen that ITV would be interested in covering a Premier League, if they broke away to form it. Dyke denies that he talked actual figures, even 'ballpark figures', but says it was clear the big clubs would get more money if they did not have to share it. The dinner was the start of what would become the Premier League.

That was the response of the biggest football clubs to the call from Lord Taylor for a reassessment of policy. Not a single supporter was asked by these directors about the rights and wrongs of breaking away to leave 72 football clubs high and dry. The Premier League chairmen always protest they were thinking of the general good of football: 'It's not just about greed,' Rick Parry was to say.

But the first person with whom it was discussed was Greg Dyke. Not Bobby Robson or Alex Ferguson. Or even the FA. The chairmen went to look for television money first. Only after Dyke had promised money did they talk to anyone in football. Noel White and David Dein were authorised by the Big Five to, as Scholar puts it, 'have a quiet word' with the FA, to ask if they would back it.

'Our previous attempted breakaways,' says Scholar, 'could be brushed off as the work of greedy chairmen of the big clubs. We needed the FA, the governing body, on-line.' In other words, the clubs needed to get the historically amateur governing body of football to give its name, and therefore respectability, to a breakaway exploitation of the game. White and Dein went along to the cream Georgian headquarters of the FA, the three lions waving in the West London breeze outside, a large picture of the Queen above the mantelpiece in reception. Bastion of the English establishment. Or the bunker, depending how often you have to spend time there.

They could surely not have expected such a warm welcome. Hughes, project director of the *Blueprint*, was supervising an array of FA staff, management and media consultants, lawyers, accountants and academics. Alex Fynn, then working for Saatchi and Saatchi, was commercial consultant, there to work out a financially sound future for the game of football. Hughes, Kelly and Millichip, then chairman of the FA, could hardly believe their luck when Dein and White arrived. Here it was, the opportunity to deliver a profound blow to the Football League. Kelly puts it in minimal terms: 'David Dein and Noel White approached us about breaking away from the Football League and it coincided with what we were doing.'

Kelly does not appear to have thought much beyond the turf war, beyond the 'threat' from the League. Neither he nor Hughes nor Millichip appears to have considered the deeper implications for the FA, with its duty to guard the ethos of football, of backing the big clubs whose sole aim, expressed over a decade, was to grab all available television money and keep it for themselves. The FA, fundamentally betraying its own traditions, blithely agreed to back the breakaway of the big clubs from the rest of football.

The Blueprint for the Future of Football, a 118-page glossy document with colour pictures, was published in June 1991. This was the Football Association's pretence at 'the fullest reassessment of policy for the game'. It was Charles Hughes' next publication, hot on the heels of his success with *The Winning Formula*. It is introduced by Graham Kelly as 'a landmark in the history of football', which is true. But it is a landmark of which the FA should be ashamed.

Looking at it now, it is a curious document, very much the product of its time. The terrible events of Hillsborough had torn away football's jocular Saint and Greavesie packaging to reveal a knacker's yard of near-insolvency, the end of custodianship. The country at large was directionless and beset by problems, just post its Thatcher-dumping, the economy sinking into recession. The *Blueprint* is wordy, full of graphs and the business jargon of the time. It has 16 sections of recommendations purporting to cover all aspects of the game, and claims to be about promoting 'excellence'. Some of its ideas, such as encouraging clubs to build stadia which they would share, were good, but never pursued. But all the guff of the *Blueprint* fails to disguise a nagging insecurity at its heart.

Nowhere does the governing body of football boast about its achievement, of having refined and founded and given the beautiful game to the world. Nowhere does it celebrate the joy of the game, the rich tradition of its clubs, the loyalty of its supporters. It has no confidence in itself or its game. It seems incredibly worried about money.

Almost its first illustrations are two graphs. One is entitled 'Slowed But Sustained Earnings Growth', the other 'Variation in Service Demand with Household Income'. Stiff as an aristocrat talking about visitors to his decrepit stately home, the *Blueprint* says: 'The country's interest in football is undiminished, and the numbers who play and watch it are unreduced.'

'Unreduced'?

Produced by the amateur governing body which had, in better days, regulated commercialism, the *Blueprint* set the tone for the complete takeover of football by business, by people who wanted to make money. By 'market forces'.

'The response of most sectors [to rising affluence on the part of consumers] has been to move upmarket so as to follow the affluent middle-class consumer,' it said in a pertinent guide to football's future. 'We strongly suggest that there is a message in this for football.'

Alex Fynn, who did not see any commercial need for a breakaway, arguing against it from the beginning, projected income of £112m a year if football were to market itself properly. At the time he was laughed at, but he has since been more than vindicated.

The FA's lack of confidence meant that the *Blueprint* was not a genuine reassessment of policy. So many things had gone wrong with what was still a magical game. It was an historic opportunity, with money coming in from the Football Trust and hundreds of millions from the television war, to reorganise profoundly, celebrate football's survival, and plan for a sound and successful future. Instead, it listened to the market forces men of the Eighties, allowed itself to be thought of as nothing more than 'a branch of the entertainment industry'. The *Blueprint*'s language has dated badly, robbing it of a dignity which *One Game One Team One Voice*, a simple call for unity, retains seven years on.

The only firm proposal which has come to fruition is the one which was already decided: the FA was going to back the breakaway of the First Division clubs from the Football League. The Premier League is the big idea nestling in the vacuum of insecurity at the heart of the FA. It would be the ruin of the Football League, which the tiny minds at the FA had come to see as rivals.

Trevor Philips, then the Football League's commercial director and co-author of *One Game One Team One Voice*, was to say: 'When we produced our proposal for power sharing, we kicked a sleeping dog.'

The cream Georgian dog, old, grouchy, flatulent, reacted by biting off the head of the Football League. The Football League was outraged, fought for its life, brought a legal action against the clubs breaking away, which they settled on the promise of £2m per season from the FA and £1m from the new Premier League. Many people criticised the greed driving the Premier League, which argued that the breakaway was somehow good for the whole of football. The Taylor Report had been a plea for grass-roots supporters to be respected, yet they had not been consulted. Most supporters of whatever club have a benevolent, sympathetic attitude towards all others, a sort of solidarity of support. They did not back a Premier League. A Gallup Poll in May 1991 had shown 68 per cent of supporters to be against it, only 28 per cent in favour; 65 per cent thought it was bad for the game, many saying it would be the death of the grass-roots. Gordon Taylor argued, like the League, for the great fabric of English football to be unified, not further fractured by the creation of yet another separate organisation, this one hogging all the money. Steve Coppell was in no doubt about the effect of the breakaway: 'All I can see this doing is making the rich clubs richer,' he said. 'Eventually that will destroy the grass-roots of the game.'

Although Hughes' document purported to have been concerned with the creation of excellence and the benefit of the England team, it turned out that the England manager had barely been consulted: 'People think there must be a lot of my thinking in this Premier League,' said Graham Taylor. 'There is none, and I'm not totally convinced this is for the betterment of the England team. I think a lot of this is based on greed.'

Taylor was disbelieving, as were many people, that the FA could so betray its history and ethos by sanctioning, let alone backing, a breakaway of the rich. But it did. In 1992 the First Division clubs resigned *en masse* from the Football League. They got their wish to go forth and negotiate a whacking TV deal for themselves, and not have to share any of the new riches with their fellow, smaller football clubs. Or even with the FA. The FA had asked for nothing back, not a penny, not a small percentage of what its own *Blueprint* had said could be a massive TV deal. There was no vision, no planning, no weaving of the Premier League into the wider fabric of the game. The Premier League chairmen could hardly believe their luck. They had taken the historic, amateur name of the Football Association and put it next to that of a lager brewer, Carling, in the title of the breakaway venture into football as a business.

The time could not have been better for the prospects of the Edwards bank account. By now, Gazza had fought and cried for

England in Italia '90, blessed by the voice of Pavarotti. Crowds had begun to rise in domestic football. Nick Hornby had written his book, *Fever Pitch*, which removed much of the stigma about football-supporting from the opinion-forming middle classes. Dyke had given the big clubs an idea of how huge the 1992 television deal would be. The money was to be massive, as predicted by Alex Fynn.

The hapless Fynn had entered the FA's bunker unsuspecting of the plots and twists lurking in the atmosphere. He had been hired as a commercial, marketing expert, and he assumed the FA wanted to do its best for football. 'I was naïve,' he says. 'I thought the desire to benefit football was on the FA's agenda, but it wasn't. They were practising politics. There was no necessity for a breakaway to form a Premier League. But the FA just wanted to destroy the power of the Football League.'

So the years of struggle to maintain equality in the League came to an end. The smaller clubs were to be left to their fate. The Football League nearly collapsed in the immediate aftermath of the resignations. And the FA's credibility, its amateur ethos, its governance of the game, finally died. A call for a reassessment of policy and a call for unity, following the unspeakable disgrace of Hillsborough, had fallen to the sectional interests of mean-minded men. The response was to back a League of the big clubs, sailing away to chase the leisure pounds of affluent middle-class consumers. Kelly even agreed to provide referees, organise the registration of players and the disciplinary system of the Premier League. Rick Parry, busy with satellites and pay per view and sponsorship deals and divvying up the cash, would not have to be bothered with the tedious business of actually running a football league, sorting out refs and naughty players.

The breakaway Premier League was, in the end, the only legacy of the call for reassessment made by the shocked, appalled Lord Taylor. The other legacy, all-seater stadia, he had to force on the clubs by law. Left to themselves to interpret the spirit of his report, there was no sense of shame. Only sectional interests and greed. The call for unity had ended up creating yet another separate organisation: the Premier League. In footballing terms, it was identical to the First Division. The only difference was that the big clubs no longer had the duty, as they did in the old Football League, to distribute some of their riches to the lower divisions. They could hog it all.

A robust generation at the Football Association, with a clear idea of itself, an ethos, a belief in the need to regulate commercialism, prevent clubs being mere vehicles for profit-making, had long given way to successors whose working lives consisted of negotiating endless committees and 93 old men. The original, amateur governing body, with its miraculous history, upper-class toffs who created a game which swept the world, was putting its name to a venture which would treat football as a 'product' to be used to make money by a bunch of businessmen.

Heads down, looking no further than the precincts of their own little desks, walls and council chambers, these inheritors of the governance of the game did not even know what they were doing. The big clubs danced in, took the name of the FA, and danced off again to make money. There was no reassessment of policy; not a single supporter had been consulted. In the end the big clubs had got their way, supported by the FA. Football ceased to be a game at all when the Premier League was formed. After Hillsborough, beneath the gloss and the talk, the sporting ethos and belief in equality were dumped by those at the top of football, backed by the FA. The result was the FA Carling Premiership, standing eagerly on the threshold of undreamt-of riches.

9

THE FOOTBALL BUSINESS

If football had had a strong governing body, proud, sure of its game and its ethos, to undertake the fullest reassessment of policy called for by Lord Taylor, it would have felt a weighty duty and responsibility to reorganise the game for the good of all who loved it. Football could never undo the damage of Hillsborough, could never bring the 96 back, or repair the loss to their families. But an effective Football Association would have looked unforgivingly at itself, wondered how the great game had been allowed to sink so low, and dedicated itself to rebuilding its soul.

It had a splendid opportunity to do so. Football was being given public money, the tax break on the pools, handed to the clubs via the Football Trust, which would amount to £200m over four years. As Lord Taylor had noted, football was still the greatest game; it had proved over a century its unique ability to excite, to 'get in the blood', its clubs were deeply embedded in the culture of English life. Even as Taylor reported, crowds were on the rise again.

The FA's own *Blueprint* said football could generate £112m a season for itself, from TV and marketing, without significantly risen match ticket prices. So soon after Hillsborough, massive, unprecedented amounts of money were flooding into football. A decent governing body would have made sure it was spent wisely. And relished supervising the overhaul.

First candidate for overhaul, though, was the FA, and it was never going to reform itself. As Graham Kelly told me, in the interview featured later in this book: 'It is the old cliché. Turkeys do not vote for Christmas.'

Which is why turkeys are not given the choice. If Christmas would have been allowed to arrive for English football, it is not difficult to see what form it could have taken. Football is only a game, a simple, great game. It is not rocket science. It is, of course, subject to social changes, changes of habit, of the pattern of community and family life. But really the *Blueprint* with its graphs and charts and chasing the middle-class consumer had it the wrong way round. Football was by far the most popular game on earth. Half of England's population were said to have watched the lyrical, wonderful, ultimately shattering drama of the 1990 World Cup semi-final against Germany. As easily as that, so soon after the Hillsborough disaster, football was again recognised for its magic. The game's popularity is a remarkable feature of modern life. Football should have had some confidence. When it was well run, well played, shown to a wide television audience, it was incomparable. Consumers of all classes would flood to it.

In England, the first necessity to bring the game up to modern needs was for unity in the running of the game, the need, offered by the Football League, for an end to the petty, arthritic rivalry with the FA and the formation of an English Football Federation, with a tight, professional management board. Had that idea not foundered on the battlements of the Lancaster Gate bunker, a new board could then have clarified its view of football, its essence, what it had to offer, and moved to manage its future.

There would have been no question of a breakaway of the biggest clubs from the rest of football. Since 1884, the Football Association had protected its game from this, and from the greed of opportunist businessmen. The maintenance of some form of sharing had ensured that the vast majority of clubs had survived a century. New money was now finally arriving which could safeguard and shore up the future for all of football. These riches would absolutely not be grabbed only by the big clubs.

A confident federation might have turned to the grasping chairmen of the football clubs and asked what they had done to deserve their positions. It would have wondered whether football clubs, loved and supported by thousands, ought any longer to be under the control of one man. These chairmen were now looking to have Government money, and the forthcoming millions from the television war, and not to share it with the rest of the game. A federation could have insisted that before the clubs were given a penny, they introduce democracy. These were, after all, the men who had presided over the fences, the hooliganism, they had been severely criticised in the Taylor Report for not caring about their grass-roots supporters. Why should they be trusted now with the rebuilding?

The clubs had failed to produce any kind of benevolent approach, mostly doing little in or for the community; with few facilities open to the public. The 'Mr Chairmen' regarded clubs as their personal fiefdoms, and they were now looking to be free to make money out of them. Democracy, ideally, would have involved taking the clubs away from this kind of ownership, which had never been intended when the clubs were formed, and for share ownership to be widened to make the clubs truly controlled by their supporters. AFC Barcelona is owned and governed by 120,000 members who elect their president, not by a single man who could use the football club to line his pockets. To the Catalonians, fiercely proud of their club, that would be heresy. And theirs is the biggest club in the world, bigger than any of English football's new plcs.

Football did have to become more businesslike, to make more money for itself and its clubs. But profit would never have been allowed to become the end in itself, the clubs would become more professional to make them healthy, to ensure their survival. Commercialism could have been introduced with some dignity; real designers examining football's 'brand-loyalty', building on the passion the game inspires, and creating emporia to do it justice. Not hiring someone to slap a legendary club crest on a pair of flip-flops. A strong Football Association could have been a fountain of positive ideas about how to build football's image and sense of itself. And it would also act as a regulator, preventing clubs from raising prices too high, ensuring at least some live league football stayed on terrestrial television, making sure profits were reinvested in the game, not pocketed.

The football, the quality of it, would have been a prime consideration. Clubs could have been encouraged to train managers properly, make use of ex-pros to build large coaching staffs to nurture players of the future. There would have been a concerted drive to do well in the return to European club competition. Clubs would also have been required to weave themselves into their communities, massively expand their public activities, reach out to a new generation.

After a hundred years of muddling through, surviving on love alone, football could have emerged from its lowest point with a sure plan to ensure the watering of its grass-roots and the flourishing of its uniquely huge population of clubs. Some pruning of the leagues, from the Football League downwards, may have been sensible. They could even have called the First Division the Premier League had they really wanted to. But there would have been no running off by the big clubs with all the money, heading off to make a few people very rich, leaving the rest of football in its pre-Hillsborough decay.

But the FA was no such body. Far from taking a grip of its game, it put its name to the breakaway of the big clubs, blessing their aspirations to make themselves rich. Even if the FA had been a robust, organisation, the early Nineties were a bad time to be standing up against greed. Football has always been a product of its time, and at that time, money had ceased to be a means to an end. In the country at large, after its decade of Thatcherism, money was an end in itself. Money was king. Everything which stood in its way; unions, taxes, most communal institutions, many basic employment rights for workers, had been run down, bulldozed, in a drive to reorganise the economy in favour of those looking to make as much money as possible. There was, the Prime Minister had said infamously, 'no such thing as society'. There were only people trying to make money and somehow, the British were told, if the rich were freed from all restrictions, it would bring prosperity to all. When, after severe civil strife – disasters, riots, strikes – the yuppie boom of the mid-Eighties collapsed to reveal a recessionary aftershock of inequality, bank-ruptcies and repossessions, this widening gap was dignified with a philosophy: 'market forces'.

The profit motive became the defining principle of British life. It is sobering to consider now quite how far it has penetrated, how many areas of life – health, education, sport – have lost their sense of what they are and become ruled according to the dictates of buying and selling. It might hurt, the people were famously told recently, but it works. Everything was subjected to 'market forces'. It was argued, without evident justification, that somehow this lack of organisation would ensure the poor were looked after, that the money would 'trickle down' from the fortunes of the rich. It was noticeable that the rich were always keenest on the idea.

The nationalised industries had been privatised, handed to the Stock Exchange, in the belief that if they were run to make a profit for their shareholders everybody would benefit. It was stuff rejected even by the Victorians as too primitive, and which had been alien for well over a century in Britain, where people grew up with accepted axioms such as: 'There is more to life than money'. Institutions had grown up to safeguard that truth, and the Football Association was part of this civic fabric, historically dedicated to preserving the kernel of its beautiful game from the tarnish of too much moneymaking.

The FA's uncertainty, lack of confidence, its *Blueprint*, has to be seen in the context of the times. Greed, pseudo-justified as 'market forces', was good. The Football Association handed football's top echelon to 22 chairmen, a motley crew. Even in the United States, the only other developed country prepared to tolerate the unmitigated fractures of market forces, sport is not organised without restraint. The National Football League knows that competition is undermined if money is allowed to rule. The league operates a franchise system, and a draft system of players, together with a cap on the amount of a club's money which can be spent on players. This is done to ensure some equality between clubs, to make sure the little club always has a chance. Recently, when Major League Soccer was started in the US, the league gave the clubs almost no independence, even allocating players to clubs rather than allow them to outbid each other in the transfer market. The English FA, the first football governing body in the world, concerned with its own turf war, simply handed their name and game to 22 clubs, sent them off to take all the money about to flood into football, and asked them to put not one penny back.

Some chairmen claim they genuinely were not motivated by greed. They too were products of their time, and 'market forces' claims to be good for everybody. David Dein, a multi-millionaire commodity broker who had bought into Arsenal in 1983, seemed genuinely to believe 'trickle down' applied to football's rich man's breakaway: 'Today's decision (to form a Premier League),' he said, 'should . . . reward all clubs, large and small.' Dein, one of the new fat-cat chairmen who has some history of at least supporting football, said recently that the big clubs have a duty to the small: 'With money comes responsibility,' he said.

But when the Premier League was formed, nothing was introduced into its structure to ensure it acted responsibly, for the wider good of the game. Dein may feel it in his bones, but many of his fellow chairmen have no such sense of responsibility. Those clubs which have floated to become public companies – Manchester United, Newcastle United, Aston Villa, Chelsea, Tottenham – now have as their principal objective the making of money for their shareholders.

In 1992, Dein would soon see where his fellow chairmen's priorities lay. The *Blueprint* had proposed a Premier League of 18 clubs, so that the top players would play fewer games and therefore be fresher for England matches. This, the only footballing justification for the breakaway, was ditched because four clubs were unwilling to clamber out of the overflowing Premiership trough into the dry gutter of the Endsleigh League.

The fans, bored by the administrative side of football and wanting only to watch the game, were mostly oblivious to the greed behind the breakaway. The newspapers spent far more time in 1991–92 analysing the damage to another footballing institution, Gazza's knee, than to the surrender of the game to moneymaking. Even now, many supporters are unaware of the difference between the old First Division and the FA Carling Premiership. But the difference is very great. In the Football League, money is shared so that all clubs can survive. The Premier League was formed precisely because the big clubs did not want to share any more with the rest. They wanted to be freed to get rich. And it was the owners who would make the money.

A new breed of financial adviser arrived – accountants, brokers, lawyers, schooled in the nihilism of 'market forces' – looking at football in the most superficial of ways. Football, according to the City, is an 'entertainment product', the clubs are 'brands'. In a report in March 1997 which was widely read by the Premier League clubs, City analysts UBS gave an account of football as they saw it. Entitled *UK Football plc: The winners take it all*, it predicted, approvingly, widening inequality; much more money for the top clubs and the disappearance of many smaller clubs. This is what the report says about football supporters:

'The football fan as a captive customer.

As a business, football enjoys a particularly valuable and often brand-loyal customer base: the fans. Many fans inherit their clubs from parents or friends or by dint of locality, and as such become captive customers (it is unlikely that they will change colours).'

Gerry Boon, of accountants Deloitte and Touche, has been one of the best self-publicists of this new breed, producing an annual survey of football finances which, although only an analysis of publicly available accounts, is given massive coverage by the mostly business-illiterate sports press.

'Journalists are very lazy,' says Boon. 'If they can go to a source for information, they will do so rather than do their own research. We saw football as an emerging industry in around 1992, and began to do this report as something of a marketing exercise. Every year I make myself available to the press. With all the football clients we have picked up since then, I'd say it has paid for itself.'

Boon's analysis of football support, 'brand-loyalty' is that it is 'demand inelastic'. 'That means you can put the prices up but the demand doesn't change. They still buy the product.'

The grass-roots supporters, loyal for a century, who had kept the game going throughout its dark times, were not to be cared for, rewarded, even respected in the new age of football, contrary to the injunction of Lord Taylor. Football took this support for granted, a 'captive market', which could be exploited. The television world saw it as captive too, Sky knowing from hard experience that football was the key to forcing people to buy their dishes. And so the first thing the Premier League did was the débâcle at the Royal Lancaster Hotel, Sugar screaming in the corridor. It sold its supporters to Sky for £305m.

The chairmen were not concerned that the 87 per cent who didn't have a dish would now be forced to pay for something they could have free. They did not even inquire into the quality of the coverage. They were not told there would be Monday night games, repeats of live 'Super Sunday' games, in full, later in the evening. The dancing girls, the fireworks were never mentioned. They were certainly not subjected to the screamings of Andy Gray, even for an hour and a half, let alone years. The club representatives turned up, were presented with two figures and voted for the higher one: £305m between 22 of them, over five years. They shrugged, shook their heads, then extended paws into the middle of the table, to grab their share.

The rest of the football world, the Football League clubs, left on the beach at Lytham St Annes, the non-leagues, the grass-roots – schools and parks teams – which were suffering severe decline in funding and facilities, could only gape as enormous money came into football to be pocketed entirely by the top clubs.

And the wider world gaped a little as well. The arrival of £300m into an industry of only 22 companies was not to be sneered at. It was pure profit, paid just for being part of the Premier League, no costs involved. Suddenly this ragged game, football, was beginning to look like an opportunity to make money. Football fans, vilified for years, were, in market forces-speak, captive. Instead of being penned in, herded about by police dogs, they could be charged more for everything, they would still buy 'the product'. And football was being hyped as never before, it was fashionable. It enjoyed acres of press exposure, amounting to free advertising.

In 1994, I interviewed Gerry Boon. He described himself as a 'missionary' for football's new business age. The Sky deal, he said, was a 'quantum leap in football finance'. The clubs were sleeping giants. 'We are now advising our clients,' he said, 'to regard football no longer as a rich man's hobby, but as an investment vehicle.'

After over a century, the FA had freed the top football clubs from all restraint and allowed them to be used by individuals to make money. The question was who would make it. Some of the old custodians, the likes of Herbert Douglas Ellis, had the wherewithal themselves to stay around to cash in on the launch into the satellite age. Manchester United had shaken off Knighton, and were floated and ready to exploit their market. Some sharper noses, Hall and Sugar, had sniffed money before the Sky deal, acquired clubs as soon as the Premier League was mentioned. But many sitting directors found themselves in trouble, drastically short of money. The Football Trust grants were limited to £2m for each stand. The clubs, wanting to build stands costing £8m and £10m and £12m, needed more money. There were few exceptions: at Liverpool, David Moores, inheritor of the Littlewoods fortune, simply put another £10m into the club to make sure it had what was necessary. Blackburn Rovers was rebuilt with the froth of Jack Walker's Jersey fortune. But no other club had such easy access, and the money had to come from the outside. This could have provided the opportunity for the clubs to become more democratic; proper public issues of shares in return for investment. But this was market forces come to football and in fact the opposite happened.

These were classic circumstances for business takeovers. There was massive public help, grants, to build stands, which would themselves make fortunes. The captive market, the fans, could be charged more, forget what Taylor said about ticket prices, and a new middle-class leisure pound could be chased. Satellite money brought present and future riches. And the clubs, investment vehicles for all this, were for sale, cheap, because they were strapped for a few million cash. Just to get them up and into the satellite era. And so a new generation of entrepreneur came into the game, seeing for the first time, money to be made.

Every single top football club, to get over the short-term cost of the Taylor Report, and enter the altogether more lucrative world beyond, has had a takeover, a flotation or financial reorganisation of some sort. These were not like the old deals, the shares hawked round pubs or money put in in return for a seat in the directors box and a name in the programme. The football clubs were investment vehicles and this was corporate dealing.

'As for the clubs,' Lord Taylor had said, 'in some instances it is legitimate to wonder whether the directors are genuinely interested in the welfare of their grass-roots supporters.

'Boardroom struggles for power, wheeler-dealing in the buying and selling of shares, and indeed of whole clubs, sometimes suggest that those involved are more interested in the personal financial benefits or social status of being a director, than of directing the club in the interests of its supporter customers.'

The next few years were a blatant flouting of Taylor, seeing more wheeler-dealing than ever before. Many grass-roots supporters would be priced out. Some of the hardest heads of the Eighties, to whom market forces had dealt the riches, took their cold look at the figures and began to profess a sudden desire to be involved in football. The idea has grown in Britain that somehow businessmen are brilliant, supremely talented people, men of vision, alchemists. But many are dreary, single-minded, lacking much education or breadth of vision, seeing life, with all its magic, purely in terms of what they can get out of it. And in England, business culture is notoriously short-term, businessmen not looking to build for the future, but to make a quick profit, a killing. It was a bitter irony that the Taylor Report, which had called for an end to football clubs being bought and sold, provided the reason and opportunity for a massive new round of trading.

In many ways football was easy business. The hard work had been done a century before. The early founders had set up clubs, carved out bits of land, formed companies only to protect themselves. People, ordinary people, had taken the game spectacularly to their hearts, propelled its astounding growth. Generations had supported their clubs, standing on terraces, loyalty an article of faith, and the clubs, for all their faults, had never thought to overcharge them, the shareholders still, even in the late Eighties, not mostly in it to make money. The clubs were companies in structure, but clubs in style, and football was a game, not a means of making money. The 'captive market' was captured when football had that ethos.

But to the new entrepreneurs, these were private companies, which they could buy comparatively in the certainty of future profits. The formation of the Premier League, for which the big clubs had been angling all those years, allowed them to take £305m and keep it all to themselves. From 1997, with television drooling over the revenues coming to it on the back of football fans, Sky will put in £670m over four years – all to only 20 companies.

Football itself barely understood all this. The FA had dimly heard in the world outside its bunker the phrase 'market forces' so they were content to assume it gave respectability to its backing of the breakaway. They agreed to do all the Premier League's donkey work, asked for nothing in return, and settled back in their armchairs. The newspaper back pages continued to believe anyone going into football must love it, and delivered gushing, humanising profiles of businessmen moving in on new targets. Barely a sports page looked closely into who these businessmen were and what they wanted from the game.

They wanted what they had always done. Business. Buy a company, build it up, float it on the Stock Market. This is not alchemy, it is not some mysterious genius; it is only boring old business. Doug Ellis says it was similar in the package holiday business after the war. You try to be in the right place at the right time and then you cash in.

As the Sky money came in, the club-companies, with new or newly financed owners, began to dedicate themselves to making money. Lord Taylor's rebuilding programme, against the spirit of his report, itself provided one of the main opportunities for profit-making. Premier League and First Division clubs had to have their grounds all-seater by August 1994. After some changes, lower-division clubs were allowed to retain terracing, brought up to the safest possible standard, by 1999. Lord Justice Taylor had called for the rebuilding to be done with ambition, with style. He had seen European stadia built with local authority help and shared by clubs, incorporating facilities for the community. He pointed to the beautiful stadia of Italy, recently seen in the World Cup, built by local authorities, to the designs of some of the world's top architects, and shared by great rivals, like the San Siro, by AC and Inter Milan. Even the FA *Blueprint* had recommended sharing superstadia.

As with everything else not to their taste in the report, the clubs chose to ignore the plea to build creatively. The reaction of nearly all clubs was the same as that at Blackburn, whose soulless new cladding is the face of the Premier League. They wanted to build stands which would make as much money as possible. Revenue streams, and entertaining. Money, by then, was becoming the heart and soul of football. The Taylor Report, an indictment delivered after the deaths of so many innocent people, a call for the fullest reassessment of policy, became, after due expressions of regret, a commercial opportunity.

Total expenditure on rebuilding stands following the Taylor Report is £620m, £200m of it from the Football Trust. Yet it has produced barely a single stand of note. Bryan Gray, chairman of Preston North End, who built an exception, the award-winning, inspiring Tom Finney Stand, explained his motivations for commissioning it: 'We didn't want to build another Taylor stand.' Explaining the phrase 'Taylor stand', he said: 'Stands were just thrown up after the report, looking to get people in, without any regard to aesthetics or design. We were not going to do that at Preston.'

Some of the bigger clubs were not so proud. At Liverpool, the new Kop compromised on leg room in order to cram more people in. A deal with the yellow arches has brought a McDonalds 'restaurant' in to garnish the Kop's bottom. John de Quidt, chief executive of the

Football Licensing Authority, cited it as a 'disappointing' example of building. 'Some of the building has been exciting. Bolton's new stadium is excellent. But many of the new stands are, I'm afraid, glorified warehouses.'

One of the surprising, inspiring exceptions is the McAlpine Stadium, a curvaceous jewel topping a hill in the dank old mill town of Huddersfield. Football here plays itself proudly into the twenty-first century, the club a tenant in a wonderful stadium built by the local authority, woven into the civic life of the town. The arrangement benefits everybody, yet has hardly been repeated anywhere. The same architects, the Lobb Partnership, built the North Bank Stand at Arsenal, but apart from these isolated exceptions the post-Taylor rebuilding has brought safety and 'revenue streams' to English football grounds but little inspiration. One of the joys of football support, going to different grounds, experiencing their individual character and atmosphere, has now been largely devalued by the uniformity of what has been produced, and the North-South-East-West names the stands have been given.

'We have,' according to Ernie Walker of UEFA, 'some of the safest, but ugliest stadia in the world now. We need to be much more ambitious.'

The prospectuses of clubs looking to cash in on the Stock Market all boast of the profits earned as a direct consequence of the Taylor Report. Newcastle United plc's prospectus, which made Sir John Hall £100m when it floated in April 1997, boasts to the City that: 'One of the central conclusions of the Taylor Report was that . . . the industry should move towards all-seater stadia . . . Premier League clubs' stadia have subsequently been transformed . . . creating a more attractive environment and opening up new opportunities in catering and the provision of executive facilities . . .'

Newcastle tells the City proudly about its 'significantly risen gate prices', 'higher revenues per seat', its 70 executive boxes and 2,336 'executive scheme places'.

The word Hillsborough is not mentioned.

Taylor had said prices should be tailored to the needs of the poorer fans who then stood on terraces for £3 or £4. This has been universally ignored, treated with contempt. Prices have been put up mercilessly, the captive market exploited, many lifelong fans priced out. In 1995, the Football Supporters Association magazine asked, 'Did anybody read the Taylor Report?' It pictured two match tickets, both for Manchester United home games against Coventry City. In February 1988, the price on the ticket, for the Old Trafford Scoreboard Paddock, was £3.20. In January 1995, the same match from the same position, now called 'L Stand', was £15.

At Ken Bates' new non-electrified paradise, 'Chelsea Village', top price in 1996–97 was £40, £25 a standard. In 1997–98, top price rose to £50. In 1989–90, before the Chelsea Village had settled around the gates of Stamford Bridge, people watched the football for an average £7.30.

John de Quidt has emerged as a critic of the greed driving the stadium rebuilding and ticket pricing: 'It is an irony that before the Taylor Report families were excluded from football because of hooliganism. Now they are excluded because they cannot afford to get into the rebuilt grounds.'

Prices generally have tripled, as football has chosen to follow the dictates of market forces, rather than the words of the good judge. Many clubs, such as Arsenal and Newcastle, went further merely than putting the prices up. They had the 'captive market' pay for the rebuilding, with 'bonds'. Supporters at Arsenal, 6,000 of them, paid £1,000 and £1,500 each for theirs. The bond entitled them only to the right to buy a season ticket in the future. These bond schemes could have provided a good opportunity to introduce democracy; Arsenal could have offered shares in return and supporters could have acquired real involvement and ownership of their club. Instead, anxious they might not be able to get into the ground in future, supporters forked out a total of £8m. A massive stand was built with all manner of entertaining in it to make money for Arsenal. But the club is still almost wholly owned by three individuals: David Dein, Danny Fiszman and Richard Carr. When it floats, each will make a great deal of money. The supporters will get nothing. Ticket prices will probably rise again.

The clubs now advertise their stands as banqueting suites and conference centres. At Chelsea, Bates, stern would-be electrocutor of the masses, has reinvented himself. Ken and Ruud, the white beard and the dreadlocks, stroll down the King's Road together, friendly bosses of the cosmopolitan Chelsea Village. The advertising for the

Chelsea Village Hotel, backing on to Stamford Bridge, sums up Bates' new style: 'The very best in three-star accommodation'. In the new South Stand at high-class Stamford Bridge, opening in 1997–98, 'membership' for the 'Galleria restaurant/viewing area' is £2,175 per seat. Executive boxes, mostly seven-seaters, are £2,900 per person.

At Arsenal, the 'business entertainer' can bring between one and 149 guests at £152 per head for a full day's experience, which includes champagne, 'hostess reception', even a football match in the middle. Arsenal's income from this and other corporate facilities in its South and North Bank Stands is buried in its £20m turnover in 1996.

Aston Villa boast about the entertainment on offer round at Herbert's, with boxes from £8,750 to £15,000 for the season and hospitality in the executive clubs starting at £1,025 per season. Villa plc made £1.2m from catering in the eight months to January 1997, and is looking forward to much, much more cash when its new catering and conference centre opens in the Holte End.

Officially, Football Trust grants were not given to build commercial facilities, such as banqueting or catering. But a grant solely for the structure of a stand could still amount to the maximum £2m. Many stands have been built with the help of the Football Trust, public money, and gone on to make fortunes for the club-companies. At Anfield, the £8m Centenary Stand contains 30 executive boxes and the 'Bob Paisley' and 'Bill Shankly' suites – the names of great managers put to venues for sales conferences and commercial exhibitions. On the wall of the Centenary Stand, near where it meets the rebuilt Kop, close to the yellow 'M' of Ronald McDonald, are the flags of Liverpool and Carlsberg, flying side by side. Beneath is a plaque: 'This stand was built with the help of a grant from the Football Trust.'

With 20 clubs in the Premier League all raising their prices to the captive market while simultaneously looking for corporate money, total income, per season, from boxes, hospitality packages and catering is close to £100m. You would think that once clubs had cleared £2m each, from conferences and rack of lamb and waitress service, they would have to pay back the grants of public money to the Football Trust, who could then apply the money to more worthy causes. But they do not. The grants were gifts, and when the National Lottery began in late 1994, pools money plummeted and the Football Trust found itself desperately short of money. The Premier League took a long time to respond, finally announcing in June 1997 that it would put back £20m, over five years, matching similar further grants of public money, this time from the Lottery, to allow the Football Trust to fund rebuilding lower down the footballing ladder. The Premier League expected hearty congratulations for its charity.

Yet an all-out profit motive never sits comfortably with safety, as the litany of disasters which plagued the Eighties proved. John de Quidt says he is reasonably confident there cannot be another Hillsborough at a top ground. But this is because the rules governing safety have been drawn so tight, not due to a change of attitude, an emergent culture of care for the grass-roots supporter.

'One of my most intractable problems,' he told an *FC* magazine conference of stadium managers in April 1997, 'has been to create the same level of commitment to safety at board level as is found among safety officers. In my six years ... I have never been able to get all the Premier League chairmen in a room to address them.'

Even now, after Hillsborough, with the football business boasting to the City about the Taylor Report, almost all the stadium managers at the conference, from all levels of the game, complained that chairmen did not see safety as a priority. Chairmen favoured commercial departments, which made them money. Stadium managers were rarely given budgets, having to beg continually for small amounts of money for basic maintenance. Steve Frosdick, a stadium safety consultant, described football as 'morally bankrupt'. 'This year,' he said, 'I have heard of a Premiership football club refusing its stadium manager £100 for a piece of equipment in the same week as it spent £1m on a player.'

The new business of football was always a safe bet as an investment vehicle, but it probably surpassed expectations. Football has enjoyed a boom, hyped by Sky, which has enabled it to believe that everything it has done has worked, that 'market forces' has been the best way to reorganise. The glamour of the game boosted by the arrival of players from abroad, tempted by huge wages, football is rampant, it is everywhere. The players are icons, showbusiness stars, paid galactic salaries. Celebrities, actors, comedians press their allegiance to this great new game, invented around 1992. Prime Ministers, unlike their predecessor in the Eighties, fall over themselves to be associated with football. The day before the general election, on 30 April 1997, John Major appeared at the Soccerex football business exhibition to pose for a photo-opportunity with the FA Cup. It may not have won him many votes, but perhaps only because Tony Blair was pressing home his credentials as a Newcastle fan.

As a result of the Sky money, the hike in ticket prices, the increased entertaining and hospitality and merchandising operations, the exploitation of the 'captive market', in a short space of time, the turnover of the football companies mushroomed. Manchester United plc, from a sluggish start on the Stock Exchange, is now one of the fastest growing 'leisure companies' in the City. As the City suddenly woke up to the great game, between 1994 and 1997, United's share price multiplied over six times.

Still, though, the 'industry' believes it can go much further. Sam Chisholm of Sky whispered 'pay per view' at the start of his courtship of Rick Parry. Football has persuaded itself that the 'captive market' will fork out to watch every game live on digital television. That, the promise that each club will make individual fortunes from television, is what has been most responsible for the City, after a hundred years of ignoring the ruffians' game, taking an interest in football. Caspian, the media company which took over Leeds United in 1996, has based its whole strategy on pay per view. Their projections are that they can make £60m a year out of it and they want it as soon as possible. Again, nobody has consulted a single supporter. As with the Sky deal, they will be given no choice. If loyal supporters want to watch their football, they will have to pay ever more money for it.

So the football clubs, never meant to be companies at all, have come to be seen as valuable investment vehicles. For those who own valued companies, there are only two ways to get money for their shareholdings, to 'realise the asset'. They can simply sell part of the company, sell some shares, but when a company is private this is difficult. The owners have to find a willing buyer and negotiate the sale themselves. At Leeds United the directors and major shareholders, Bill Fotherby, Leslie Silver and Peter Gilman, did sell out in this way, in the summer of 1996, reorganising the Leeds shares then selling to Caspian, walking away with £5m each.

But flotation is in many ways a much better means for an owner to get his money out of a company. The company is placed on to the Stock Market, with a much increased number of shares, still owned by the same people in the same proportions. The value given to it depends on the assessment of those working in the City as to how valuable the company is, how much it will make its owners in the future. When the company floats, a shareholder does not have to sell his whole shareholding, and he can remain involved, still working in the company. He does not have the hassle, if he wants to sell some of his shares, of finding a buyer himself. The shares are traded publicly, and an owner can sell a few at a time, realising a part of his asset, getting some cash, whenever he wants, when the price suits. The majority of shares in public companies are bought by institutions, insurance companies and pension funds, looking to make money through dividends or through seeing the valuation of the shares increase in future. Martin Edwards has sold five times, making £6m on the float in 1991, £1.2m in 1995, £4.4m in 1996, £16m two months later and a further £5.57m in July 1997, a total of £33m from offloading some of the United shares he and his father accumulated years before. He still has 15 per cent of Manchester United plc.

All of those floating, Tottenham Hotspur, Manchester United, Newcastle United, Aston Villa, Chelsea, Sunderland, Sheffield United, Millwall, Preston North End, Queens Park Rangers, Leicester City, have become non-footballing companies in order to float. The football club is a mere subsidiary of this holding company. This is done specifically to avoid the FA's Rule 34, which preserves football clubs as sporting institutions. The Football Association has watched as its clubs have specifically reassured the City that the FA rules apply only to the football club subsidiary, not to the plc holding company whose shares will be traded. So Rule 34 (a) (v), which says that if a club is wound up, its property must be distributed to other local sporting clubs, no longer applies. This rule, historically protective of football clubs being bought, wound up and the grounds sold off at a profit, is still invoked to warn off sharks. It became an issue at Brighton in 1996, when it was discovered the clause had been removed from the articles of association. But now the FA's own rules do not apply to its biggest clubs. These 'leisure companies' can now be asset-stripped, a real danger, given the likelihood that major conglomerates will buy football companies as 'profit centres'. If the corporate strategy changes, nothing is to stop the clubs being liquidated and the grounds sold off. Or, if a floated club has a bad period, with crowds dropping, the ground could become more valuable than the company itself, which can then be wound up, the ground sold off.

When the club floats, it is the holding company which goes on the Stock Exchange to be traded. Originally Newcastle United Football Club had had 2,000 ten-shilling shares, a history of the backing of a community for its club. These were the shares bought up by Hall in his battle with McKeag, hoovered up from as far away as the Australian outback. Newcastle United plc floated 143 million 5p shares. The 5p is 'face value', the official price. But the Stock Market's valuation is based on its reckoning of the company's value. Newcastle's price on flotation was £1.25 for each 5p share. When the club floated, it was valued at £180m.

Of the 143 million shares, 40 million were new, taken up by institutions in the City. At £1.25 each, this raised £50 million for Newcastle United plc in new money, used to pay off debts, and, the company said, to fund youth development. Taking into account these new 40 million shares, Cameron Hall's share was 57 per cent of £180m–£102m for the Hall family. Shepherd Offshore's shareholding amounted to 7.3 per cent of £180m–£13m – for Freddy Sheperd.

Many reasons have been advanced to justify the flotation of football clubs. The most genuine advantage is that new money can be raised, by issuing new shares and selling them on the open market. At some clubs, notably Preston North End, this was a true reason for the float. The club had been taken over by a local company, the Baxi Partnership, which did not need to cash in on its ownership. Its float on the Alternative Investment Market allowed new investment, while Baxi retained 40 per cent control of the club itself.

But the great rush to flotation began in 1996-97 with the ground rebuilding programme having mostly been completed, undermining the argument that the flotations were necessary to get money into football from outside. Often the flotations have been presented as if the clubs are doing it for the good of the fans, giving them an 'opportunity to invest' in their club. In every club prospectus, flotation has been given a populist window-dressing: 'To give employees and supporters a greater opportunity to invest in Manchester United', was an example from 1991.

This is disingenuous; a sales pitch. It amounts in reality to an invitation to supporters to give their money to the existing shareholders. Many recently, encouraged to put their hard-earned money into their clubs as an expression of support, have seen their value plummet.

The other promise is that it gives supporters 'a say' in the running of clubs. This is one of the justifications advanced by Tony Fraher, of the bank, Singer & Friedlander, who has become another of the missionaries advocating the City as the answer to football's necessary reorganisation: 'Supporters,' says Fraher, 'get the right to go to the AGM and ask questions.'

'Anyone who says flotation gives supporters a say is a hypocrite,' says John Bowler, chairman of Crewe Alexandra. 'It gives them no say whatsoever. The supporter has a handful of shares, no power.' In fact the floated football clubs become much more remote from their supporters, controlled according to the City institutions' demands for dividends or share growth, both earned through profits.

Company structure in itself has always arguably been inappropriate for football clubs. It is something of a historical accident that the clubs were formed into limited companies. But at least democracy would have been more real with the clubs still private companies. Supporters could have invested in them, in return for shares, without seeing their value subject to the changing perceptions of pension fund managers in the City. In fact, this and other reasons for flotation have mostly been advanced to sugar the true reason for a float, as admitted, honestly enough, by Maurice Watkins, Manchester United's solicitor, about United's float: 'The main advantage was to release cash to shareholders.'

The shareholders, who bought their shares before football was a business, a means to make money, have got their cash out. Martin Edwards, Doug Ellis, Watkins himself, are men sitting on enormous personal fortunes created by football's boom. At the time of writing, some 18 clubs have floated. 'I'm struggling to understand why these clubs are floating,' says Darryl Keys, a director of Singer and

Fiedlander, formerly a missionary for the business age whose closer experience has turned him into a critic. 'Flotation is supposed to be done to fund long-term capital development. But in football's case, the flotations have come after the rebuilding of the grounds. In my view, the reason comes down to greed in most cases; the entrepreneurs cashing in.' When the 'football businesses' came to the market, the City generally welcomed them with open, friendly valuations, looking with a kindly eye at this new, strange game, arrived recently from the working classes. It was told about television and the certainty of pay per view, that football had a 'captive market', sitting at home with Sheffield United scarves on and 'Blades' tattooed on their arms, who, like sheep, would fork out £10 for each televised match if forced to do so.

Then, at the end of the 1996–97 season, the City was shocked to find that the emerging football industry has a century-old system of movement between its divisions called promotion and relegation. And that since 1992 the gap between the Premier and 'First' Division has become a galaxy. The 20 Premier League clubs will be sharing £670m of Rupert Murdoch's money over the next four years, the 72 in the Football League only £125m. And the City decided that this made the value of companies like Sunderland plc half what they had been on flotation, each share down from £7.50 to, at the time of writing, £3.85.

Chris Akers, of Caspian, owners of Leeds United, talked openly in April 1997 about doing away with promotion and relegation altogether, as this would make better commercial sense and inject stability into the Premiership 'sector'. Such is the vision for football of some of its new bosses.

The City, looking for short-term profit and the growth in value of shareholdings, appears to base its judgements on surprisingly scanty evidence. Little has emerged which suggests they know much about football at all. In February 1997 a brief press release by Coopers & Lybrand accountants described the football 'sector' as overvalued. Mark Palios, formerly a professional player with Crewe Alexandra and Tranmere Rovers, and a partner in Coopers, said that the City did not understand football, or how poor the management is in football clubs. This small announcement wiped hundreds of millions of pounds off the value of football shares, beginning a gradual dawning of reality in the City. Even the champions, Manchester United plc, the world-wide 'brand', more supporters in Singapore than Stretford, suffered a dip in share price in 1997, from £7.20 to, at the time of writing, £6.10.

Other football clubs, including Newcastle, Spurs and Aston Villa, suffered a drop. Clubs such as Sheffield United suffered a dramatic fall when they failed to get promotion, worth around a third what they were when the City still fancied Blades to go up. The City is interested in football only to the extent that boys looking at figures on pieces of paper reckon they can make money out of it. This is the fate of football now, cast to the winds of the market. If pay per view fails, either because too much of the 'captive market' has been alienated, or because the market is not as captive as the clubs assume, the City could lose interest, plummeting its perception of football. To football lovers, this would be a disaster, but the City is used to taking gambles. Some succeed, some fail. And although to football the amounts bought up by pension funds on flotation are massive, to the funds themselves, football is merely a small new industry, worth a punt.

Here is how the major English football clubs have been wheeled and dealed since the Taylor Report. For the clubs floated on the Stock Market, the value given is the one quoted at the time of writing. Valuation of those still privately owned is difficult, necessarily imprecise, and subject to change. The values given are estimates based on comparisons of floated clubs of similar size and on discussions with City bankers and analysts.

Club	Reorganisation	Value
Manchester United plc	Floated on Stock Market 1991	£429m
Newcastle United plc	Bought by Cameron Hall Developments 1992 for estimated £3m	
	Floated on Stock Market 1997	£181m
Arsenal	Gradually bought by David Dein and Danny Fiszman since 1983	£200m
Liverpool	Still privately owned by David Moores	
	Refinanced by £10m rights issue 1995	£180m
Aston Villa plc	Floated on Stock Market 1997	£99m

Club	Reorganisation	Value
Chelsea	Boosted by investment from Matthew Harding. Floated in 1996 on the Alternative Investment Market as Chelsea Village plc	£177m
Sheffield Wednesday	37 per cent taken by Charterhouse for £17m, 1997	£46m
Wimbledon	Sold by Sam Hammam to Norwegian investors 1997	£30m
Leicester City	Planning to float on Stock Market	£25m
Tottenham Hotspur plc	Floated on Stock Market 1983 Taken over by Alan Sugar for £8m in 1991	£97m
Leeds United	Sold to Caspian Group plc for £30m in 1996	£70.5m
Derby County	Taken over by Lionel Pickering in 1991 25 per cent taken by Elektra for £10m 1997	£40m
Blackburn Rovers	Taken over by Jack Walker 1990	£25m
West Ham United	Terence Brown bought 38 per cent for £2.5m in 1990 Remainder owned still by Hills and Cearns families. Private placement with Nomura 1997	£30m
Everton	Bought by Peter Johnson in 1994 for £10m Rights issue 1997 raised £10m	£100m
Southampton	Reverse takeover January 1997 into Secure Homes	£25m
Coventry	Taken over by Bryan Richardson 1993, £8m investment by Geoffrey Robinson and two others in 1995	£20m
Sunderland plc	Floated on the Stock Exchange 1997	£28m
Middlesbrough	Taken over by Steve Gibson 1994 Owned 68 per cent by Gibson's company Gibson O'Neill, 32 per cent by ICI	£25m
Nottingham Forest	Taken over in 1997 for £16m by consortium headed by Nigel Wray, including Singer & Friedlander, with Irving Scholar as consultant. Planning to float	£40m
Bolton Wanderers	Reverse flotation into Mosaic Investments 1997. Renamed Burnden Leisure plc.	£50m

Most top clubs which have not floated appear to be preparing to do so. Arsenal has seen its shares shifted between David Dein and Danny Fiszman, and the board is deciding on the future of Highbury before going ahead with flotation. It is almost certain that Arsenal will float in the future, and when it does, Dein's will be one of the more spectacular personal football fortunes. He bought his first stake, 15 per cent, in 1983, joining the old Etonian family who sat on the Highbury board. 'I'm delighted,' said Peter Hill-Wood, Arsenal's then chairman, 'but I still think he's crazy. To all intents and purposes it's dead money.' It is the comment to sum up the difference between the two generations of club owners; the custodians, who never looked to make a penny out of football, and the new entrepreneurs, who saw in it the potential to make a fortune. Dein has now accumulated a 33 per cent stake in Arsenal, which would net him, if the club floated, £66m.

Leicester City is, at the time of writing, deep into discussions about a 1997 float. Everton is certain to float if Peter Johnson can achieve some stability and success, depending on the future of the proposed new stadium. Even Coventry City has reorganised itself into a holding company structure. Its shares are held in trust and it is therefore impossible to discover the proportions in which they are owned, but there seems no question that a float will come when the time is right.

A question hangs over Liverpool. Major shareholder David Moores is, in the Littlewoods tradition and as a genuine fan, temperamentally unsuited to flotation, but there is very great pressure now and a fortune to be made, and speculation that a float is being actively discussed at Anfield. Only Middlesbrough appears to be an exception, where Steve Gibson, a local man, a supporter of the club and football fanatic, has consistently said: 'I will not see this club run by faceless institutions in London.' These are admirable sentiments given that Gibson picked up Middlesbrough cheap and would stand to make a fortune if it floats.

The flotations, in the absence of real analysis in the football media, have been presented wide-eyed as a feature of football's boom, rather than as evidence of greed. The influx of foreign players, the rise in crowds, the City's valuations of the clubs, all of these are put forward to argue that all football's changes must have been for the best, that 'market forces' have worked, that the Premiership is a great success. There is an argument, mostly naïve and not based on an examination of the circumstances which produced the boom, that the new chairmen have done a great job, that they have turned football round. The truth is much more troublesome.

Most of the money has come in from outside and was coming anyway. If the breakaway Premier League had not happened, more of the money would have had to have been shared, and more clubs would have benefited. As it was, the Premiership, 22 clubs, carved up the satellite and Football Trust money between them, which it could then borrow against. Despite that, at the same time, they hiked up ticket prices. The amount of money actually invested in football by the new owners has been comparatively small. Generally they bought their shares in clubs for a few million from the old custodians, perhaps put some more money in in the form of loans, getting their payback with interest and salary. This took the clubs over the initial rebuilding, in order to get to the riches available on the other side. On flotation, the shareholdings have been valued massively higher than they were bought for, making the businessmen huge capital gains. The argument that flotations have been done to bring in new investment from the City is not justified by the comparatively small amounts which have actually been raised. Some argue, again with scant knowledge, that these men took a risk and therefore deserve a reward. But football was not much of a risk. It was the greatest sport in the world, proven over a century to have phenomenal support. It had been mismanaged and undervalued for years, and now the Sky deal was coming.

'Yes, I must admit,' Peter Johnson told me, 'I didn't think Everton was much of a risk when I bought it.' His capital gain, in four years, is £46m at the time of writing.

The Premier League clubs argue, as do most other rich people, that this, nothing standing in the way of their own enrichment, is the best way to run the game. No sharing, little regulation, no restriction on ticket price rises, no requirement that any games be seen on terrestrial television, no watering of the grass-roots. For the rich to get richer and hold all the power. The City, and a growing number of advisers looking to get some of the new football coin for themselves, have had two decades of everything their own way, and they appear genuinely to believe that running everything only for profit works.

Tony Fraher, an urbane, persuasive man, told bewildered football journalists on the launch of Singer & Friedlander's football fund in February 1997 that all was well, the marriage between the City and football was made in synergic heaven. 'The City will introduce better management into football, and it will be in everybody's interests to have a well-run club. What we're doing,' he said, whether tongue in cheek or genuinely misguided, 'will help bring football back to its roots in the community.'

There is truth in the argument that football needed to introduce financial discipline. Clubs needed to sort out their commercial operations, to get a better television deal, to get corporate money in, to produce decent merchandise. But the individual clubs should have been encouraged to do this within the framework of a game which ensured the money was spread for the greater good of all, and that grass-roots supporters were protected. Making money is one necessary part of a healthy organisation, but it has become clear that the public company, floated on the Stock Exchange and therefore run by City institutions, is not an ideal structure for a football club. The need for dividends overrules the desire for footballing greatness, and it is almost impossible for tradition to be safeguarded, for benevolence, if the sole aim of a football company is to make as much money as possible. The concentration of money in the hands of the rich has not been justified by club success in Europe or any real improvement in the England national side. Indeed, English clubs' performances in Europe have mostly shown a deep inferiority to continental technique, which has been produced from quality coaching, not a belief in instant managerial transformation and a drive for profit alone. In the wider game, already the inevitable consequences of running anything for the untrammelled gain of the rich are becoming clear. Inequality is the deepest stain on football. While the top clubs wallow in wealth many Football League clubs are in trouble. The grass-roots are parched, worse off than ever.

The City supports this, fully expects the rich to get richer and some clubs to go out of business. All structures, the governing body, the sharing of money, the ethos of football as a game, which previously ensured this did not happen, have been removed.

In *UK Football plc: The winners take it all*, co-written by Julian Easthope and Guy Feld of UBS, the analysts predict that the gap between the big and small clubs will continue to widen. Pay per view they describe as 'a footballing gravy train'. They think there will be some takeovers of football clubs by large corporations: 'We expect more corporate activity in the sector as media and possibly leisure companies grow to understand the value of the rights and franchises possessed by the top clubs.'

I asked Easthope if football was not in danger of being wrenched apart like any unregulated industry, like the food industry for example, in which corner shops, homely, friendly, local places, have been thrown to the wall by the relentless national march of Tesco, Sainsbury, Safeway, Asda. The footballing equivalents, clubs built with a century of love, holding lifetimes of memories, the Bournemouths, Brightons, Hull Citys, threatened with insolvency, while Manchester United, Newcastle, Arsenal, Liverpool, talk about the money to be made in a European Superleague. Easthope did not disagree; in fact he approved of this prospect.

'There is consolidation in any industry,' he said.

'I think the big clubs have a really great future,' said Feld. 'But I'm bearish about the small fry.'

There is a phrase for supporters of Wrexham, Hereford, Northampton: 'Bearish about the small fry.' From phrases such as these, spoken casually by boys in the City, cherished local institutions are laid to waste. The FA and Football League knew a century ago that 'market forces' would inevitably produce 'consolidation', although they probably called it greed then. They decided they were concerned for the good of all, and for the inherent quality of the game, so they arranged for sharing of money. A sport needs governing, the commercial imperative to be balanced by other values. The City has nothing to tell football about how to run itself; it cares as much for Crewe Alexandra as for some corner shop in Crewe. In England, though, with market forces rampant in every area of life, the FA seems to have forgotten the reason for its existence.

Football in the Nineties, an 'industry' given over entirely to money-making, has produced some benefits; the rebuilt grounds, the foreign players, although both of these have serious downsides; the grounds rebuilt dismally, the atmosphere destroyed, and the foreign players taking much of football's new wealth into their own bank accounts, and cutting down the opportunities for home-grown players.

The disadvantages are becoming clear. While the likes of John Hall have personally become £100m richer, many areas of football are desperate for small amounts of money. For a century, the game muddled through, crying out for unity, planning, some reform, some investment in the grass-roots and the distinguished fabric of the game. The disgrace is that now, the time of greatest ever wealth, is the time of least redistribution. Football has fallen to the dogma of its day. 'Market forces.' Bearish about the small fry. Consolidation.

I asked the FA's lawyer, Nick Coward, whether Rule 34 should not have been updated, to allow investment from outside, but to ensure, as the FA used to do, the integrity of football clubs. 'This is a different time,' he smiled. 'The market will decide what happens to clubs.'

The market is already deciding. It has allocated fortunes, unbelievable fortunes, in a handful of years, to people who saw the chance to make a killing from clubs which people used to keep going for years without a thought of profit. The ethos, the heartfelt desire to play, to watch, to support, is being drained from football as it becomes a commodity, a branch of the entertainment business. Lord Justice Taylor had called for a total reassessment of policy, but what happened was a total abdication of responsibility in favour of exploiting the game to make money. The game of football has become a business, an 'industry'. In many ways it is similar to the privatised utilities: gas, water, electricity, trains, which were owned by the public, sold cheaply to City institutions, and have since produced 'fat cat' directors and made such excessive profits that they are subjected to a windfall tax. In some ways, football has been cast more extremely to the winds of the market because, unlike the utilities, there is no regulator, no Ofwat, Ofgas, Oftel, established to preserve fair prices for supporters, to ensure that profits are invested in the long term.

Football was simply taken over, the people's game effectively privatised. Margaret Thatcher, putting the whole of Britain through the same transformation, never liked football, had wanted to confront it, crush what she saw as its dangerous excesses. Lord Justice Taylor stepped in to put a quiet stop to the identity card scheme. But his report provided the superstructure for businessmen looking to make money.

Football was Thatcherised in the end, but not in the way contemplated, by her harsh, punitive hand. It was, ultimately, a more standard Thatcherite transformation: the embracing of 'market forces', the chase for money, carrying the game away from its hundred years' sense of itself, from any belief in custodianship, community, accelerating away from the grass-roots supporter. Pricing ordinary people out. Looking to attract business, the corporations. Revenue Streams. Conferences. Banqueting. Making huge money for the few, punishing the many with higher prices. No longer sharing, and failing to look to the long term and the struggling grass-roots. Jack Walker, who created from three-sided scratch the corporation which most epitomises the FA Carling Premiership, handed Thatcher her ultimate symbolic triumph over working-class football. In Blackburn, the poor northern town, with its permanently Labour council, Jack Straw the local MP, Jack Walker made his own most admired politician honorary vice-president of Blackburn Rovers. You can see her in the programme, if not in the ground: Baroness Thatcher of Kesteven.

Football looks to persuade the public that all changes have been for the good. But great changes are taking place, and many, and the widening inequalities in the game, are clearly damaging. The glossy ups of the new age are obvious, screamed out by Sky TV, bombarding subscribers with the pitch that the Premiership, 'undoubtedly', is 'the best league in the world'. But football is a subtler, more delicate phenomenon than a mere product to be used to sell satellite TV, a 'dish-driver', to use the jargon. As the initial bubble of the Premier League bursts, it reveals profit and commercialism where the heart and soul of football used to be. Like so much else in Britain, football needed to become more businesslike, and it ended up no more than a business. There have been a few very big winners. The losers, watching aghast as the money pours in and is devoured by greed at the top, struggle to have their protests heard above the clatter and din of hype.

10

FOOTBALL'S FAT CATS

In preparing for this book I asked most of the Premier League chairmen for an interview. They are all-powerful in football now, having managed to sneak into Lancaster Gate by the front door and take all the FA's authority away, while it was looking. The rest of the game has to knock on the Premier League's doors begging for crumbs. And the Premier League drives a hard bargain; it always wants something in return. People who plead for some of football's great new wealth to be redistributed to the wide, traditional pyramid of the game, have to persuade the Premier League that it is in the big clubs' interests. They cannot just ask them to give it, even though some individual shareholders have so much more, personally, than whole strata of the game.

I wanted to ask the chairmen about what they have done, about how they have turned football into a business, and also ask the question that is genuinely puzzling about much of this breed of chairmen-owners. Why do they want so much money?

Most people dream, a dream exploited by the Lottery or pools, of one day having maybe a few hundred thousand pounds. It would ease insecurity, banish worries about the next gas bill, fix things up, buy some luxury. Maybe sort a few other people out for some cash. Free the mind from all the worry. But the moneymaking in football is beyond that, way beyond it. These are enormous personal fortunes, unimaginable to most people.

Yet few of these men have ever given their justifications for how much they have taken from the people's game. So many people give themselves to football, to watching, playing, running teams, out of love, without a thought they will ever make a penny from it. But these men have taken charge of great, historic football clubs and, for the first time in football's history, made personal fortunes out of them.

Anyway, Martin Edwards refused. Sir John Hall never replied. Alan Sugar's personal spokesman, Nick Hewer, is very obliging, lets you see the newspaper cuttings, tells you what a nice guy Alan is, how he only bought Spurs so he would have somewhere to take the family, but an interview isn't on. Jack Walker never talks. Robert Coar is left in Blackburn, taking the orders from Jersey, and he obliged. David Dein gave me his number but didn't seem too happy about it and the Arsenal press office took four months to reply that he did not see it as 'the sort of project he wishes to undertake at the present time'. Sam Hammam was different; he hadn't sold for £30m at the time I contacted him; I wanted to talk about Wimbledon being the grafting exceptions in the rich man's league. He rang, but said he was sorry, he couldn't do justice to it on the phone. Ken Bates never replied. Peter Johnson said yes, which was good of him. So did Douglas Ellis. It was striking, with both Ellis and Johnson, who had been so purposeful about making the most of their financial chance, that neither would say they had deliberately made so much money out of the game. It was 'an accident', or 'just a row of noughts'.

Here is a list of how much these businessmen have personally made out of football in the very recent past.

The list is is not definitive; there are many more who have cashed in, but these are the main shareholders of the major clubs, with values at the time of writing. The amounts they 'invested' – usually the price of acquiring a shareholding – were put in when the clubs were private. They have therefore never been publicly disclosed. Some have been publicly estimated and come to be accepted. Some of the investment figures are estimates; where I have written 'undisclosed' this means not provided by the club. The current worth of their shareholdings is, in the floated clubs, the value at the time of writing. The other clubs listed are those likely to float; the valuations are estimates based on the proportion they own of their clubs and the expected City value of the club given in the previous chapter.

Name and Club	Investment	When	Current worth of stake
Manchester United			
Martin Edwards	£600,000	1978	£64m, already cashed in £33m
Amir Al Midani	£500,000	1986	£8.5m, already cashed in £8.2m
Maurice Watkins	£50,000	1977	£11m, cashed in £1.1m
Newcastle United			
Sir John Hall and Family	£3m	1989-92	£103m
Freddy Shepherd	£300,000	1980s	£12.7m
Leonard Hatton	Undisclosed	1992	£6.7m
Arsenal			
David Dein	£300,000 est	1983	£66m
Danny Fiszman	£8m est	90s-1996	£90m
Richard Carr	Undisclosed	Undisclosed	£40m
Aston Villa			
Herbert Douglas Ellis	£500,000	1982	£33m, cashed in £4m, 1997
Peter Douglas Ellis	Undisclosed	Undisclosed	£1.6m
Sir W.S. Dugdale	Undisclosed	Undisclosed	£2.7m
Chelsea			
Ken Bates	£1 plus guarantee of debts	1982	£50m
Wimbledon			
Sam Hammam	£100,000 est from Ron Noades	1981	Sold 80 per cent for £30m, 1997
Leicester City			
Ken Brigstock	Undisclosed	Undisclosed	£2.9m
Roy Parker	Undisclosed	Undisclosed	£2.4m
John Elsom	Undisclosed	Undisclosed	£2.5m
Martin George	Undisclosed	Undisclosed	£2.7m
Tottenham Hotspur			
Alan Sugar	£8m	1991	£50m

Leeds United

Leslie Silver	£1m	1980s	Sold for £5m, 1996
Peter Gilman	£35,000 plus guarantee of debts	1992	Sold for £5m, 1996
Bill Fotherby	£35,000	1992	Sold for £5m, 1996

Now owned by Caspian Group plc, a media company, which bought Leeds United in 1996 for £30m. Value now £70.5m. Shareholders: Richard Wright, Chris Akers.

Everton

Peter Johnson	£20m	1994–97	£66m

Southampton

Roger Everett	£15,000	1984	£7.25m
Guy Askham	£3,500	late 60s	£963,000
Ian Gordon	£2,650	1988	£721,000
Brian Hunt	£2,650	1988	£721,000
Keith Wiseman	£2,650	1987	£721,000
Mike Richards	£2,650	1987	£721,000
Lawrie McMenemy	£500	1996	£136,000

Sunderland

Bob Murray	£250,000	1986	£11.2m
John Fickling	£600,000	1995	£3m
Peter Reid	£300,000	1996	£1.35m

Nottingham Forest

Nigel Wray & others:	£16m	1997	£40m

The total worth of these 34 individuals and the Nottingham Forest consortium, swollen in the satellite age from mostly small amounts of money put in to buy shares in football clubs comparatively recently, is £925m.

11

THE REBUILDING PROCESS

In 1996, Football Came Home. Back to England where it was born. Three lions on the chest and all that. The national game rehabilitated, cleansed, reborn. Everybody praised football then, wanted to be associated with it, to sing its praises. To wave a flag of St George and sing along with the two comedians, Skinner and Baddiel, cheerleaders of replica shirt-supporting football in its new business age. What an age away Hillsborough seemed; the terraces, the pens, the policing, the crush. Who could believe it was only eight years ago, people dying at an FA Cup semi-final? The rebuilt grounds were a central, vital part of the national celebration: the new safe, mostly boring stadia, full of boxes, good enough now to host major international championships. Anfield, Old Trafford, Elland Road, St James' Park, Villa Park. Hillsborough itself qualified as a venue, sharing Group D with the City Ground. Graham Mackrell, who had been the 'safety officer' at the ground on 15 April 1989 was 'centre director' of the two grounds. The disaster was not mentioned in the 'factfile' on Hillsborough in the Euro '96 brochure. And what a tournament it was, everybody was agreed, a triumph, the whole of football rebuilt, Hillsborough left far behind. Football had come home.

Six months after the tournament, on Thursday, 5 December 1996, ITV screened a film, *Hillsborough*, by Jimmy McGovern, writer of *Cracker*. The film revealed that for the people most affected by the Hillsborough disaster, it was not a faded memory at all. They had lived with it every day since it happened, a tormenting, tortuous, grief-stricken whirlpool. Still a major, awful part of their everyday lives. It turned out that while the football clubs had rebuilt after and on the back of the Taylor Report, cashed in and come home, the families of the people who died at Hillsborough had been unable to move on, to rebuild their lives. For eight years they had experienced the flipside of 'market forces' Britain, dragged through a very different, but altogether familiar, British landscape.

In the wake of the disaster, some of the families had gone to the Taylor inquiry, which had started on 15 May, only a month later. They had made friends, found some solace in sharing their grief. Liverpool City Council social services organised a drop-in centre. Then there was a letter suggesting the families have a meeting and form a support group, ready for the emotional and legal strains to come.

At first, Phil and Hilda Hammond had not wanted to go. 'You just have your own grief,' explains Hilda of her feelings. 'Now, we families have all relied so much on each other for so long, it seems incredible, but at the time, I didn't really want to meet them all.

'Then, as time went by, I felt I wanted to meet a mother who had lost a 14-year-old son, like I had. Those whose children were grown up had a slightly different grief. They had known what their children looked like as adults, what they had achieved. I was desperate to meet someone whose son had been killed at 14. That was what made me go in the end.'

People were tentative, quiet, at the first meetings. Then one night, Jan Spearitt, whose son, Adam, had been 14, made contact with Hilda. 'Jan felt the same way I did. She'd seen our name and address in the papers and she said that so many times she'd felt like getting in the car and just driving over. Since then Jan and Eddie, her husband, have helped us so much, and I'd like to think we've helped them.'

The Spearitts, like the Hammonds, also had a younger son, Paul, nine. The two families brought their remaining children together. Paul and Graham, then 11, never discussed the losses of their older brothers, but they played together, became best friends, stayed over at each other's houses.

The Taylor Report, with its findings of negligence and police culpability, its criticism of the police allegations of drunkenness, was not admitted in evidence to the inquest when it began under coroner Dr Stefan Popper in Sheffield in November 1990, because the evidence had not been given on oath. The coroner's court, in which the cause of a death is established by a jury, is an anachronistic mix, barely reformed from its ancient origins, the focus of constant calls for reform. The coroner, paid by the local council, does not act like the judge in a criminal case. Uniquely in the English system, the coroner is the investigator of the death. He controls the gathering of evidence and the taking of witness statements, done on Dr Popper's behalf by the West Midlands Police under assistant chief constable Mervyn Jones. The coroner decides what evidence should be put before the jury. The families of the dead have no right to ask to see this evidence beforehand, or to see the evidence the coroner has gathered but decided not to put before the jury. Legal aid is not available to ensure that the families of the dead have legal representation. The Hillsborough families had to pay to be represented; the Hammonds joining with 42 other familes to pay £3,000 each into a fighting fund of £126,000, to have solicitors and a single barrister represent them collectively at the inquest. The police and Sheffield City Council were represented by solicitors and barristers paid for out of public funds.

In total, nine barristers were employed for interests other than the families; acting individually for Sheffield Wednesday Football Club, Eastwoods, the engineers, Sheffield City Council, the South Yorkshire Police and one each, paid for by the Police Federation, the policemen's union, for police officers Duckenfield, Murray, Greenwood, Marshall. The Police Federation itself had a lawyer there, representing the police collectively. These barristers often acted together to cross-examine survivors giving evidence.

The coroner decided to hold 95 mini-inquests, at the rate of eight a day, in which the circumstances of each death were outlined in a strictly limited way. The Director of Public Prosecutions, also assisted by the West Midlands Police, was at that time still considering whether the negligence of the club, council and police amounted to a criminal offence, most probably manslaughter. Because of that, and the right of people not to incriminate themselves, the mini-inquests were limited to the movements of the dead supporters up to their deaths. The families could not ask a question which might touch on liability for the deaths. Before the mini-inquests started, Popper and Mervyn Jones went in and out of the court a number of times to enable cameramen and photographers to take their pictures. Once inside, each family, called in to the mini-inquest, heard the name, age and address of their loved one read out. This was followed, in every case, by a blood alcohol measurement. There was then a statement by the coroner, a presentation by the pathologist, a summary of witness statements and a presentation of photographs and television coverage by the West Midlands Police. They could barely ask a question. Then it was over.

'I came out of there,' says Hilda Hammond, 'and I said: "I feel like I've just been to the theatre." '

The medical evidence as to Philip's death was that he had died in hospital, from haemorrhaging as a result of a rib piercing his lung. They were told that an 'unidentified doctor' had treated him. Hilda, a senior nurse, wanted to know what treatment had been given. They were not allowed to ask.

At the start of the general inquest, into the whole course of events at Hillsborough, the coroner announced he was going to restrict the evidence to what happened before 3.15 p.m. on the terrible day. The medical evidence, he said, was that 3.06 had been 'the latest time when the real damage was done'.

'. . . The overwhelming evidence,' he said, 'was that once the chest was fixed so that respiration could no longer take place, then irrevocable brain damage could occur between four and six minutes.'

The time he chose, 3.15, was the moment that the first ambulance arrived on the pitch. He said it provided a 'convenient marker' because it could be seen on television. But the symbolism was powerful: all attempted medical help, what happened to the injured or dying in ambulances, hospitals, in the hellish gymnasium, even on the pitch, after 3.15, was to be excluded. The decision seemed utterly unsupportable, given that many people had lost consciousness in the crush but been taken to hospital and saved. One man, Andrew Devine, was in a coma, being cared for by his parents at home in Allerton, Liverpool. He was to wake up, begin to communicate with his parents, in March 1997, aged 30, nearly eight years after the crush which caused his brain damage. Nevertheless, 3.15, nine minutes after the most severe crushing, remained the limit of the coroner's inquiry.

The individual causes of death were never fully investigated, the course the dying had followed, who had tried to help them and how.

For the families, the deaths of their loved ones became little more than the backdrop to a general account of what happened at Hillsborough that day. And the job of the nine barristers, there to represent their clients, was to persuade the jury against a finding of unlawful killing. It was to avoid their clients being blamed for the deaths.

The police waded straight back in with the story discredited by Lord Justice Taylor, about the disaster having been caused by Liverpool supporters arriving drunk, many without tickets. Taylor, in his report, had contrasted the openness of the junior police officers – 'alert, intelligent and open' – with the approach of the senior officers. They, he said, had been 'defensive and evasive witnesses'.

The families, travelling from Liverpool to Sheffield and back every day for 93 days – the longest inquest ever in Britain – had to sit silently through the police rolling their stories out again about drunkenness. At Hillsborough, uniquely in all the disasters which rattled their deathly roll-call in the Eighties, the dead, as part of their post-mortems, had blood samples taken to check their alcohol levels. Even Jon-Paul Gilhooley, who was ten. Almost none of the dead had excess alcohol in their bloodstreams. Yet drink continued to be played out as a major issue at the inquests, just as the blood alcohol measurement had been deemed to be the most important characteristic of the deceased at the mini-inquests.

In *No Last Rights*, a thorough account of biased media coverage of Hillsborough and the injustice of the legal processes, the authors, Phil Scraton, Ann Jemphrey and Sheila Coleman, quote the coroner's explanation for the unprecedented decision to take blood-alcohol measurements: 'I felt it was a justifiable investigation given where it happened and all the circumstances surrounding it . . . the alcohol level was something which sprang to mind as something which could possibly be relevant.'

Phil Hammond, along with all the families, sees a terrible purpose and consistency in the whole course of the legal process, beginning with Duckenfield's lie and continuing, almost with a life of its own, throughout the aftermath. There had been the taking of blood samples, completed within 48 hours, looking for alcohol. Then, within 72 hours, the police, feeding the 'Truth' lies to *The Sun*: 'Right from the minute Duckenfield, with people dying all around him, lied to Graham Kelly, instead of taking responsibility and admitting he'd ordered the gates to be opened, the police line was set. They were going to blame the supporters for deaths which their own policing had caused. They were going to say that our loved ones died because drunk Liverpool supporters had come late, forced the gates and poured into the ground. When they knew it was all lies.'

A barman was called to the inquest, saying fans had drunk his pub dry, been out of order, ripped a cigarette machine off the wall. His testimony was carried widely in the press. The families called the manager of the same pub, who said it was nonsense, he'd have the Liverpool fans back any time. It had been a normal, big football crowd, in fact happier than normal, it being a sunny day, and a semi-final. His testimony was not widely carried.

The second, major part of the police's case that they had not been culpable was that the camera showing the Leppings Lane terrace was not working. This, they said, prevented them from seeing what was happening. They did not have binoculars either. And for a time, they said, the radios weren't working. Taylor had never mentioned this. His Interim Report is clear: 'The officers in the control room could be expected to keep a close watch on pens 3 and 4. They had a direct view of them from an elevated position through their window. Although they had no field glasses, there was the zoom facility on the TV camera.'

At the inquest, Police Constable Trevor Bichard, who ran the CCTV system in the police control room, gave the evidence about the camera, Camera 5: 'My recollections are that the particular camera had been faulty ...You were getting what is called flare. The camera was not being used as much as it would normally be because of the substandard picture ... It was set and left in that position.'

The control room operated five cameras. Two video machines taped the cameras in sequence, staying on each one for a few seconds, unless the police overrode that and directed the tape themselves. The coroner, assisted by the West Midlands Police, said that no film could be found of the Leppings Lane terrace at the crucial time. The first film of it began after 3.02. To this day, no film has ever been produced of the Leppings Lane Terrace between 2.30 and 3.02. At the inquest Bichard said the tape was recording pictures from Camera 5, and that there should be film of it, but that the picture was poor. The night of the disaster, two video tapes were stolen from the Sheffield Wednesday control room. It turns out that they would not have shown the Leppings Lane terrace, but nobody has ever been caught for the theft of tapes from a disaster scene. And nobody has ever been shown the film of Leppings Lane at the crucial, terrible time.

In the absence of film, the police pursued their line that they could not see clearly that people were dying and in need of help, rather than invading the pitch. This was the main foundation of their aggressively argued case that they were not criminally negligent in opening the gates, then failing to react to the disaster as it unfolded before their eyes. The coroner said that 'the assessment of the terraces', was 'a very important factor, maybe the single most important factor in the whole inquest.

'The total sum of evidence from the control room, that is Mr Duckenfield, Mr Murray, Mr Goddard and Mr Bichard was that none of them noticed any problems with the pens until three o'clock.'

Eddie Spearitt gave evidence about the death of his son Adam. They had gone to the match together, arrived at around 2.30, and seeing the crush outside Leppings Lane, stayed away behind it. Eventually they had entered the ground through Gate C when it was opened. Eddie told the inquest about the absence of signs, stewards or police directing them away from the crowded pens. He and Adam had ended up at the front of pen 4, close to the emergency gate. When the crush came, he said, it was 'like a vice'.

'I turned Adam round to me. He was obviously in distress. There was a police officer just slightly to my right about five or six feet away and I started begging him to open the gate. When I say in my statement that I was screaming, I literally mean screaming. Adam at this time had fainted and my actual words, although they are not on a statement, were, "My lovely son is dying", and begging him to help and he didn't do anything. He just stood there looking at me.'

Eddie described the desperate efforts he had made to try to save his son. He had tried to lift him by the lapels over the ten-foot fence. Failing, he tried to punch the fence with his bare hands, succeeding only in making his hands double their size and full of holes. 'No one opened that gate. Right at the beginning when I was begging the officer to open the gate, if he would have opened it then I know I could have got Adam out. I know that because I was there and know what the situation was.'

Eddie and Adam Spearitt had both lost consciousness in Pen 4. Eddie was placed on a ventilator in intensive care and he recovered. Adam was pronounced dead at 4.45.

The families sat through all this, the harrowing evidence from survivors trapped in the crush, the sight, the sound, the smell of people in agony and dying their last all around them. The survivors' traumatic evidence was picked at in forensic detail by the army of barristers ranged, they felt, against them. The families' own representatives were often apologetic and unassertive, advising the families to contest the inquest procedures all together at the end.

'Some of the families sat through all 93 days, every day in Sheffield,' recalls Phil Hammond, 'and their loved ones were mentioned only once, in a roll-call of the dead.'

Philip was mentioned only once in addition to that, in passing by one of his friends, giving evidence about the crush, when he said: 'I lost sight of Phil.' The Hammonds never found out what happened to their son in hospital, before his body was brought back to that gymnasium, a polaroid put on the board for his uncle to search through.

The coroner spent 17 pages of his summing up dealing with the allegations of drunkenness. He then instructed the jury that they could only decide the deaths were accidental, or that the dead had been unlawfully killed, or pronounce an open verdict. '... the word accident straddles the whole spectrum of events,' he said, '... from something over which one has no control ... to a situation where you are in fact satisfied that there has been carelessness, negligence ... it does not mean that nothing has gone wrong ... bringing in this verdict does not mean that you absolve each and every party from all and every measure of blame ...'

The families watched as the jury returned on 28 March 1991 with a verdict of accidental death. They were stunned. Bewildered by what they had been through. The callousness of the police on the day, the infuriating, unjust procedures of the coroner's court. Hilda Hammond says it changed her whole view of the country: 'Before that, I believed in British justice. We all did in our family. One of our worries is that Philip was so law-abiding that if he'd got out of the front gate at Hillsborough and a policeman had told him to get back, he'd have done it.

'I thought they would find the truth of how Philip died, how they all died, and that if anybody was found to be to blame they would be punished. We would at least know then, and we could mourn for Philip, with all the legal procedures out of the way. We could start to come to terms with what had happened. I was so naïve. The whole aim of it all seemed to us to have been to clear the police. And if that meant blaming the innocent Liverpool people, fine.'

In *No Last Rights*, the authors itemise each Orwellian twist and turn of the inquest, describing it as a 'grave miscarriage of justice'. Every single legal procedure was to go against the families and in favour of the police. The South Yorkshire Police, Sheffield Wednesday Football Club and their engineers, Eastwood & Co, admitted they had been negligent. Yet the Director of Public Prosecutions decided that nobody should be prosecuted.

The full, calculating coldness of English law came to visit the families, wearing its blackest shawl. Families who have lost a child get a standard Government £3,500 bereavement payment. Those who have lost adults get nothing from the Government. Damages from those who admit negligence are assessed strictly according to financial loss. There is no compensation for pain and distress. As most of the dead were children, not breadwinners, there was no financial loss to most families. In the Hammonds' case, for Philip's life, they were paid the cost of his funeral, the value of his watch. They were given refunds of his £6 match ticket and £8 coach fare.

The families tried test cases for greater compensation. Trevor Hicks sued for the pain his two daughters, Sarah, 19, and Victoria, 15, must have suffered before they died. It was found not to have been proven that they suffered any pain. The families sued for their own traumas, for the interruption of the relaxed ordinariness of an English Saturday afternoon in spring, to see their loved ones on television, being crushed to death. That case became a curiosity piece in a law student's training, the ruling that relatives watching on television do not have sufficient 'proximity' for a claim of 'nervous shock'. Only those suffering from grief and post-traumatic stress disorder who, like Eddie Spearitt, had been there, physically, alongside their dying loved ones, could receive compensation.

In November 1996 the families watched as 14 police officers, on duty at Hillsborough, were awarded £1.2m compensation for 'nervous shock'. They said they had suffered depression, irritability, nightmares, anxiety since the disaster. Some had been unable to work since. One, PC Anthony Bevis, 47, said the police were unprepared for Hillsborough, 'abandoned by the senior officers': 'I felt a betrayal by the senior officers whose job it was to command.

'I suffered from guilt for the fact that I should have been able to do more, particularly when a young man begged me to save his brother.

'Nothing was coming over the radio. No senior officer was in command.'

The Police Complaints Authority recommended disciplinary action against Duckenfield and his assistant, Murray, but Duckenfield had retired on the grounds of ill-health. They decided it would be unfair then to discipline Murray alone. He retired with his pension in 1992, aged 50, also on the grounds of ill-health.

In November 1993 the families pursued a judicial review application, asking for the inquest to be reopened due to the coroner having imposed the 3.15 p.m. cut-off, failing to inquire into the circumstances of the individual deaths, devoting too much time to the drinking allegations, exhibiting bias to the police in the selection of evidence and witnesses, and incorrectly instructing the jury. The families lost.

They were long, bleak, grim years, the persistent legal defeats compounding and confusing and deepening their sense of loss.

'It has been like a whirlpool,' says Hilda Hammond.

Sucked into what they felt was a profound injustice on top of the senseless deaths, the families wanted to consider further legal challenges. There were a number of possible avenues: further appeals against the coroner's decisions, possibly private prosecutions against the police for manslaughter, and, possibly, charges of perjury and conspiracy to pervert the course of justice. At the very least, they thought such actions might uncover some of the truth of what had happened that day, and how the police, South Yorkshire and West Midlands, had pursued their case, from the beginning. How the tapes went missing. What the truth is about the cameras and the control room.

But they were short of money. There had been a Hillsborough appeal, which raised £16m nationwide, but it was applied to a whole range of causes, mostly not to the families themselves and it was not allowed to be used for legal services. There was a fighting fund, but little money came in. Attempts to keep the issue alive in the media generally foundered on lack of interest and the continuing public myth that the disaster was somehow caused by the Liverpool supporters.

Periodically, some loudmouth would follow *The Sun*, to reinforce this allegation. Bernard Ingham, who should have had little to say about the policing at football matches, included the tragedy in a list with the civil riots and violent strikes which cursed Britain under the rule of his boss. Later, in an article in the *Daily Express*, Ingham wrote that the deaths had been caused by a 'tanked-up mob'. The remarks were disowned by the paper's editor.

In 1994, Brian Clough had a go in his autobiography, talking about Hillsborough having been caused by latecomers without tickets.

The Hillsborough familes, with Colin Moneypenny, of Liverpool City Council's Hillsborough Disaster Working Party, keeping a watching brief, found the media reluctant to give their denials as much space as the famous mouths which had sounded off.

The media was never interested: it had discovered football; the FA Carling Premiership, Fantasy Football, Cantona, Shearer, Keegan. It barely had the intelligence to cover the profound changes taking place in football, let alone attend to the complex, traumatic whirlpool in which the families of those who died at Hillsborough were now embroiled. The football world, off to planet corporate, did not encourage even the mentioning of Hillsborough in its new polite company.

Jimmy McGovern met the families when he was working on a character for *Cracker*. His character, Albie, had been traumatised by his father's death in 1993, which Albie believed had originated in heart problems caused in the crush at Hillsborough, after which his father's spirit and love for football had been crushed.

'My view of Hillsborough,' says McGovern, 'is that it was an inevitable consequence of the Thatcher years. She waged war on working-class institutions, like the unions, at the same time as awarding the police big pay rises. The police began to act with contempt towards the very people they are supposed to serve. They were always wary, fearful, where groups of working-class men congregated. You can see that most clearly in the miners' strike, in which the policing was ruthless.

'By 1989, the unions had been smashed. But there was another forum where the working class congregated, and that was football, the working-class game. And you could see the same treatment there; the working-class scum – pen them in, contain them. It was assumed that if they were football supporters they must be hooligans.

'That was my character in *Cracker*, Albie; he began to kill people who assumed things about him.'

McGovern's research came to the attention of Ann Adlington, the Liverpool City Council solicitor who has worked tirelessly on behalf of the families, effectively in her spare time, ever since the disaster. 'I wanted to be sure he was going to do justice to the plight of the families,' she says. 'They had been trampled on enough.'

She had McGovern meet the families, and *Cracker* was shown to them in a private screening in November 1995. The families liked it, but they made McGovern promise to make a film about the real-life miscarriage of justice which had sucked them in for five black years.

'I prided myself on having read everything about Hillsborough,' says McGovern, including *No Last Rights* and a previous report by the same authors. But I didn't realise many of the details of the injustice until I met the familes. I promised to do whatever I could. After *Cracker*, I was hot. Granada commissioned it immediately.'

Hillsborough, the film, was strong and true and crystal clear. Faced with a television programme by a well-known writer, the media now covered the continuing shame of Hillsborough, trailed it, wrote features about it. The film blew away the lingering defamation on the Liverpool supporters, told the real truth about the disaster, the police construction of the case, the taking of blood samples, the infamy of *The Sun*. The trauma and outrage of the inquest. And, most emphatically, the grief, of young lives lost. The tearing, torturing despair of grief.

It showed, so soon after Euro '96 had displayed a rebuilding embraced by politicians and every celebrity in the kingdom, that no rebuilding had been allowed for the families of the Hillsborough dead. They were still stuck on the events of that terrible day, and the legal twists which have kept them there, still going over what happened, fighting for the truth.

'Jimmy did in two hours what we'd been trying to do for seven years,' says Phil Hammond. 'We could only get a bit out here, a bit there. He'd got the whole nation to sit down and watch. But it was only a fingernail of what we've been put through.

The full extent of the tragedy of injustice, piled on the loss of his son, is clear from Phil Hammond's work. After a couple of years, he was elected secretary of the Hillsborough Families Support Group. The back room of the family home in Aigburth is full of papers, files, documents. Full of Hillsborough. That one day, the worst of his and his family's life, dominating still.

'We've had to put our grief on hold,' he says. 'We can't come to terms with it because we still don't know what happened. Say, for example, Philip had been killed by a drunk driver. At least if that driver was caught and punished, we'd know what happened and hopefully that the driver wouldn't be doing it again. We could never get over it, but at least we could come to terms with it. But with this, we can't.'

He has an encyclopaedic, heartbreaking knowledge of the Hillsborough ground on that day; he knows the layout in minute detail, the names of the policemen, the times, even the names of the ambulancemen. The ferocity of the detail twists the scale of injustice.

Jimmy McGovern's researchers discovered the existence of Roger Houldsworth. He had designed, installed and maintained the Hillsborough CCTV system, and was in charge of the separate control room, on behalf of the club, which watched pictures from the same cameras. He said he had made a statement as long ago as May 1989 that the cameras and monitors were working perfectly. He had assumed his statement would go to the inquest jury, but now realised it had not.

Then, Yorkshire TV released to the families tapes which the South Yorkshire Police had passed to them soon after the disaster, before the inquest. The tapes show Camera 5 working; tilting, panning, zooming, filming the Leppings Lane terraces. They do not, still, show the crush time, between 2.30 and 3.02.

Faced with the evidence of the camera working perfectly, apparently contradicting PC Bichard's evidence to the inquest, the South Yorkshire Police issued a statement, by Assistant Chief Constable Ian Daines, on April Fools Day 1997, saying: 'The camera which took the pictures was indeed in working order, otherwise there would have been no tape to submit in evidence.

'What officers have previously explained is that the live transmission of the pictures into the police control point at the time was of poor quality . . . It has always been assumed that the interference on their screen was caused by television equipment being used to transmit live coverage of the FA Cup semi-final.'

This was never mentioned at the inquest. I asked ACC Daines for clarification of when the acount of 'interference' had 'previously been explained'. He said it had been explained at the inquest. I pointed out that PC Bichard had said, clearly, that the camera had not been working. 'This is playing with words,' said ACC Daines. 'Camera not working and interference amount to the same thing to you or I.'

A doctor, Ed Walker, contacted Phil Hammond following the screening of Jimmy McGovern's drama to donate his fee from writing a review of the programme to the family support group's legal fighting fund. Dr Walker said he had treated people injured at Hillsborough at the Northern General Hospital, Sheffield, after 3.15. People were acutely ill, then, but still alive. He had made a statement at the time, criticising the reaction to the disaster, saying that people needed urgent resuscitation, that they could have been saved. This contradicted the medical evidence accepted as 'overwhelming' by the coroner, that people could not have been saved after 3.15. The pathologist giving evidence to the inquest, Dr Wardrope, had asked Dr Walker to stand by to give evidence to the West Midlands Police on 15 June 1989. Dr Walker was never contacted, and his evidence was not put to the inquest.

After McGovern's programme, Dr Walker had gone on the radio, mentioning that he had treated a young boy. Hilda had tried to contact him through the radio station but he had not got the message. When he rang Phil to donate his fee, Phil asked him if he was the doctor who had been on the radio. He was. The Hammonds found, seven years after the tragedy, the doctor who had treated their son. Ed Walker recognised the description; Philip had just been on a skiing holiday, he was brown, his hair very blond. He had been one of the first, said Dr Walker. He had still had some breath, and a pulse, when he arrived at the hospital. The doctor had tried to resuscitate him but failed to bring him round.

'That was the first we had ever found out about what treatment Philip had,' says Phil Hammond. 'We had been told that an "unidentified doctor" had treated him. Now it turns out that that doctor actually made a statement and that the West Midlands Police knew he had. But he didn't give evidence to the inquest. We now want to know why this doctor was never called. And it proves that the 3.15 cut off was totally wrong.

'Now we know how our son died, but I want to know if he could have had treatment earlier, and if he had, whether he might have been saved.

'I wouldn't have cared what state my son was in when he came back to us, if he'd been alive. Even if he'd been in a coma, whatever. He'd have been here, we could have looked after him, we'd have been able to give him a cuddle.'

In June 1997, following representations by the families to the new Labour Government, Home Secretary Jack Straw announced an 'independent scrutiny' into the effect of this evidence. Lord Justice Stuart-Smith, who, as secret services commissioner, scrutinises MI5, has been instructed to consider whether the video evidence and that of Dr Walker and Roger Houldsworth merit a potential quashing of the inquest verdict, and, possibly, criminal charges. The families believe there is a case for charges, of perjury and conspiracy to pervert the course of justice, against police officers, for the investigation of the disaster and their testimony at the inquest. The families believe the new evidence is too strong to be ignored. 'They can't sweep this under the table now,' says Phil Hammond.

In May 1997, with McGovern's programme having awoken public consciousness, the Hillsborough Family Support Group organised a concert at Anfield in aid of the legal fighting fund. It was a great day and it has raised good money for the potential future legal costs. But it is about the only time since the tragedy that the families' shattered lives have been even acknowledged by the football world. The contrast between the rebuilding of football into a business, making its floating fortunes from the banqueting centres built with public money on the back of Hillsborough, is stark.

In 1992, only three years after the hell of 1989, Hillsborough was used again for an FA Cup semi-final. Many believed that the FA was bringing it back as a venue so soon after the disaster so that it could be part of its bid, its complement of grounds, to host Euro '96. At the game, between Sunderland and Norwich, a revolving advertising board flashed up the message: 'UEFA '96: The Pitch is England's.'

Still, to this day, there is no memorial at Hillsborough to those who died. When Phil Hammond asked for one, he was told he could put a plaque on one of two sites: a wall outside the men's toilet in the Leppings Lane end or a beam right in the middle of the dark tunnel.

'We've had nothing from them all these years,' says Phil Hammond. 'Football's name was being dragged through the dirt at the inquest, with the police saying football supporters were drunk and misbehaving. We were there to defend our own loved ones, not the whole of football. Liverpool Football Club should have had a barrister there to represent them and the good name of their supporters. Challenge all those lies.

'The clubs have all done all right out of Hillsborough. They were forced to rebuild their grounds, but they saw it as an opportunity. They got public grants to build the stadia. And they've put prices up, unbelievably. Two of my lads at work can't afford to get into Anfield any more. The clubs have made the fans pay. They've had their money back off Hillsborough.

'You would think the football world might have supported us, but everything is money now with them. There is no memorial at Hillsborough. Sheffield Wednesday don't want to know about it. I think the new Kop should have been named after Hillsborough in some way: the Remembrance Stand, perhaps.'

Colin Moneypenny, of the council's Hillsborough Disaster Working Party, believes that 'the football industry' should have paid all the families' legal costs, right from the start: 'Hardly a word or a penny of the vast wealth and high profile which came to the top level of the game as a direct result of the disaster has been redirected to the families. Football has emerged from the terror of Leppings Lane as a high-fashion industry, bowing its head to frivolity, trivia, and most of all money. The many difficult, controversial questions about the disaster remain unanswered. The disaster has been strictly off the agenda of "New Football".'

A day of protest was organised at the live Sky match between Liverpool and Spurs at Anfield in May 1997. Forty thousand supporters and both teams held up red cards saying 'Justice for the 96'. At the time, one of the most spectacular, moving sights ever at a football match, Sky were showing adverts. Andy Melvin, executive director of football at Sky, denied that they knew there was to be a protest. But he also revealed the lack of interest in anything but the surface gloss of the game which has made Sky's fortune: 'It is vital – no matter how worth while the cause – that television is not used as a vehicle for promoting such demonstrations . . . If we get involved in one cause or protest or demonstration . . . then it would have serious implications on television's role in sport.'

So, although Sky claims not to have known about the Hillsborough justice demonstration, Melvin implies that if they had known they wouldn't have shown it. *The Sun* spread the first, most pernicious, damaging and lasting lies about Hillsborough. The families believe that *The Sun's* front page was a serious factor in the denial of justice, fed by the police, establishing the myth about Liverpool fans misbehaving. Yet *The Sun's* infamy did not prevent the Premier League awarding its television contract to Sky, the televisual incarnation of a Murdoch tabloid. Sky's general football coverage has been a screen version of *The Sun*, with the same lack of capacity for analysis or recognition of the substance of things. 'The view at Sky,' one of their journalists told me, 'is that *The Sun* has four million readers a day so it cannot be doing much wrong. Sky's football coverage follows *The Sun*. I've had lots of good stories about deeper issues which they haven't been interested in using.'

Football, Sky-fuelled, has moved on, to corporate pastures new, greener and richer than the old grass-roots. Treating the Taylor Report as an opportunity, to rebuild itself in the Thatcherite dream, monuments to 'market forces'. The post-Taylor stands, catering for the rich, parking luxury company cars, partaking of football for corporate entertaining. Putting the prices up to the rest, to the lifelong fans.

'If you want to exclude working-class scum,' says Jimmy McGovern, 'you just price them out. It's the easiest way.'

Football, come home in 1996, turned into a business, having made fortunes for a few entrepreneurial owners, praised by everybody, sung to by a couple of comedians. Meanwhile, the Hillsborough families, whose loved ones went off excited to a football match in 1989 and never returned, have been dealt the flipside of the same Thatcherite project. Hillsborough, joining Zeebrugge, Clapham, King's Cross, Bradford, Manchester Airport, and all the the others in the roll-call of

Eighties disasters. The families suffering at the hands of tabloids, ignored by the rest of the press. Left to struggle alone in the underbelly of 'market forces' Britain, their grief swirling in the black nightmare of a continuing procedural whirlpool.

12

FOOTBALL'S LEAVING HOME

Blackburn Rovers' Ewood Park is where they bought up and knocked down the houses of neighbouring people to make way for carparks for corporate entertainment. Nuttall Street's terraced houses have long been bulldozed. No trace is left of Kidder Street, flattened to provide 905 spaces behind the popular Blackburn End for P-Reg silver BMW 740is, gleaming Jags, broods of Mercs, resting for a few hours once a fortnight within a compound of steel railings. At the Manchester United game on 12 April 1997, the Blackburn End carpark hosted a monumental Rolls-Royce with a personalised number plate, its chauffeur sitting out the whole match reading the paper. Alongside was a lugubrious Bentley Hooper Turbo, sporting in its interior, draped casually across black leather upholstery, a new-looking MUFC scarf.

Inside the ground, the entire centre section of the Jack Walker Stand seemed, as ever at Blackburn, to be filled with the drivers and passengers of these saloons. Many of them had name tags, the sure sign of a corporate affair, together with the other trademarks of business entertaining: uneasy, overly polite body language, restrained chat and a no-after-you etiquette on reaching their seats. The armoury of commercial manners, known by some as 'corridor skills'.

Before the match, Ewood's tannoy announcer tried to whip up the crowd: 'Let's hear it from the Blackburn End,' was acknowledged with a cheer from the barmy army in their replica shirts. 'Let's hear it from the Darwen End,' brought a celebratory response from United fans in

Championship-winning mood. 'Let's hear it from the Jack Walker Stand,' was greeted with polite, half-hearted applause from a standful of suits.

It was one of United's key games on the way to the 1997 title. The final score was 3–2, but they won it with grace and ease. Flowers saved a penalty from Cantona in the first half, and Ewood was jubilant in the rare Blackburn sunshine, five minutes of joy. But after 32 minutes, Cole scored. United had lost away to Dortmund in midweek, but they were still quicker, playing smoothly in a class above. Their kids were, as always, awesomely competent; Butt, Scholes, the Nevilles, putting never a sponsored foot wrong against sluggish opponents. McKinlay equalised, a long shot, but just before half-time Scholes swatted a clinical second into the corner. The barmy army drifted into silence for most of the game, struggling to raise a chant, barely protesting even when United fans, standing up throughout, sang the inevitable chorus to a quiet, suited Ewood Park: 'Where were you when you were shit?'

As is the way in the Nineties, the away fans, who formerly could never be heard at England's hair-raising football grounds, stood up and made all the noise. United fans produced the song of the season, to the tune of 'You Are my Sunshine'.

'You are my Solskjaer, my Ole Solskjaer,
You make me happy when skies are grey,
Alan Shearer, was fucking dearer,
But please don't take my Solskjaer away.'

Blackburn were yards slower, a planet different from United. Only Hendry, playing out the season with a ruptured groin to ensure his team were safe from relegation, seemed at all committed. Brian Kidd and Alex Ferguson did gleeful dances on the pitch after United's goals, near to the Blackburn badge, lime-chalked into the turf: *Arte et Labore* – Through Skill and Hard Work.

After the game, the corporate crowd came drifting out the back of the Blackburn End, middle-aged mostly, clutching the odd programme or gift. Blackburn had lost, but these people looked as if they had had sturdy, serious afternoons, a job satisfactorily done. They walked obliviously through what used to be houses to where they had parked their luxury cars.

Chris Walder, North West regional marketing manager of accountants KPMG, explained to me how corporate entertaining works, how it fits into doing business in Britain in the Nineties. Marketing departments, he said, target companies who have potentially lucrative work, and marshal information about their executives. They find out what their interests are; who likes opera, theatre, football. When the time is right, usually after initial meetings, they might invite a football-supporting director to a box. 'It doesn't get you the work,' says Walder. 'It is a matter of relationship building, strengthening a tie. It is a strategic part of the marketing mix.'

This is why the suits always appear to be having such a dreadful time at football matches. Why they have name tags and apparently stilted, awkward conversations: by definition, they don't know each other very well. The whole point of the afternoon is a 'getting to know exercise'. And the company entertainment budget must justify itself with work-getting; serious salesmanship is passed round with the bread rolls. They can't just sit back and watch Beckham. According to Walder, firms run courses to instruct young employees how to behave at such events.

Muller, the fruit corner company, former sponsor of Aston Villa, has a large box at Villa Douglas Park. They use it, they say, for their national sales managers to entertain buyers from the major supermarkets. Orders from these buyers are, clearly, worth millions of pounds. 'The box is a very valuable business tool,' they explained. 'It gives Muller sales managers an opportunity to get close to their account customers and gain valuable feedback about the company's products. It allows Muller to build stronger relationships with its trade customers.'

I asked Muller whether watching behind a glass screen had its negative side. They said there was a loss of atmosphere, but it was compensated by the 'comfortable surroundings'. 'Given that the hospitality box is used as a venue to discuss business matters, comfort is an important consideration.'

In the Blackburn End carpark that day, one of the first groups to come out was the party entertained by Matthew Brown, brewers of McEwan's Lager. Gary Scunthorpe, central Manchester account manager, said the brewery had boxes at ten different football grounds around the country. Some brewers had a box at every ground. Three or four carparking spaces on what used to be Kidder Street came with theirs. He used the box to invite mainly pub landlord customers. 'If you're very close to getting a customer's business, it may make the difference, just tip them over the edge,' was his assessment of its usefulness. 'And there's always another brewery out there who is going to invite customers. In a way we're just keeping up with each other.'

Another smart, suited man, who did not give his name, said he was from a major Unilever company. He had hired a 20-seat box, which came with 'a number' of carparking spaces, and invited some regular customers. 'I've never used a box actually to get business,' he said. 'I'm probably using it wrongly. I use it for existing customers to say thank you for the business they've given us.'

A foursome came out next. They looked utterly miserable, like children, forced to play together by their parents, who had then spent a long, dismal afternoon comparing stamp albums, waiting for their mums to come and pick them up. One of them, glasses and a green suit, said he was from the Royal Bank of Scotland. Entertainment was a growing part of doing business, he said, not just at the football, also at rugby or golf. It was difficult, he said, to assess its effectiveness as a business tool. He really shouldn't be talking about it to a journalist anyway, he said, and I would have to phone his regional manager in Preston, otherwise he'd get into trouble.

Some stayed to chat. Joe O'Malley and Derek Atherton, managing director and marketing director respectively of Woodstock Leabank Office Furniture in Bredbury, Cheshire, had been entertained by Colin Mustoe, a supplier, from Senator Office Furniture, holder of a £24,000 box at Blackburn. Joe stood urbanely in the carpark, his long cigar ashing slowly down. They were football fans, United fans, but they were clear this was business. It wasn't as enjoyable as going to a game with friends. 'It's a good, informal opportunity to get to know a supplier, it helps to cement the relationship. We have seven season tickets at Old Trafford and we do the same, give them to our sales people.'

They had enjoyed a three-course meal before the game, with drinks, then watched it from behind a glass screen. In common with all these box-frequenters, they actually didn't like watching a game behind glass. 'It's . . . artificial,' said Joe. 'There's a button to turn the crowd noise up and down.'

They were not snobs or cold-hearted men. It was just business. They admitted they preferred going when it wasn't business, when you could just have a laugh and watch the game. Joe said he recognised a danger that football was changing too much: 'They're squeeezing out the youngsters. I went to United when I was ten, on my own, and when you do that, you stay a supporter all your life. Football clubs have to think long term, make sure the youngsters, the next generation, are not being priced out. At the moment, they are being squeezed.'

I went straight from there to the Fox and Hounds, the pub opposite Ewood Park, across the Bolton Road, which has been hard-core Rovers since long before 'Uncle Jack' 'put something back' into his town by turning its football club into his corporation. Black and white pictures, action shots of Rovers in the Seventies, decorate the walls. Landlord Derek Howarth, Rovers shirt on his huge frame, had pinned up Warsaw, Rosenborg and Moscow scarves, swapped on Rovers' unsuccessful route-one tour of Europe the previous season. He introduced me to some fans: Bill Jeffries, 47, a retired lock-keeper; Ray Nulty, 50, a self-employed plasterer; and Steve 'Dinger' Bell, 43, a self-employed joiner. Local men, they'd supported Rovers all their lives; they could remember being taken as children and they had been steadfast fans ever since. 'My Dad used to sit me on his shoulders in the Blackburn End,' said Steve. 'He'd put me over the wall when he went for a pint.'

Bill remembered being taken to the 1960 FA Cup final by his Mum and Dad. He'd always supported Rovers, throughout years in the Second and Third Divisions, supporting the likes of Fazackerley, Garner, latterly David Speedie. He told a story of dedication. 'In the Sixties – 1969 it was – Rovers had a League Cup game away at Arsenal in midweek. On the Saturday they were playing QPR in the League. We were only 19, we couldn't afford to go there and back to London twice in a week. So we stayed down in London, we slept under the deckchairs in Hyde Park.

'On the Saturday it was pouring down. We went to the ground, the team arrived, but the game was called off. They just turned the team coach round and went back to Blackburn.' He paused, smiled. 'And we tapped 'em for a lift.'

He sipped his pint: 'There's loads of stories like that.'

This is true. Every football supporter seems to have a fund of outlandish loyalty tales, of support for the club taking him beyond the reach of logic or reason. Don Price, a Manchester City supporter, tells one about a friend who went on the pre-season City tour to China a couple of years ago. He was with a small group of City fans, who were going on to Hong Kong to live it up before going home. But then, while they were in China, they were told City had hastily arranged another friendly back home, soon after their return. Don Price's friend cancelled his ticket to Hong Kong and went home early, so he could make sure to be there a couple of days later, at City's pre-season friendly at Scarborough. Price said the same thing as Bill Jeffries: 'There's loads of stories like that.'

Football support, from the very beginning, was always partisan, a matter of loyalty. It came to be handed down the generations with the city air. Football was never entertainment; it was always more than that. The clubs were institutions of belonging. Most football supporters struggle to explain the game's grip on the emotions, channelled into one club they support all their lives. They talk of their first game, remembering the spectacle, the silver illumination of floodlight, the smoke, the elemental swell of the crowd.

'When I was young, about nine or ten, my parents had a shop near Anfield,' says Sheila Spiers, Liverpool fan and now vice-chair of the Football Supporters Association. 'A friend of mine and I used to walk in for free with about 20 minutes to go, when they opened the gates to let people out. We used to climb up there to the top of the Kop and catch the last minutes of games.' She pauses to think. 'It's just that there is no other emotion like it.'

Mick Johnstone, 48, a Middlesbrough supporter, regular at Ayresome Park since he was 15, tries to explain it: 'For a start, I love watching football. I love the game. And 'Boro?' He shrugs. 'It's in the blood.'

It is what so many of them say. In the blood. Bill Jeffries says it: 'It's part of you, the club, part of where you're from. You feel like it's representing the town, and you're representing the club. It's history as well, our club is steeped in history and you're part of that when you go to support them. It's in the blood.'

Lifelong home and away loyalists, the men in the Fox and Hounds were fighting a losing battle against rising prices. Bill had paid £489 for season tickets for him and his son Stephen, 13. Stephen had a Rovers scarf on, adorned with 40 or so badges: 'These are from all the clubs we've been to together,' said Bill. 'I want to be able to give my son what I've had, that experience of football. But it is getting too much.'

The previous week Rovers had played Chelsea at Stamford Bridge. Tickets at Bates Electric Fence-free Village plc had been £25 each. It had been around £120 for the day out.

'This is a poor town,' said Steve. 'You have to work hard for your money. I scrape to afford season tickets for me and my lad. My wife works part-time for BT. She paid for the season tickets this year, on the plastic.

'The players, they're making £15,000 a week. I don't make that in a year. I have to work my nuts off to clear £200 a week. And the same, I guarantee you, goes for everybody in this pub.'

They all nodded. Blackburn's a poor town. Steve was getting angry: 'If I made £15,000 a year, I'd be laughing. I'd buy all my friends a season ticket.'

They felt seriously let down by the players. They were not like the chaps in the carpark outside, partaking of their football in the middle of pleasant afternoons strengthening a business tie. They had watched millionaire players, wearing the colours of their club, capitulate resignedly to Man United. They made an exception for Hendry, their warrior. 'He gives everything,' said Steve. 'But the others – that was absolutely disgusting. They're not even trying, they're not working for their money. At work, I have targets, tough ones. If I don't meet them, I don't get paid. The players? They're not producing. But they're paid obnoxious amounts of money. And the money comes from us.'

Alan Shearer, it would be fair to say, was not their favourite person. 'He's the kind ruining football,' scorned Steve.

They each knew many fans who had gone to Ewood Park in the old days, stood with them in the Second and Third Divisions, who, when the ground was rebuilt and the 'snotters' arrived, found that prices went up too far. 'I'm lucky,' said Ray. 'I'm working so I can afford it. But a lot of people aren't working. They can't afford to go any more. People who have supported Rovers all their lives. And it breaks their hearts.'

'I'll tell you what it's like,' said Steve. 'Money's so tight that me and

Ray have been budgeting for this day, to come out and have a few drinks after the Man United game, for three months. And look what the players are on – it's obnoxious.

'The time is coming, soon,' he said, red-faced, outraged, 'when I'm going to cut Rovers out of my life. You can only shuffle the cards for so long. There comes a point where you have to sit down and say, right, that's it, I can't afford it. It might hurt, really badly, but you have to just cut it out. Find something else to do on a Saturday afternoon.'

'It's just a business now, Rovers,' said Bill, mournfully.

The only research which has been done into the changing nature of football spectating, the arrival of corporate and middle-class spectators to replace financially excluded poorer supporters, suggests that the 'new fans' will not be as loyal as those football has for a century taken for granted. John Williams, of Leicester University's Sir Norman Chester Centre, carries out an annual survey of Premier League supporters, funded by the Premier League itself. In 1996, Williams found that 'new' football fans were drawn disproportionately from high wage brackets, particularly those earning more than £30,000 a year. They were, he found, less passionate about their football than those of lower income who were still managing to afford to go to the games; 34.5 per cent of fans earning £10,000 or less a year described their club as 'one of the most important things in my life', while only 9.9 per cent described supporting as 'just one of the things I do'. At a salary above £30,000, only 17.5 per cent of respondents described the club as 'one of the most important things in my life'; more, 18.6 per cent, described it as 'just one of the things I do'. Williams found that some richer new fans are buying season tickets, at £300-odd, just to be sure of entry to the big games. For less appetising fixtures, they are not bothering to turn up, simply leaving the seat empty.

Williams is sanguine about the changes. 'People used to support because of their locality, out of a sense of loyalty, kinship and ritual. I think that has been broken, not just because of pricing. Society has changed, the communities have changed and internally the game has changed. It is much harder to establish and maintain the strong relationship.

'We may be moving away,' says Williams, 'from the time when somebody supported one club all his life. People are beginning to move their allegiances.'

But the Premier League clearly does not accept this view, that its traditional relationship with supporters is weakening. Its 'football businesses' continue to rush to the City boasting of a 'captive market', which they will next exploit with pay per view. This is a paradox at the heart of the football business, of the 'market forces' rhetoric which says that making money in the short term is how everything should be run. Flush with profit and capital gain, the new owners are too busy to recognise they are undermining the very support which brought them into the game in the first place. Painfully, reluctantly, football's uniquely loyal, lifelong fans are having the game wrenched away from them. The 'captive market' is slowly being released.

In Middlesbrough, the renaissance under new owner Steve Gibson was effected with the move to the new Riverside Stadium, built with the help of £15m public money. When the stadium opened in 1994, the club, freshly promoted under then highly rated young manager Bryan Robson, imposed a season ticket-only policy. Ian Muter, 34, had supported 'Boro through its bad times, the dark days of 1986, when receivers had locked the Ayresome Park gates. The days before 'Boro went shopping for players in São Paulo or Turin, when they had to look closer to home, trawling the local leagues. Where they found a 19-year-old called Gary Pallister working part-time as a clerk on the docks and playing for Billingham Town in the Northern League Second Division. His wages, £100 per week when Middlesbrough signed him, were paid by a local scaffolding firm, a kind of sponsorship. It is not believed the same firm was asked recently to weigh in for Ravanelli's wages.

Ian Muter applauded the Riverside success story, thought it was wonderful. But he was unemployed, still is, and could not afford a season ticket. 'I just thought it was a shame,' he says, 'that lifelong supporters were being priced out at a time when the club was enjoying such a great spell. I felt it was of fundamental importance. Football isn't just entertainment to people, something they can just drop. It's part of their culture, their identity. Suddenly working-class people were being denied access to something which was a very important part of their lives. Suddenly it was all season tickets and Sky TV. Next it's going to be pay per view. There has to be some balance.'

Muter organised a petition to Middlesbrough Football Club. The modesty of its request is heartbreaking. Muter, concerned not to appear to be carping at a time of 'Boro's Brazilian rebirth, did not ask for prices to be reduced, only for some tickets, in a small section of the new stadium, to be sold on a match-by-match basis. He even produced a business plan, arguing that 'one-off' supporters who could save up to go to the odd match would be more likely to visit the shop and spend money than people who went to every game.

Helped by two friends, he aimed for 3,000 signatures, a tenth of the Riverside capacity. 'I got some people making crass remarks, saying they had taken out a loan, why couldn't I do the same. You can't get that sort of credit when you're unemployed. But a lot of people were supportive, including many away fans.'

He went out in all weathers, in the underpasses near the ground, until 2.40, then he used to go home and listen to matches on the radio. 'Radio 5 has been a godsend to people like me, who have effectively been disenfranchised from football.'

His 3,000-signature petition was delivered to the club in 1996. It made no difference. I met him when 'Boro had just lost in the 1997 Coca-Cola Cup final, before they lost in the FA Cup final and went down. Wembley tickets had been £38, impossible. He'd watched the game on a screen in a pub: 'It's different after a couple of years of not going. You don't feel the same. I was sorry we lost, of course, but it's a more remote feeling.

'But I'm an optimist. I think it will come full circle. I think the bubble will burst. I think the Hillsborough families will get justice, and when they do, it'll be a good time to have a full debate about the way the game is going. They should look at democratising the game so that the supporters can decide issues. And somebody has to start campaigning against this pay-per-view nonsense.'

Mick Johnstone, a bus driver, is hanging on in there watching the football, as are many working class supporters. He works six days a week, 48 hours in all, at £5 an hour, clearing around £180 a week. His season ticket in 1996-97 was £270 in the East Stand Lower at the Riverside. He has two daughters; one is 18, so her season ticket is full price, another £270. His other daughter is 16, hers was half price: £135. With petrol and some food and drink, football has become a very expensive pastime. They try to avoid the shop. 'The girls know we can't afford to get the shirt and the latest gear.'

Middlesbrough's two Wembley finals took hundreds of pounds off the Johnstones as well, eating into the credit card. The tickets for the cup finals were £38 each, and they'd had to stay over in London. The match programmes were £5, the Wembley drinks and hot-dogs shameless: 'You know it's a rip-off there,' he says. 'You just try not to buy anything inside Wembley.'

He is, he says, determined to afford season tickets next year. His 18-year-old daughter might have a job by then, before she goes to university: 'It's priorities. We haven't had a holiday now for a couple of years. We've channelled all our leisure money into Middlesbrough. I've always been a fan, it's a big part of my life. It's my major hobby. I want 'Boro to be successful.' Johnstone says he believes supporters are 'investors', not customers. 'A customer won't go back and buy a lousy product again, but a supporter does. He always goes back. He believes it is important always to go, to support the club, to help it back to the good times. But the football investor gets nothing in return.'

From the FA's *Blueprint* onwards, football has increasingly regarded this fervent support as old hat, silly talk. It calls itself 'a branch of the entertainment industry' now, believing that makes it sound clever, sophisticated. Football saw society changing, but it did not look to fulfil its traditional role, as purveyor of magic, focus for community loyalty, in a new era. As John Williams said, that would have been difficult. And the football business has not shown itself prepared even to admit it has difficult problems, let alone act to solve them. The concept of supporting a team loyally is being weakened, as are the reasons for that support: that the team is local, that you went as a child, that support is in the family, that you can afford to get in to watch the team live, with your friends. A younger generation is consuming its football differently, as entertainment, glamour, the players as icons. Support is becoming a matter simply of consumer choice, opting for the best product on offer at the time. A survey of young people by market researchers BMRB in 1996 showed that 27 per cent of seven- to 19-year-olds nationwide who call themselves football supporters support Manchester United. And United are actively, aggressively marketing themselves to get more supporters wherever they are in the country; their club magazines stocked in newsagents everywhere, their merchandise erupting in shops in every town, building on the exposure on Sky and other new football media.

In this gradual replacement of traditional supporters with a new affluent and more casual consumer of football 'entertainment', the current boom is germinating within it the seeds of decline. It has taken over a 'captive market', and fostered in its place a 'customer-base' increasingly supporting only the winners. These are the conditions for 'consolidation', for the complete dominance of just a few massive football companies, probably in some European Superleague.

Tony Simpson, director of Team, a marketing company, has been substantially involved in the new age of football and has been very disappointed by the thinnness of the imaginations at work. A Birmingham City fan himself, he believes that football support is being inexorably undermined. As a fan, he feels outraged, as if something precious is being callously destroyed, but even as a marketeer he believes football is getting it wrong: 'The clubs already had tremendous loyalty, from traditional supporters, growing up with it, with this crazy sense that they had to support their team, even if they were no good. But the clubs now have a very shallow view of their brand, they do nothing to encourage a feeling of belonging. All they are looking at is the bottom line. The next generation is very unlikely to enjoy the same feeling of support. And the new supporters may well get bored of football. Then the clubs will be finished.'

The Premier League refuses to recognise that its full grounds and hyperbolic media exposure mask structural problems, but it has now found it can no longer ignore one aspect of the change. It has, it officially admitted in 1996, destroyed the atmosphere. Paul Johns, who runs 'supporter panels' at each Premiership club, found in 1995-96 that 60 per cent of supporters felt the atmosphere was not what it used to be, and over 30 per cent were unhappy with it. In only four years, the Premier League and the new barons of football had managed to silence one of the most spectacular experiences of modern life. Still, the Premier League puts this down not to 'snotters', consumerism or pricing out of fans; Johns argues it is solely down to all-seater stadia.

Rick Parry asked that something be done about it. There appears to be a concern that people might stop going if the atmosphere does not pick up: 'It will be less attractive as a spectacle', and because television likes a noisy crowd in the background. A working party was assembled, including Johns, and Mel Highmore, the Ewood Park stadium manager. Highmore, a wise, gentle man, former community policeman in Blackburn, recognises to some extent the scale of football's atmosphere problem: 'I'd compare it to the slum clearances of the Sixties, when people were moved into high-rise flats. It made conditions safer, but it destroyed the fabric of their communities. It has been the same with the removal of the terracing.'

But the depth of the analysis has not been matched by an appropriately profound solution. The working party went over to Italy, had a look at the games without inquiring too far into the cultural roots of Italian football support, found that fans there congregated in certain ends and brought drums. So the working party made similar recommendations, that 'ends' should be allowed for singing, clubs should plan entertainment, have theme days. And bands are to be officially sanctioned. Sheffield Wednesday supporter John Hemmingham first began to take a trumpet to home matches in late 1993. The club encouraged him, advertised for musicians, and drummers joined him. Football has now grabbed at this as the simple solution to its having killed the atmosphere. Bang a drum.

In autumn 1996, only months after Football Came Home, John Hemmingham's phone rang. It was, to his utter astonishment, none other than David Davies, the FA's head of public affairs, wondering if Hemmingham might try to get the crowd going at England home matches. On Wednesday, 26 June 1996, England versus Germany in the semi-final of Euro '96, the biggest game played in England for 30 years, it turned out that 14,000 people had been on corporate entertaining packages, selling at between £299 and £359 each. For those whose companies were not paying, Wembley prices had been £50, £60, £70 and £90. During the tournament the sense of occasion, the flags of St George and the playing of Skinner and Baddiel's ditty had seen the atmosphere through. But with the euphoria over, England matches were dead. Davies had not thought to reduce prices, perhaps shave corporate entertainment. He offered Hemmingham and his boys free tickets to come and drum up some noise. This band is now a fixture at England internationals, their tickets paid by the game's governing body which sold its game to the corporations and saw it drained of its ethics and its soul and its heartbeat.

The FA never had the imagination or the will to see that the wellspring of atmosphere was the feeling of belonging, of connection between supporter and team, and that it had to be preserved. They handed the game to undeserving entrepreneurs who have lined their pockets in the boom, while creating the conditions for decline. The FA did not even consider democratising the clubs, insisting that before they were to get a penny of Government or football's television money, they would have to involve supporters. Democracy, of ownership or of running the club, would be a safeguard, deepening the sense of belonging and ensuring that football remembered who it was there to serve. It is clearly the true nature of football clubs; they belong to their supporters, without them they are nothing.

Mick Johnstone tried to organise a supporters' trust at Middlesbrough in the bad days. He was told if he raised £250,000 he could have a seat on the board. They were ready, he and a few hundred other supporters, to organise an appeal, raffles, dinners, discos, to raise the money. Steve Gibson stepped in just as the movement was beginning.

When Bournemouth were in financial trouble at the end of 1996, Trevor Watkins, a solicitor and lifelong Bournemouth supporter, looked to do just that, to put in place a supporters' and community trust. This put the club in the hands of people whose loyalty will last much longer than that of any potential white knight new chairman coming in on an agenda of his own to put money into the club.

Watkins looked to the example of Northampton Town, where a supporters' trust has raised £60,000 for a club which was in administrative receivership in 1992. In return for its investment, the supporters' trust now owns 18,000 shares, 8 per cent of the club, and elects a director to the board, currently Brian Lomax. The club, Lomax says, is secure now, partly because it only rents the new Sixfields Stadium, opened in 1994 and built by the council. This saves Northampton from the major expense of upkeep and from being prey, like many lower division clubs, to asset-stripping businessmen interested in the ground. The supporters are entitled to monthly open forums with the manager, directors or players. 'Supporters feel they have a real stake in this club,' says Lomax. 'They are not just brought through the gates and fed bullshit by the board. The club is woven into the community, and there are many great advantages to that.'

In an age in which football has forgotten what it is, in which it has been happy, for short-term profits, to undermine its own magic and strength, Lomax makes an eloquent case for the need to preserve the game's roots. 'I'm not a religious man,' he says, 'although I did study theology at Cambridge. It taught me that human beings have a fundamental need for mythology, and symbolism. We create rituals which fulfil our craving for solidarity, for expressions of comradeship and loyalty. In a world which is losing its sense of human togetherness, there is a very great requirement for places in which solidarity can be found. I believe that that is what football support is all about.'

He discovered it the hard way. Growing up in Cheshire in the Fifties, Lomax was Altrincham's only away fan. He used to cycle to away matches, miles and miles across the county, age 11. The team came to know him, their only supporter, and eventually the players used to take him with them. In 1960, Altrincham was taken over by Noel White and Peter Swales, business partners. Lomax defends Swales vehemently because of the job he did at Altrincham. 'I loved what they did,' he said. 'They loved the game, and they turned Altrincham into giant killers, into a top team. It was the crowning glory of my boyhood.'

He has contempt for Francis Lee, for the bloody manner of his Manchester City takeover from Swales and also for the half-hearted gesture of putting a fan on the board, beleaguered fanzine editor Dave Wallace. When Wallace criticised Lee's choice as City manager of Alan Ball, the man who had previously taken four different clubs to relegation, Lee told Wallace that he was there to represent the board to the fans. Wallace said no, he was there to represent the fans to the board. The position of fan on the board was quickly established. 'Hypocrisy,' says Lomax. 'That wasn't a real supporter on the board. It was a gesture. And when he did something Lee didn't like, he was removed.' And City, under Alan Ball, were duly relegated.

Lomax, living between Coventry and Northampton, drifted away from football for a while, eventually going again on Boxing Day 1982. He thought his son might be old enough to go with him. Coventry were away so they went to watch the Cobblers. 'I got into it again, although my son didn't. Then my nine-year-old daughter, Emily, asked if she could come. She came to the FA Cup third round match between Northampton Town and Aston Villa, January 1983.

She was enraptured. She was absolutely bowled over. She went home and away with Northampton for the next nine years.

'I believe there are certain very important values in life, and that football support embodies them. There is a sense of pilgrimage, of going to a sacred place; there is loyalty, sticking with something through good and bad times, and a feeling that you do not deserve the good times until you have suffered the bad. My daughter grasped this immediately, even as a young girl. I took her to Altrincham, and they were losing 2-4 to Runcorn. It was pouring down. I said we should go and stand under cover, but Emily wouldn't. She said: "No, if the boys are struggling out there, then I will too". '

'It's about emotion, you see, about sharing and comradeship, about the whole being greater than the sum of its parts. These are very deeply rooted human needs and they translate into other things. I believe that that is at the root of people's love for football and loyalty for their clubs.

'That was why I stepped in to help the club really. My daughter loved the club so much I couldn't bear to see it die. Now I feel I am helping to safeguard it.'

Lomax says people have to think through what football is: 'It's nonsense to say it is a business, or that it is entertainment. People can take or leave entertainment. Football is much more fundamental than that. Supporters aren't customers and football is much more than a business. People don't seem to understand that, that something can be run in a proper, businesslike manner, but be more than only that. At Northampton, we have a commercial department. And the commercial manager's job is to make as much money as possible, within the boundaries we set him. But it is only a department, not the whole point of the club.

'I compare the Premiership to snooker. Ten years ago, people loved snooker, it was on television all the time. Now the audiences have halved and they struggle for sponsors. The Premiership, with a few big clubs, is becoming like that. And in the grounds it is trying to be like golf or rugby where most of the support is corporate. This is very sad, and profoundly wrong, the loss of identity of the supporter with the game.'

The world is currently in love with football and football believes it can do no wrong, but great changes are taking place. Lifelong supporters are being gradually, casually, excluded by a new generation of businessmen–owners, who feel a duty to make money, not to their clubs' heritage and support. The game is being dragged out of reach of those, of whatever class, who loved and nurtured it, before it was ever considered a commodity, a satellite 'dish-driver'. Football should make its money, capitalise by getting some money from the corporations, but it should not sell its soul to them. Even the corporates want the plebs there to create a bit of atmosphere, as long as they can turn it down behind their glass screens. As football turns itself into a commodity, it is losing its magic, the spontaneous, communal miracle, the thrilling roar of its crowd, its clubs' unique appeal to loyalty. Beneath the current boom, the moneymaking, beneath the cheerleading of a couple of jesters, football is leaving home. It is heading for a small number of football companies, entertaining business customers in plush, silent stadia, echoing to the tedious knell of a drumbeat.

13

A DREAM COME TRUE

Alan Shearer could not have pleased the crowd, or the press, any more than he did that day, 6 August 1996, when he was presented to the journalist and brewery assembly at St James' Park, the Toon Army standing outside in the rain. This was a flawless display of smiling and right answers, the consummate professional delivering his message to the media. Awed, apologetic journalists rose, gingerly took the mike and asked real testers: 'How important *is* the number 9 shirt to you, Alan?' or 'How *are* you feeling on this dream day for you, Alan?' Whatever, Shearer, media training in evidence, provided just about the same soundbite: 'I'd play in any number to be honest,' he said, 'but it is a dream come true to be wearing the Newcastle number 9.'

'It's a dream come true,' he repeated, to rapturous applause, 'to play in front of Newcastle supporters and in front of me Mam and Dad.

'At the end of the day,' he said, 'I'm just a fan like the people outside.'

Alan, he wanted everybody to know, was an overgrown Newcastle supporter, still a child really, wanting only to play for his hometown club wi' his Mam and Dad watching from the stands. He stuck to the line with admirable consistency. He was like a modern politician 'on message'.

When he had dealt with this public grilling, The One And Only did some 'one-on-one' interviews for the cameras. He was interesting to watch; guarded, body braced, eyes watching, scrutinising questions for hidden danger. He'd pause for an instant, relax, then deliver the message. It was a dream come true, he told the nation's media, all he'd ever wanted since he'd been a child.

John Hall beamed coldly, Keegan kicked about, hands in his suit trouser pockets, giving the odd sorrowful interview to whoever asked. Some kids milled about in front of the platform, yelping for an autograph. Shearer calmly did his work in front of the cameras. Then he came over and signed some autographs with a practised hand.

'I touched him!' one kid went running back screaming. 'I touched Shearer!'

He went outside then, the sheet-metal worker's son from Newcastle, out to the Toon Army. They were ecstatic and completely wet through. Four hours they had been waiting, putting up with the rain and DJ Alan Robson, the Sincerest Man on North-East Phone-ins. But they seemed not to mind at all; it was worth it, for a sight of the returning hero. Many men had brought the kids along. They would always be able to say they had been there, the day that Shearer signed.

Shearer came to the foot of the stage in his white polo shirt, ready to go on. He was po-faced, professional, head down. Robson announced him: 'The one and only Alan Shearerrrrr!' and the black and white-striped crowd roared, hands above heads in the drizzle. Shearer turned his smile on then, and trotted up on stage with it. It was a little wider than the one he does on the Braun adverts. He gave his two-handed wave, arms aloft above his head, and they all went wild.

He was handed the mike. It was a dream come true, he said, it was all he'd ever wanted, he was a Geordie, one of them. He was on stage for a couple of minutes, at most. As he left, the job done, he clicked the smile off again.

The Toon Army, strangely, seemed satisfied, mooching slowly away in the unremitting rain. Nobody would entertain any treachorous talk about the fee, £15m, maybe being too high, or whether Kevin really needed another striker – he already had an expensive half-dozen. It was magic, everybody said, the whole thing, a brilliant signing. They'd had a glimpse of Shearer, now they were off. Tremendous.

To me, it was shocking. Why did he seem so cold? Saying it was the best day of his life, a dream come true. It didn't look like it. It looked like he'd gone ahead and done a media call, like he was saying what professional footballers said. It was a dream come true. You played for the love. You felt for the club. As if he was feeding the myth which makes football go round. He looked as if he was doing his job, followed his media training.

But this was different. There was no need for it. This wasn't the standard footballer moving for the money and having to justify it in sentimental terms. This wasn't Chris Sutton explaining his move to Blackburn: 'A nice town, similar size to Norwich.' Ravanelli, £42,000 a week, going to Middlesbrough 'for the challenge of English football'.

This was really a sentimental moment. In Shearer's case the myth was true. He really had supported Newcastle since he was a lad. He had dreamt, as a child, of one day being the Newcastle number 9. It really was what he had always wanted. Yet now, still only 26, he seemed not to feel it any more. Where was the emotion of childhood dreams realised, a heartfelt communion with the Toon Army?

The football world is embarrassed by Gascoigne, its greatest talent, who has been through some of the best managers in the game: Jack Charlton, Arthur Cox, El Tel, yet emerged unpolished. Still mad, burping. With personal problems obvious, blatant, money probably exacerbating them, not solving anything. But Shearer is different. The football establishment loves him. The ultimate professional, player's player. They think he is 'a great advert for the game'. Presenting the right image. Glenn Hoddle, appointing Shearer as England captain, said: 'He conducts himself well, handles the press well.'

This display, to football, is handling the press well. Emerging from the world of millionaires and agents and deals, and being an advertisement for the game. Feeding the myth: it's all about being a fan, about having Mam and Dad watching from the stand.

Surely Alan Shearer felt his dreams as a young lad, a sheet-metal worker's son, growing up a Newcastle fan. Dreaming of playing the game for a living, the thrill of it, the impossible joy of it, the glory, the fame, the money as well. He was determined to make it. He left home at 16, went the length of the country, to Southampton, to start. There he went into digs with a strange family and under the hard paternalistic control of Dave Merrington, head of youth development. Football suddenly not a game any more, but a profession, starting on £20 a week YTS.

Merrington ran a noted scheme at Southampton, producing many outstanding footballers: Shearer himself, the Wallace boys, Le Tissier, Kenna. Merrington, a Geordie himself, was perhaps the ideal man for the job, combining the brutal knowledge of a central defender with born-again Christianity. It was Merrington, then at Burnley, of whom Willie Morgan, the former Manchester United winger, famously said: 'You could tell when Dave Merrington became a Christian. He'd still kick you, but he'd apologise afterwards.'

Merrington was strict, he kept them going morning and afternoon. Tuesdays was 'Crash', agonising fitness training. They cleaned the pros' boots. Some pros treated them like rags, others had time for them. They all loved Jimmy Case. He talked to them as people, gave them advice, gave the best tips at Christmas.

Merrington was concerned to give the boys an all-round education; he sent them to Southampton Technical College, to learn sports management, before this became standard practice for YTS footballers. He took them to a centre for the homeless, where they would see another side of life. 'We wanted to develop their characters,' says Merrington, 'for them to become rounded human beings.'

But Merrington drummed into them the underlying hard truth of professional football. Only a few would make it. They had to work hard, and even then it might not be enough. Football was a profession, more than a game. It was a man's game, a hard business.

Football was always hard. For a player, it was unthinkably, unjustly hard in the early years. The Professional Footballers Association, the players union, was formed to fight grim battles, working men struggling against real exploitation. Players were treated by the backers of the early football clubs in the manner of industrial relations of the time, like factory fodder; given a few quid and no rights or security. Billy Meredith, the great Welsh winger who suffered and observed callous treatment during his legendary career at both Manchester clubs, resurrected the union in 1907 after a previous attempt had foundered. In 1900, the FA, uncomfortable with professionalism, believing it to be corrupting the sporting ethic, the players becoming mercenaries, had imposed a £4-a-week maximum wage. Meredith's friend Di Jones, playing for Manchester City in a pre-season friendly, sustained an injury which became infected and he died. City denied all liability because it had been a pre-season friendly. Jones's widow and children were left destitute. Yet Meredith, strikingly, still loved the game despite its injustice to employees. 'My heart was always full of it,' he reminisced at the end of his life.

The maximum wage lasted, incredibly, until 1961; justified self-servingly by clubs and League on the grounds of maintaining equality between teams and loyalty from players. Footballers became gigantic figures, heroes to boys and men, but personally suffered meanness and injustice. Tommy Lawton, one of England's greatest ever centre-forwards, who performed in the Thirties and Forties to crowds of 60,000 at Everton and Chelsea, wrote in his autobiography, *Football is my Business*: 'I have enjoyed my span in the game, and if I had my time over again I would still be a professional footballer, with the hope I might make a little bit more money. What I shall do when my legs begin to go back on me, I don't yet know.' He ended up, after 23 caps for England before and after the war, running a pub.

The maximum wage increased a little, to £20, in the Fifties. It was more than the average working man made, but it still wasn't much. Jimmy Armfield, an outstanding full-back who captained England, played his whole 19-year career at Blackpool. There was nothing to gain from moving on. Those were the days of travelling to away matches by train, the directors in first class, the players in third.

'We didn't mind,' stresses Armfield. 'It was just the style of the time. We were working class. We lived in our communities, we didn't have to live in a goldfish bowl like footballers do now. Even when I was England captain, barely anyone would recognise me outside Blackpool. We loved our careers. We loved playing the game.'

Armfield trained as a journalist well before his playing career was over. Top players made enough to set themselves up in something when they'd finished. Tom Finney still runs a plumbing business in Preston. But many players, led by Jimmy Hill as PFA chairman, had had enough of the artificially low wages. Hill eventually forced the abolition of the maximum wage and the removal of the enslaving 'retain and transfer' system after a court case brought in 1963 by George Eastham of Newcastle.

John Barnwell, then a young player with Arsenal, now chair of the League Managers Association, remembers, when the maximum wage was lifted, Arsenal's manager going up the team coach with envelopes, mostly offering the players £25 per week. The players threw their envelope out of the window. 'I saw Tommy Docherty throw his out of the window,' recalls Barnwell, 'so I thought I'd better throw mine out of the window as well.'

These were football's industrial relations: the clubs, still Victorian in spirit, trying to screw the players with low pay and short-term contracts, the players loving the game and the crowds, but growing tired and cynical. The wages lid was blown off by Fulham paying Johnny Haynes a fortune, £100 a week, almost immediately. Players began to make better money then, but it was hard, negotiating with wheeler-dealing managers. The clubs wanted to pay as little as possible and be able to get rid if the player didn't perform.

Jon Holmes came to know the Leicester City players in the early Seventies, when he was a young man selling insurance in the city. He offered to do the negotiations for some of them. One day, he introduced himself to manager Jimmy Bloomfield as a player's agent. 'It was a bit scary,' he says. 'In the early days the whole thing was a bit harum-scarum. But if the clubs complained, I used to say: "How is it that you can have as many advisers as you want, but the player isn't allowed one at all?"'

Holmes won better deals and the confidence of the Leicester players. In the late Seventies, he began to work for a talented, pacy young striker called Gary Lineker. Over the years, they have gone on to make each other a fortune. Lineker's boyish image smiles from a mosaic of magazine front covers on Holmes' office walls: 'I always say to my players they should do right by the game. That means promoting the right image. If they do that, the game will do right by them, look after them.'

Holmes believes he was one of the first agents in the English game. Harry Swales was around also, bringing Kevin Keegan out of his youth at Scunthorpe and into Hamburg, Brut adverts and the first lifelong, golfing financial security for any player. The clubs did not like agents, but there was nothing they could do. Their own historically ruthless attitudes led the smarter players to agents for self-preservation.

The late Seventies were more easy-going. There was a little more money around; the game was still hard, but players who established themselves enjoyed some stability from more enlightened managers. Top players made enough, maybe up to £12,000 a year, to be comfortable, buy a house, put a bit away, buy a business when they finished. Peter Lorimer, one of the stars in the great, grim, Revie Leeds side, went to the Commercial Inn in Leeds as celebrity landlord when he finished, the pub destination of many players of his era. He is still there. 'As long as we weren't being ripped off, we were not too concerned about the money,' he says. 'We loved playing the game, loved winning trophies, and were all friends off the park as well. We still play in charity matches now. I can't imagine today's players still playing for fun in their fifties.'

But there were tough stories as well. Some players did not have the strength to cope with the complete step down to obscurity from the pedestal of crowds and fame, having to start another career from scratch. The PFA gives grants for retraining, seeing ex-players into jobs as driving instructors, financial advisers. Some found it hard to cope, down on their money and luck. Tales abound of problems: depression, alcoholism, hard times.

Mick McGuire, executive at the PFA in charge of representing players, says that when he played, 1971-87, for Coventry, Norwich and Oldham, he was happy with what he got: 'My main consideration was to play in the First Division. Money wasn't the priority at that time. My only concern was that the club appreciated me. At Norwich, John Bond would renew my contract every year and I was happy. I didn't get into negotiations. I bought a house, saved some money. Now, it has changed. Players are much more aware of maximising their opportunities.'

Wages rose steadily throughout the Eighties, pushed up by more money in the game and more insistent agents. Even before the 1992 Sky deal, at least one English player was on £1m a year. By the end of the decade several English players were destined not to have to work again. The footballer's occupational pension had come in by then, paying out a tax-free lump sum at 35, now to a maximum of £82,000, and a proportion of a player's salary for the rest of his life, according to the length of career.

Alan Shearer, a young lad arriving at Southampton, a family club, in 1986, was determined to make it in football. Dave Merrington explains the difference between those who make it and those who don't: 'They have to reach a certain technical standard, of skill, and fitness. If they reach it they have a chance. After that the most crucial factor is mental toughness. Football puts extreme demands on players, and not everybody is cut out for it.

'We used to tell them the importance of dealing with it, the intensity of the arena, and how to deal with the press. Alan Shearer always had that toughness. He always coped very well.'

Leroy Whale was the only local boy, living at home with his parents, amongst Alan Shearer's Southampton YTS group, 1986–88. He was a good striker, outstanding as a junior, it was his dream to play for Southampton. Now 27, he remembers those two years as the best of his life; Merrington strict at the time, but, looking back, brilliant. 'Money isn't important when you get there. You're only 16. You're looking for the fame, being known as a player. Then you talk to the pros, they're talking money, all the time, the money.'

They had a laugh, he says, him most of all, playing tricks on the pros, larking about. 'Underneath it's ruthless though. It's always there, the knowledge you're not all going to make it. When push comes to shove you look after yourself. There's a hard edge to it. It's horrible really, professional football.'

In 1987–88 Leroy played superbly up front with the outstanding Alan Shearer and Rodney Wallace. They won their league, the South-East Counties Division Two, winning 25 out of 28 games, scoring 100 goals. Shearer, an England youth international by then, bagged 50. Leroy Whale scored 35. Despite a glut of strikers at the club – Steve Moran, Danny Wallace, Colin Clarke – they gave Shearer his debut at 17, in April 1988, while he was still an apprentice. Shearer scored a hat-trick at home to Arsenal, romping to a professional contract with his soon-to-be trademark smile.

Leroy Whale was sure he'd get a contract, everybody said he would. Manager Chris Nicholl called them in one by one. Leroy's friend Rod Wallace came out with a nice deal, a couple of hundred quid a week to start. Leroy was wondering how much to ask for. Chris Nicholl told him the club had too many good forwards. There was no budget left. Leroy could stay on till Christmas on expenses only, but there was no contract. 'I was absolutely gutted. That was all I ever wanted, to play for Southampton. Suddenly it was gone.'

Since then he has watched his old striking partner become the consummate modern professional. Leroy has made a living the hard way, working his way up in a billboard company, starting as a fitter's mate. He has always played non-league, for Basingstoke, Yeovil, more recently Fareham, a cult player, giving everything, an old-fashioned crowd pleaser.

'Nineteen was the worst time of my life. I was working outdoors, coming home really tired, finding the training in the evenings very hard. I'd speak to Rodney, he'd have just had a new contract, a pay rise, a nice big car. It was hard.

'I don't regret it now, though. I'm happy, I've done well in my job, been promoted to project manager. I've made a living in the real world, which I think a lot of footballers don't understand. I'm proud of having played in that youth team. But it shows how narrow the mark is between making it and being out of the game.'

Young Alan Shearer was single-minded. He asked Kevin Moore, a respected senior player, to advise him on his first contract. 'I told him to ask for half of any transfer fee which the club got for him in the future,' says Moore. 'Then to concentrate on making himself as valuable as possible.'

Shearer didn't take the advice about the contract, but he dedicated himself, always, to becoming as valuable as possible. He stayed four years, playing 105 full games, scoring 23 goals. By 1992, still only 21, he was the hottest young player in the country, just picked for England. And in 1992, the Premier League had come into its first whack of Sky money.

'Sky was a quantum leap for players' wages,' says Mick McGuire. 'It multiplied the commercial opportunities, with the game changing its image. It was no longer the working–class game.'

Players' agent Paul Stretford, who acts for the likes of Stan Collymore, puts the effect of the Sky deal more simply. 'It meant there was more money in the game and therefore a bigger pot for us to go at.' Kenny Dalglish, flush with Walker money, trailed Shearer for a long time, talking to his agent. Manchester United came in for him late on, but, running a balanced wage structure in a dressing-room of stars, United were not in the tax-exile's league. So Shearer went to Blackburn. He gave 100 per cent there, scored goals, made his name. Won the FA Carling Premiership, just. And was paid a reputed £500,000 a year.

It seems wrong to traditional supporters, to whom football means unconditional loyalty to one club, that to the modern player it is so clinical a business. But the Sky money poured into a game which had not prepared itself wisely. It was an industry of historically adversarial employment relations. Football was a short career, the players had to try to make as much as they could while at the top, doing deals with poker-faced managers or stolid chairmen. In the Seventies and Eighties the context of club, fans, tradition, smoothed the edges of the business. The players, in a tough, homely atmosphere, had some affinity with their club and its crowd. They played for a living but they knew what football was about, what it meant to people. Mostly they felt the same way themselves. For the likes of Shearer, though, football has changed completely since he queued up on the Gallowgate End as a 12-year-old to watch the Coming of Keegan. Football in 1992 was thrown utterly to the winds of 'market forces'. The players, advised by their agents, now do their deals to a backdrop of anonymous stands, corporate sponsorships, with floating clubs making fortunes for their owners. The money has flooded in and much of the soul has been squeezed out. Clubs complain that players are greedy, that they are taking too much money out, but the argument is hollow. The clubs have put no framework in place to show the players a more rounded way to think about football. They have led by mercenary example.

Shearer's *Diary of a Season,* the account of his championship-winning year at Blackburn, 1994-95 is, between the lines, a fascinating insight into the life of today's top player. It mixes reports of games with Shearer's considered thoughts on modern life and how to behave as a model pro. It is quite deliberately a 'great advertisement for the game', but it makes it seem so empty:

Monday, 22 August 1994:
I pick up my new car, a Mercedes 280, having traded in my two-year-old BMW for it. I suppose I'll get stick from the lads but Lainya [Shearer's wife] will drive it mostly since I have a sponsored Rover for my own use. I don't train today because the hamstring is still a bit sore.

Friday, 23 September 1994:
Tim [Flowers] drives us to the ground in his new Land Rover Discovery. He's like a kid with a new toy, which naturally

encourages Mike [Newell] and myself to tamper with all the gadgets in sight.

But the larks do not stop there.

> Monday, 1 May 1995:
> I beat Mike Newell on the final hole of the golf course, which means he has to dip into his pocket and pay for the round. It is a good time to be playing him, though, because he has just taken delivery of his new BMW car and seems to be in a hurry to get home for a drive in it.

If the Premier League gave a proportion of its money to rebuild the decaying fabric of the rest of football, less of it would be available to pour out in astronomical wages to players. Non-league clubs might have decent grounds, municipal pitches might have changing-rooms, football's money might be spent on football rather than on the saloon car industry. But the chairmen won't do that, competing instead with each other to bid the wages up, while arguing the players should be happy with less. In 1995-96, half the Premier League's turnover, £172m, went on players' wages. Agents, free-market middle men in a historically exploitative industry, take a lot of money out too. Jon Smith, of First Artist, Les Ferdinand's agent, estimates that the 39 agents licensed by FIFA to operate last year in England made around £500,000 gross, on average. That's £20m a season, of football's money.

Average Premier League players are retiring now at 35, with enormous private investments to buffer their occupational pensions. They absorb their values from the industry in which they work. The concept of loyalty is mostly anathema. 'To the clubs you're just a commodity,' Les Ferdinand told me. 'They'll sell you at the drop of a hat.' He understood his profession; a few months later Shearer's striking partner was sold to Tottenham, Newcastle United plc recouping £6m just before their accounting year end. 'Some players stay loyal to one club, but not many any more. You have to get the best deal for yourself.'

The Chris Sutton transfer of 1995 was the one which first spectacularly bid the post-Sky wages up, the players and agents diving in for their deals. But even that, said to be around £500,000 and rising, is not excessive at all today. Mick McGuire says there are three main brackets of players' salaries. 'The average player in a lowly Premiership side is on £150,000 a year. A decent player in the middle order, you're talking £250,000 to £300,000. Top players are on anything from £500,000 to £1,500,000 a year.'

The very top players are on more than that. Ravanelli has famously been quoted as having taken £42,000 a week from Middlesbrough. The players have become rich beyond the imaginings of the traditional supporter. The Merrington approach is rare in football; most players are given nothing to do in the afternoons. There is no attempt to create rounded characters. Football in the Nineties has an air of flash, and the players are advertisements for the game. Stories abound of players losing sense of themselves in the all-encompassing atmosphere of money.

There are on-field tussles, all players talk of them, opponents pushing them back, sneering: 'Fuck off, how much are you on?' A defender in a top Premiership club recalls one striker, a famous international, who used always to wave his wallet around. 'Add a fucking nought to your wages,' he used to say, 'and you're getting fucking close to mine.' 'A mortgage?' was another favourite, 'what the fuck's that?'

At half-time during one game, the manager, a big name, was giving the striker a talking-to, for not funnelling back. 'What are you going to do about it?' asked the striker, sitting in the dressing-room, the team around him. 'Fucking sell me?'

Alan Shearer finished his 1995-96 season early, to have a minor groin operation. He did not say then that he wanted to leave. He went to Euro '96 and concentrated on making himself as valuable as possible. When he came out, top scorer, he went to Jersey with agent Tony Stephens.

Jack Walker offered more money, and Shearer thought about staying another year. Kenny Dalglish, on £300,000-a-year as Blackburn's director of football, told Shearer he couldn't lose whether he stayed or went. Shearer and Stephens had a long chat with Alex Ferguson, and he nearly went there. It is believed, though, that Blackburn would not sell to United. Newcastle were circling, and Blackburn told them they could have Shearer for £15m. Newcastle, already planning to float, paid up. They summoned the obliging press to scurry up from London, to fill the papers with SHEARER COMES HOME and the sheet-metal worker's son line. Even at the press conference, Shearer, trying to show he was moving for the love of the club, said: 'I decided to join Newcastle before the money was even mentioned. I told Kevin I wanted to join, then the money was sorted out over the next two or three hours.'

Later in the year *The Daily Express* itemised Shearer's income. According to the paper, he was on between £24,000 and £30,000 per week, depending on win bonuses, making an annual salary of £1.5m. His signing-on fee was £500,000 a year. In endorsements, Stephens has found the Shearer smile worth £2m from Umbro, £750,000 from Lucozade, £250,000 from Jaguar, in return for driving one of their top of the range cars. The clean-cut image of the England captain is worth £1m a year to Braun. A total of £5.5m in a year.

Modelling the England kit, an Umbro creation, costing £70, brought out immediately after Christmas 1996, Shearer slipped up. He was asked whether it was right for it to be so expensive. The obvious line to take would have been to say the kit was good quality, or he hoped that parents would be able to afford it. But perhaps he did not think of it in time. 'That's life,' he shrugged. Which it is, to him. Market forces. If the FA can charge £70, fine.

The modern player is in danger of losing the feelings of previous generations of footballers, the context, the relationship with supporters, the meaning of being a footballer. Some, who worked before, came up the hard way, say they appreciate what they have more than those who came straight through apprenticeships, who have known only the incubation of football clubs. Gary Pallister laboured in the Middlesbrough docks, Stuart Pearce was an electrician for Brent Council, Chris Waddle worked in a sausage-seasoning factory. 'I look at some of the young lads at clubs,' says Waddle, 'and I think they could do with working. They don't know how lucky they are.'

John Beresford, left-back at Newcastle, visits schools in deprived areas of the city. He goes home to Sheffield a lot, sees his old mates, many of whom are on the dole or struggling from job to job. 'I'm aware I'm very lucky,' he says. 'There's nothing better than going out with your old mates and have them wind you up. It's the best thing for reminding you who you are.'

Chris Armstrong, now of Spurs, was working in a burger factory when Wrexham, his home town club, rescued him in 1989, paying him £150 a week. 'It's your dream job,' he says of making it. 'You can't believe you're playing football for a living.' Some players, he says, become cynical about the game, looking only for what they can get. 'You try not to. With me, if I ever get tired of any aspect of being a footballer, I just think back to working in a factory, and realise I'm in the best job in the world.'

But these are individual histories, players who are big or rounded or strong enough to see there is more to life. Football does nothing itself to cultivate such human feeling, to guard against greed; quite the opposite – the players are exposed more to that than any other ethos. There is a growing chasm between player and supporter, and many supporters are now coming to resent the players, not look up to them. Players' wages are given more publicity than the capital gains of floating chairmen, and the myth-making is wearing thin. Supporters increasingly know that players move only for the best deal. It is the free market. It has no capacity to guide in any other way, and it is paying beyond what is decent.

The PFA could set up a footballers' charity foundation, send some of this money around the community. That would be a good advertisement for the game. And the clubs, if they had any ethos, if they were not just investment vehicles now, would build in work for players in the afternoons; community work, media work. They would employ more coaches, giving players a future in the game afterwards. But Merrington's ideas never were the norm. He himself was put out of a job when Southampton, preparing for their flotation, brought in Graeme Souness as manager, a big name for the City. For a time one of football's most distinguished and best youth developers was threatened with having to leave the game, before he was given the post of chief scout at Wolves.

The players are only symptoms of football's more general loss, commodities simultaneously overpaid and ruthlessly dealt with, in danger of losing their love of the game, loyalty to the club, the bond with supporters. Shearer, modern football's model professional, seems to me a tragedy of sorts. Big money has liberated footballers from oppression, haggling, insecurity at 35, but the obsession with it has driven out many good things too. Shearer has more money than any one person should have in a sane world, a Jag and all the other trappings. But on the day he achieved his childhood ambition, on the day he became Newcastle United's number 9, he seemed like he was doing a job. Remembering his media training. Smiling the smile. As if the hard business of realising his dream had, at only 26, removed his capacity to dream at all, replaced it with agents and negotiations and deals and the crisp, dry matter of contract.

14

LOW TIDE IN LYTHAM

When you ring the Football League, if the person you want is out, they never seem to take messages. They always ask you to ring back later. The strong impression is that the receptionists are on stern instructions to save on the phone bill. A visit to the League's 'headquarters' only confirms the air of old-fashioned penny-pinching. The League sits in prim, respectable Lytham St Annes on the North-West seaside, its wealthiest members having run off some years ago to the City of London, to find its streets paved with gold. The League's accommodation is in a row of gloomy looking hotels near the seafront. Inside, it is a far cry from the Georgian pomp of the Football Association. The FA's reception, with its leather armchairs, pictures of the Queen and the Duke of Kent, is bursting with silverware: platters, vases, trophies, ceremonials from other football associations handed over at internationals. There is an enormous gold ball from the Brazilian Football Federation, a massive glass vase from the Swedish FA with an engraved map of Europe; the whole of Lancaster Gate is an international swap shop of gold, silver, pewter. The League's reception has more the air of a down-at-heel B & B. The receptionist sits behind a wooden counter with an 'ENQUIRIES' sign above. A tiny cabinet in the corner contains a few mementos; a vase from the Anglo-Italian Cup, an ornamental bull from Hereford United. The League's gift from UEFA to commemorate Euro '96 appears to have been a small barometer, which is tacked on to the wall. The place fits in perfectly with St

Annes itself; its faded, left-behind air evoking an age when foreign travel was impossible.

Even in its heyday, though, before the First Division became so swollen with self-importance and desire for money that it ran off to become its own Premiership, the League never went in for the pomp of the Football Association, with its public school, amateur tradition. From the start it has had more pragmatic needs — to provide professional clubs with fixtures, and therefore with regular income and the means to survive. The idea of William McGregor, Aston Villa's modest, well-loved shopkeeper-chairman, the league was formed in 1888 by 12 clubs from the North and Midlands whose backers were not looking to make money for themselves out of football. But they were concerned from the start with pounds, shillings and pence, not the swapping of engraved tureens.

The League, framing the intensity of one-off games with a neat, season-long structure and an ultimate prize, was a success from the start. In 1892 a Second Division was formed, and the first was joined by Newton Heath, forerunners of Manchester United, whose chairman would later suggest 'putting small clubs to sleep'. Small Heath, later Birmingham City, were founder members of the Second Division, as were Crewe, and early northern professional clubs Darwen and Northwich Victoria. The first Southern team, Woolwich Arsenal, joined the following year, 1893, along with Liverpool and Newcastle United.

From the start it was seen that professionalism, although necessary and unavoidable, had within it the capacity to undermine competition. The big city clubs, in some cases formed later than those in the smaller towns, began to power their way to the top, taking advantage, simply, of their bigger catchment areas and consequently higher gates. There is a fascinating piece of sour grapes about this in *History of the Blackburn Rovers Football Club: 1873-1923* by Charles Francis, from 1885, a gripe, from one of the first clubs to be caught paying players, which echoes deliciously down the years: 'About this time the Rovers had an unhappy experience at Manchester. In a match with Newton Heath, who were all imported professionals and big fellows, the "Blue and Whites" were knocked about like ninepins. Their science was unavailing against brute force. The Rovers lost 2-1, but it was conceded that physique and not skill had decided the issue.

In fact, so secure a hold had professionalism already obtained that it was then forecast that "the most successful team of the future will be the one that has the greatest amount of money at its back, and that can afford to pay for the finest talent in the land".'

In fact, that theory would not quite be allowed to take hold until 1992, when 'Uncle Jack' arrived to test its validity. From the beginning, it was seen that 'survival of the fittest', as market forces was then called, would mean smaller clubs going bust, now called 'consolidation'. So, even before the turn of the century, the Football League was formed with a keen sense of the need to regulate market forces.

But professionalism shook football out, with some smaller teams finding it difficult to attract big enough gates. As other clubs and leagues formed, the stature of teams came roughly to be defined by their catchment areas. Unlike other countries where a football federation could plan from the beginning a formal 'pyramid' of football, in England the leagues grew more by evolution. A rough pecking order emerged between these leagues, to be followed in later years by systems of promotion and relegation which tied the minor leagues to the Football League. The First Division, soon to attract huge crowds and create footballing memories and legends, was therefore only the top of a ladder which had been gradually created by the efforts of hundreds, thousands, of clubs. The two divisions expanded gradually thereafter. In 1921 the Football League formed two new Third Divisions, North and South. In 1958 the regional groupings were made national, into the Third and Fourth Divisions. Crowds, in this heyday of football, were enormous; gates of 20-30,000 were not unusual in the late Fifties and early Sixties even at the lower division clubs, particularly for FA Cup ties.

Tensions between League and FA grew over the post-war years; the cultural differences stewing with money worries in stale committee-room air, catalysed by the issue of club and country. Eventually the League began to get more of its men into positions of power at the FA, a constant tactic in the Sixties and Seventies. Within the League, relations were reasonably stable until the Sixties. After the First World War, the gate levy, 4 per cent of the season's total distributed equally to all clubs, was a subsidy of the smaller clubs by the bigger, and away teams were still entitled to a contribution from the match gate.

The concept of owners making money from football was barely even considered then; the clubs were mostly sustained at the lower level by earnest effort, and, quite often, investment by the directors. As a cash-rich business, football has always been prey to corruption, and no doubt there was some fiddling of gate money – the phrase in football for being on the fiddle is 'having your own turnstile'. But it was mostly low level, and certainly nothing compared to the fortunes being made legitimately, with the blessing of the FA, out of football at the top level today.

The principle of equality, of the rich subsidising the poor, came to be tested by the influx of more money into the game. First, in 1960, was the League Cup. Then, in 1965, the BBC paid £5,000 for the rights to show its 6 p.m. early Saturday evening highlights package, *Match of the Day*. This money was distributed equally around the whole League, around £50 a club. But television and sponsorship was to provide the battleground for all the talk of breakaway, the big clubs becoming increasingly dissatisfied with the principle of equality. The new chairmen, Martin Edwards, Irving Scholar and those of the other big clubs, wanted the money and the power, not to share and be constantly outvoted by the two-thirds majority required by the Lytham rulebook.

The League hung on, through the breakaway threats of 1981 and 1985, by ceding a little more power, a little more of the television money, to the big clubs. The principle of equality lasted, though; it was accepted throughout football that the big clubs were nothing without the small, that they shared the same history, the only difference was the size of their catchment areas. It was a higher good, whatever the rows, for the framework of 92 clubs to be sustained by some sharing of the wealth earned, by accident of location, by the big clubs. The continued threats of breakaway were resisted because no interpretation was possible other than that the big clubs were greedy. Subsequent events have proved that to be true.

The League was shocked at the reaction of the FA to its proposals for unity in *One Game One Team One Voice*. The League fought a desperate, futile battle against the breakaway. On 6 June 1991, the League threatened legal action with 'top City solicitors', who would be instructed by Arthur Sandford, the League's chief executive, 'himself a solicitor'. On the day the deadline ran out, 12 June, the FA announced its own High Court action to seek confirmation that it did have the authority to form the Premier League. 'The proposed new structure,' said Graham Kelly, who had served 20 years at Lytham, 'with appropriate arrangements for the sharing of revenues, will benefit the national team and the national game as a whole.'

The League warned of widespread financial difficulty, with some clubs facing extinction. The League disputed the argument that the Premier League was necessary to take the game forward, or earn more money. Calling it 'divisive, élitist, and not in the best interests of football', Sandford pointed out that the *Blueprint* had stolen many of its ideas from *One Game One Team One Voice*, and now proposed to steal the top clubs as well. The sole football reason for the breakaway, the proposal to have 18 clubs, was defeated by the greed of those who feared they might be excluded.

On 31 July 1991, the High Court ruled in favour of the FA having the power to form a Premier League. The only contractual tie the League could insist on was its 'three-year rule', that clubs had to give three years' notice before resigning from the League. The League announced an appeal, but two weeks later a meeting of the Third and Fourth Divisions accepted that the rebels would to break away. 'There was no mood of pessimism,' said a statement, bravely. 'Rather of resolution to let those clubs stew in their own isolated juices.'

Which, of course, they have done ever since, finding the FA Carling Premiership a particularly rich gravy of which, so far, they have been unable to get enough. The League and FA settled the legal action with a 'tri-partite agreement', which is still in force today. The Premier League pays the Football League £1m a year, the same as it was paying in 1991 by way of the reduced 3 per cent levy on gate receipts. The FA agreed to pay the Football League £2m a year. This may seem a poor deal by the League, but it also retained three-club promotion and relegation to and from the Premier League, and the Coca-Cola Cup. Both of these are beginning to annoy the Premier League, which has too much money to be bothered with the Coca-Cola Cup, and whose shareholders feel unnecessarily endangered by three-club relegation. The League, though, insists on its binding agreement, which includes the provision that the League will not be 'financially disadvantaged' by the Premier League.

Some hope. Since the very beginning of the Premier League, the

Football League clubs, like the non-league and amateur grass-roots of football, have been able only to watch as 22 clubs have feasted on all the money, leaking much of it in wages to players, many of them foreign, and releasing next to nothing to the rest of the game. The Football League, though, likes to put a brave face on. Spokesman Chris Hull puts it like this: 'The fact that the justification for the Premier League was 18 clubs, which didn't happen, means that people can make their own minds up about why the breakaway went through. But we believe there is no point looking back and harping on about that. What is done is done. We look to our own competition; we have some great names and stadia, a complete geographical spread of clubs, and good commercial deals now. Our gates were up to a total of 12 million in 1996-97. We're going from strength to strength.'

Nevertheless in the last few years the plight of the smaller clubs has been one of the few issues to have been recognised as a stark contrast with the riches of the Premiership. How, it has been puzzled, can the top football clubs, their owners and players, be wallowing in such grand fortune, while the likes of Brighton, Bournemouth and Hull City were threatened with extinction? Even the Labour Government has raised concern about that.

The picture of the Nationwide League, though, is more complex, the truth lying somewhere in between Chris Hull's professed optimism and the pessimism engendered by some clubs' plight. The League is indeed full of historic names, and not all of them are in financial difficulty at all. The bigger clubs are aiming for Premiership moneymaking for their owners: Birmingham City under porn king David Sullivan, Sheffield United under its Manchester-based plc owners, and Manchester City, under its former player turned entrepreneur Francis Lee.

By contrast, many clubs, perhaps as many as 20, are in serious financial trouble, with hardly a light at the end of the tunnel. The old, debt-laden boards of Premiership clubs were replaced by money men tempted by Sky, but in the Football League the Murdoch money did not arrive until recently. In five years, the Premiership gave not one penny away to any of the rest of football, besides the £1m in the tri-partite agreement.

It remains true, though, that many of the lower-division clubs could be financially viable, that there are more deserving cases for subsidy, and some have been run badly. This includes Brighton and Hove Albion, which was in millions of pounds of debt when it was taken over in 1993 by Bill Archer and Greg Stanley, two men who provoked outrage in the town by proposing to sell the ground with no provision made for the football club. It was found that they had removed Rule 34 from the articles of association, which they claimed had been an oversight, potentially allowing them to profit from the sale of the Goldstone Ground. The fans mounted a tremendous campaign, attracting solidarity from football fans nationwide not prepared to see any football club go under. The two were eventually replaced by a consortium led by Dick Knight and the club retained their League status on the very last day of the season with a to-the-death duel with the unfortunate bulls of Hereford.

Most commonly clubs are in trouble because they have overreached themselves in signing players, not bringing enough money in to cover a high wage bill. Unfortunately, though, the lower divisions are also prey to constant takeover. The clubs have never been democratised, simply being handed in various states of penury from one businessman to another, and many supporters live in constant apprehension about the intentions of people who arrive from nowhere wanting to take over a club. Mike Appleby, membership manager of the Football Association, one of those who works hard and honestly for the welfare of football in an organisation which has badly let him down, says that lower division and non-league clubs are prey to asset strippers. The football clubs are, to a hawk-eyed businessman, failing companies which can be bought cheaply, sitting on acres of potentially prime land, often in town centres.

Rule 34 is still invoked at this level, and Appleby says the prohibition from profiting on the sale of the ground has actually deterred some intended takeovers. But he says it needs tightening up. He believes that people actively scour the country looking for likely football clubs to take over. 'I say to supporters who think a businessman has come in from nowhere to rescue them, look care-fully at who this businessman is, and what he wants.'

At many clubs in the League, even successful ones, supporters have their worries about the people who arrive to take them over.

These worries, that football clubs, longstanding, cherished

institutions, may be used as mere fronts for business, usually property development, which blight the prospects of the lower divisions. The League is a rag-bag of ownership, its clubs suffering periodic takeover by men of dramatically varying abilities and motives. But there are some jewels, well-run clubs, people believing, still, in football for its own sake, not merely as some short-term profit-making venture.

Bryan Gray, chairman of Preston North End since June 1994, brings to the football club an enlightened approach, music to the ears after the pile-it-high nihilism of the Premiership. Gray's philosophy derives from a career in the Baxi Partnership, a heating company, the largest employee-owned manufacturing company in the country, which has been a major employer in Preston since 1866. Gray, Baxi chief executive, says that his company wanted to 'put something back into the community'. And, listening to him, it sounds true, and as if he has thought about the implications of that for longer than a second. 'The club has a very rich history,' he says. 'It was a founder member of the Football League, very successful in the past. Everything we are doing, in terms of the team, the design of the new stand, the club store, is being done to build on that association of the club with quality.'

This is not a charitable approach; making a profit is integral to the philosophy, but it is profit for a purpose, for the club. It is seen as part of building a healthy football club to have sound commercial activities, and Gray has presided over a turnaround in the club's finances. Preston is a floated club, having gone on to the Alternative Investment Market in 1995. But Gray says this was done to raise money, not for Baxi to cash in. With a turnover of £100m, it really doesn't need to, and the fans can be reasonably sure it is around for the long term. Gray argues that the 40 per cent Baxi ownership and large supporter shareholding preserve the ethos of the football club, which is to serve its supporters, to build and be successful. But the transformation, unlike the dash for cash elsewhere, is gradual, dignified. The Tom Finney Stand, a £4.7m combination of industrial power and spotlit cool, was completed in March 1996. Preston were promoted to Division Two two months later.

Gray believes that good design is integral to a football club's sense of itself and projection to the community. In a stark contrast to the demolitions at Ewood Park, he says: 'We want to be a good neighbour. Even people who do not like football may feel proud of the stand, as a well-designed Preston piece of architecture. That way the club builds up goodwill in the town.'

They talk here about brand, but not in an exploitative way. They speak of it as if they know what it means and how it fits in. It does not mean taking a club crest and slapping it on to the bottoms of teddy bears, or pint pots, or flip-flops: 'That's Blackpool seafront stuff,' says Gray. 'It cheapens the brand.

'A brand is about being associated with certain values. In our case, Preston North End was a founder member of the Football League and has been very successful in the past. So our core values, with which supporters and people in the town associate us, are longevity and success. This can be reflected in merchandise which supporters feel proud to buy.'

The store, crafted by merchandising manager Steve White, a designer and lifelong North End fan, is a haven of dignity from the tat palaces at other football clubs. Minimal, restrained, the store stocks kit designed by White and manufactured by the club itself. White has also brought out a range of clothes, leisurewear, branded with a discreet 'PNE' logo, the Preston terrace chant. The store and its goods introduce into football merchandising a quiet respect for the loyalty of football supporters to their clubs. It sees football support as a dignified, worthwhile part of late 20th-century life, not as at other clubs, the province of the great unwashed.

Football here is in the hands of people who look at more than the bottom line. Gray believes that the Nationwide League is not a charity case; that the clubs, bearing their town's names, can all do more to weave themselves further into the affections of their communities, and that way ensure economic survival: 'We have some advantages, given our history, and that Preston is a big town with a wide catchment area. But every professional football club has a fund of loyalty in its town. If the club produces merchandise which is well-designed and good value, people will be glad to be associated with it.' He is impatient with the amateurishness of the football world: 'These really are not very difficult ideas. They're absolutely basic to any good businessman.'

It is sobering to reflect on how many truly good businessmen, with experience of running institutions, businesses, for the long term, rather than hurtling around for the cash, have actually arrived into football. Few Premiership chairmen speak with any dignity about their clubs, or betray the slightest hint of respect for their supporters, whom they seem quietly to despise, or at least fail to understand.

John Bowler, chairman of Crewe Alexandra, widely recognised as one of the best-run clubs in the League, is another with experience of business for the long term, not the quick buck. Bowler, now retired, was formerly regional director of Wellcome, the pharmaceutical company, which he says retained an ethos, a scientific and educational culture, integral to its business of making money. He is a critic of the dash for cash in the Premiership: 'The big clubs must recognise the importance of the national game, not lose sight of their responsibility to it. At the moment it is poor, very disappointing; the huge money at the top not filtering through to the grass-roots.'

Bowler also made a careful assessment of his club when he arrived at Crewe as a director in 1987, but his conclusion was the polar opposite of Gray's at Preston. Crewe did not have a large catchment area from which to draw support, and so building the club could not be based on attracting large support. Financial viability was going to be difficult to achieve purely through the turnstiles: 'The key part of our growth had to be developing players. They would come through and improve our squad, but also, by selling players to bigger clubs, provide the capital to develop our ground. We were lucky that Dario Gradi came along at that time. He liked what we were doing, and he has stayed.'

Gradi's production line – David Platt, Rob Jones, Geoff Thomas, Neil Lennon, Craig Hignett, John Pemberton and several others – has paid for three new sides of the Gresty Road stadium, on its way to becoming all-seater for 14,000. The club, finally promoted to the First Division via the 1997 play-offs, boasts excellent training facilities and a thriving community operation. A joint charitable scheme with the local authority provides football sessions for kids of all abilities, not just those Dario fancies for his school of excellence. Bowler points out that this is what football clubs should be doing: 'It is the ethos and culture of our club to contribute to the local community. There is a genuine feeling here that our club belongs to the community. But I would be a liar if I said it did not bring us benefits, in terms of encouraging support for our club, from the community and business.

'Benevolence is unfortunately not as high on football's agenda as it should be. In the higher echelons of the game, it has been taken over by people whose priority is to business, rather than businessmen who are interested in football. They have to be persuaded not to go for short-term gain.

'Many people seem to look for a quick fix in football. They think you can buy success. They only think that because too few people in football's history have tried another way. Experience has shown me that there is no quick fix. You have to work hard, know what you are, what your limitations are, work closely with the local community. You have to think long term.

'In the long term, the big clubs are beginning to alienate their own supporters, by looking to maximise revenue without sufficient discernment.'

You can drink deeply of such thinking. Any thinking at all about what a football club is and how it should best serve its supporters and community, is faith-restoring in the face of the Premiership's consumerism. The presence of Brian Lomax's supporters' trust at Northampton Town and now the newly democratised Bournemouth, also provide rays of hope in the exploitative profanity of the modern football business. Trevor Watkins, who put the scheme together for a community-based trust at his beloved Bournemouth, is clear that freeing football clubs from the hand of a single owner is the way forward: 'I stressed to the Football League that this sets the parameters for the future of football; to buy the club for the community.'

Huddersfield Town, tightly interlinked with the council, which owns the splendid McAlpine Stadium, is another good example, the football club woven into the town, one participant in a major civic venue. As at Northampton, the council's bearing of the cost and risk of the stadium frees the football club from one of its major expenses, and also its major temptation to an asset-stripper.

So although the Nationwide League has been abandoned by the greedier, big city clubs, whose breakaway is no more valid now than it was in 1992, the League is not in itself in too desperate a plight. It has a deal now with Sky: £125m over four years, small beer compared to the fat cats, but still substantial money. The problem clubs need to be reformed, as, perhaps, does the League itself, but in principle the traditions of competitive football in the smaller towns and cities of

England can, with hard, dedicated work, be safeguarded. Further community involvement is believed by many to be the way forward, building a relationship between clubs and their local people.

In June 1997, after five years of feasting and floating, the Premier League finally decided to give some money to the lower divisions. Following its latest Sky deal, £670m over four years, it coughed up £20m to the Football Trust for grants to stadia in the lower divisions, then £20m to the 72 Football League clubs to develop youth policies. It is, of course, small change, and enlightened self-interest, the Premier League seeing that it gets players from the lower leagues, soon to be free following the Bosman verdict, and £2m from each Premiership club is barely the cost of a single player. Even this, 6.2 per cent of its television money, may not have emerged so quickly without the election of a Labour Government pledging to tame rampant market forces, including those currently ruling football.

The Football Trust had been badly hit by the Lottery's decimation of the pools and had been crying out for money for nearly a year. The Trust, a good, dedicated, if somewhat naïve organisation, which funded the Premiership's post-Taylor banqueting palaces without seeking to claw back its grant money once millions were being made, begged and pleaded with the billion-pound Permiership to make a donation. When the £20m finally arrived, to be matched by the Lottery, it was accompanied by an ominous statement from spokesman Mike Lee, of Westminster Strategy, the press and lobbying firm employed by the Premier League: 'The provision of Lottery monies means that a new partnership with the Government can be developed in the future.' There they were, the Premiership billionaires, seeking to prepare the ground for getting more public money.

Mike Lee also likes to claim that the League has not been abandoned by the Premier League; that the Premier League offered to do a joint TV deal with the League, which instead did its own deal with Sky. Lee Walker, head of broadcasting at the Football League, says it was not that simple, that the Premier League came late into the League's renegotiations of its TV deal. 'Nothing was ever explicit,' he says. 'And we were on a tight deadline with ITV, we couldn't wait.'

In any case, a joint TV deal is not the same as unity, as redistribution, the historic safeguard for the fabric of English football. The breakaway may not have killed the Football League, but it has been a blow from which the League has struggled to recover.

'Of course our clubs must become more financially viable, more businesslike,' says Lee Walker. 'But you have to realise that when we as the Nationwide League, containing some of the most famous and distinguished football clubs in the world, go out to get sponsorship, we are seen by definition as second best. And the continued hype of the Premiership is bad for the Nationwide League, particularly amongst the younger generation, who are growing up supporting the likes of Man United, uninterested in their local clubs.'

St Annes is one of those North-West resorts where the tide seems always to be out. There is a pier there, standing on stilts, a fading, peeling relic of amusement. The Football League is left in the town, abandoned by its bigger members, nurtured in the League for so long, who broke away as soon as the money became really big. The Premier League cannot take the credit for the football boom; the money has come in from outside. Had there been no breakaway, the money, probably more, would still have come pouring in from a frenzied television war. And there would have been redistribution.

There is no justification, still, for the money being creamed off at the top. The Football League, for all its faults, its dowdiness, the unwieldiness of its decision-making, is a great body, the first league of its kind in the world, which has kept so many clubs alive for so long. It was responsible for building Manchester United, Newcastle United; Aston Villa was its founder member. An ethos, of football as part of the community, of running a club for the love of it, of supporting out of loyalty, all of these survive in the Football League. At a time when football is awash with money, a handful of people must not be allowed to bathe in it all, leaving the rest of football marooned in the dry sand, on rocky, peeling stilts.

15

THE END OF HISTORY

There is little of particular note in the approach to Northwich Victoria FC. The club is surrounded by nondescript housing estates, close to a museum dedicated to the mid-Cheshire town's major industry – salt. You turn right into the ground just before Kwik Save, past a pub, down a narrow cul-de-sac, to Vics' green main stand, proud, but looking in need of a bit of work. Few football supporters will ever hear much about the club; it is one of those vaguely familiar names, to be found in the Vauxhall Conference if you look hard enough. Yet this little cul-de-sac in middle England is a place of footballing pilgrimage, foreign camera crews periodically landing on general manager Dave Thomas when they are making films about the history of the beautiful game.

Northwich, like the Lancashire cotton towns, was an early, eager recipient of the new game of football, Northwich Victoria founded in 1874 by middle-class men who had been introduced to the game at universities. Patriots, they called the club after the reigning Queen. The following year, with football taking off, and Vics' ambition growing, the club went looking for a new ground. They inquired about a field close to the centre of town, used for drill by the Cheshire Rifle Volunteers. The volunteers gave permission, and Vics first marked out the field for their friendlies in 1875. They play in the same place today, the Drill Field. It is the oldest continuously used football ground in the world.

It was at places like this that football was born, marked out and given to the world. These are the birthplaces of Pele, Cruyff, Beckenbauer, of all the matches and memories and worldwide passion of the international language of association football. Yet the foreign football audiences seem to care more for the game's source and wellspring than the English football 'industry' itself.

Northwich, one of the first clubs, founder members of the Football League Second Division in 1892, bobbed in the early years of football to find their true level. Too small to compete realistically, the club struggled to make ends meet in the professional game, finished bottom in 1894 and dropped back into amateur Cheshire football. Their star player, whom they'd plucked out of Welsh local football, was snapped up by Manchester City. He was Billy Meredith, at the beginning of one of football's greatest, most eventful careers.

Catchment area still roughly determines a club's rightful place in football's odd-shaped ladder. The smaller city and larger town teams, Dover, Northwich, Bath, play in the Vauxhall Conference, formed as the pinnacle of the non-league in 1986. Below, with the promise of promotion to the Conference, smaller towns in the North play in the Unibond League's two divisions, while those of the Midlands and South play in the three divisions of the Beazer Homes League. Below these are the ICIS League in the South, the Midland Football Combination, the North-West Counties League, the Northern League. Each of the member clubs, many with a hundred years' history, is a world in itself, a local temple of myth and legend, its own list of great games, most fondly remembered players and characters, periodic crises. Each is the place of generations of homage, a small, dignified part of the fabric of football.

One of Northwich's quirks is a bitter rivalry, the kind that splits families, with the other local club, Witton Albion. 'It's stupid really,' says Dave Thomas, 12 years Vics' general manager. 'Fans in Northwich hate each other, they think it's like Man City and Man United. They don't realise that nobody outside the town gives a toss.'

You would think, in this time of football's hype and pre-eminence, of its new, satellite wealth after a century surviving on gate money, that it might have marked the Drill Field, its oldest ground, with some sign of distinction. In fact, the opposite is the case. The Drill Field is more a monument to dogged survival, to the hard work of its succession of custodians, than to football's recent reinvention of itself.

It is squashed by semi-detached suburbia at one end and a Kwik Save carpark at the other, elbowing sharply almost into the pitch. The main stand is old, haggard, tries its best. Cups of tea are served at half-time in paper cups. Opposite, the stooping Dane Bank stand is flanked by two grass verges, one of which, completely dug up, looks like a slag heap.

In 1993 the ground nearly disappeared, like so many others, into the early, dismal history of the English superstore. As developers wrestled with planning permission, the struggling club rallied, was rescued by loyal fans dipping into their pockets: £100,000 from an appeal, matched by a loan from Tetley's, saved the ground. According to Thomas, developments at the top of the game, the arrival of the Premiership and the demands of Sky, have made life harder, not easier, for clubs lower down.

They have been critically afflicted by the Football Trust's moratorium on grants, announced in December 1996, due to the decline in pools income caused by the National Lottery. Northwich were awaiting a grant to rebuild the Dane Bank side of the ground. Now the Lottery, FA and Premier League have finally put some money in. But it is late and it may not be enough. What the Lottery gives, it takes away; at this level it has destroyed carefully built local lotteries which were a vital source of cash. 'We had a lottery making a few hundred vital pounds a week,' says Thomas. 'That has been seriously damaged since the National Lottery started.

'One of the biggest problems for clubs at our level is that our gates are badly affected by Sky matches. We can hardly schedule a midweek match which doesn't clash with some game or other. In European weeks, football's on television every night. Given the choice, many people who'd normally come down to watch their local team will stay in and watch a glamour game on telly. Which is all very well, but we at the grass-roots are losing money as a direct result of the Premiership and nothing's coming back.'

On European week in mid-March 1997, Northwich Victoria's rivals Witton Albion suffered their lowest ever gate, 220. While Premiership clubs have provided floated fortunes for their owners, the non-leagues, the backbone of the game, have seen none of the new money. The Vauxhall Conference, offering promotion to the Football League, has become, oddly, a magnet for rich backers, injecting wage inflation where it can be ill-afforded. Max Griggs, the Doc Marten shoe magnate who in 1992 amalgamated two Northamptonshire village teams to create Rushden & Diamonds, is only the most spectacular example, the Jack Walker of the Conference. It remains to be seen whether these backers have been tempted in by footballing hype, or whether they will be staying for the long term.

I went to a match at the Drill Field in November 1996, Northwich v. Walsall in the FA Cup first round. Not a glamour tie maybe, but here, a world away from tannoy announcements, suits with name tags and megastores, it felt like the heart and soul of football. This was football on a terrace with a programme and a Bovril. Here, at local level, are wags in the crowd, supporters, fierce, some of them, not consumers of 'entertainment', who can be here for no reason other than a sense of kinship with the club.

Northwich's part-time players fulfil the John Motson, Road-to-Wembley cliché about welders, joiners and carpenters, but this glosses over the tough realities of football for many players, the fine line between full-time and part-time status. At the end of every season, the PFA sends a fat circular out, listing hundreds of professional players who have been released. Northwich, perusing the list, picked up several ex-pros, including Wayne Fairclough, 27, brother of Chris, released by Chesterfield at the end of 1995-96. If Chesterfield had kept him another year, Wayne might have enjoyed a glorious FA Cup run, culminating in a semi-final against Middlesbrough. As it is, he is unemployed, travelling from Nottingham to Northwich for little more than his expenses, just to keep playing.

Steve Walters, 24, is a Dario Gradi graduate, a former England youth international, who was at the FA School at Lillieshall in the same year as Andy Cole. His promising career at Crewe was brought short by a blood disorder. Still a crafty, skilful midfield player, Walters' Vics income now supplements a wage from his regular job stacking shelves at Iceland. He is partnered in midfield by Eddie Bishop, a welder and old-style midfield general, who formerly plied his footballing trade with Chester and Tranmere.

The cup tie was a potential giant-killing which would have been especially welcome against Walsall, whose manager Chris Nicholl formerly played for Witton on his way to more glamorous employment and international status. The last time he set foot on the

Drill Field was 30 years before, when he starred in Witton's 6-1 humiliation of Northwich. This time, after a rousing, committed battle, he was happy to escape with a 2-2 draw. Afterwards, drained fans and glowing players went drinking together in the Vics social club.

It was a reminder of what football has always been, of how and why it grew, until the stockbrokers took it over; a real experience, an emotional, not economic relationship between supporter and player, everybody giving of themselves for the football club. Dave Thomas, working alone in a cramped office in the oldest football ground in the world, is sanguine: 'It's a struggle to survive. We're battling away. But I do think clubs like ours should have a bit of help, to make sure we can keep going into the next century.'

Below the Conference, the stories are harder, the problems deeper. In the last three years the Northern League, the second oldest in the world after the Football League, has lost teams. Southbank went out of existence in 1994. Darlington Cleveland Social packed it in halfway through the 1996-97 season. Ferryhill have struggled for two seasons without a ground.

Graham Craggs is secretary and treasurer of First Division club Billingham Synthonia, two miles away from the depressing ostentation of the Wynyard Estate. The club was formed in 1923, deriving its unique name from synthetic ammonia, one of the early products of ICI, from whose works the players were drawn. He says most clubs are surviving on a shoestring. 'As soon as the Lottery started, our own cash draw went down week by week. In the end we scrapped it. Gates are down – it's very hard to schedule a match to avoid clashing with a TV game. And all the publicity goes to the Premier League. People have never heard of us.'

Craggs has been involved with the club, unpaid, for 13 years, nine in his present role. At the end of a season he has occasionally to dip into his own pockets to pay his players their wages, of £20 and £30: 'I feel a duty to keep the club going, for the love of the game. I wouldn't want to let the players down. It would be wrong and disappointing if we went out of business.'

Craggs, a vessel inspector at the ICI chemical plant, is currently looking at a Lottery bid to turn the ground into a big sports complex, available for community use. 'That's the way forward for football generally,' he says. 'Gone are the days when people would come out of the mines and steelworks and play football. It's more of a family atmosphere, we have a hard core of local supporters. It would work very well as a sports facility with the community.'

The Lottery, though, is a haphazard vehicle of redistribution. In every club, school, local authority in the land, Lottery bids are being developed in a desperate attempt to fill glaring gaps in public provision. For the time and cost of these bids, a fraction of real money will emerge: 'I'm sure if we're successful the other 39 teams in the League will get nothing.'

Introduced ostensibly to fund sports, the arts, charities, the Lottery has in fact sucked money out of all these areas of life, which made money in more immediate ways. Now, innumerable hard-up bodies are spending valuable time on futile applications. In non-league football, every club has been hit, yet it is uncertain who will be compensated, and by how much. Craggs is another, giving his time and money, who looks askance at the fortunes washing through football at its highest level. 'It's a classic case of the rich getting richer and the poor getting poorer. They should feed a percentage of the television money down to the grass-roots. At Middlesbrough, they're supposed to have been paying Ravanelli £42,000 a week. I could make that stretch for five years. It's obscene at the top. It's them and us. And we're the us.'

Nationwide, the story is the same. At a time of football's greatest wealth, clubs are going out of business, quiet, agonising, slow deaths, despite the efforts of a population of volunteers, forsaken by those who could really help. In the ICIS League, secretary Alan Tursey reports the same twin curses: Sky and the Lottery. In the Beazer Homes League, secretary Denis Strudwick has had several clubs fold in recent years. Dartford went in 1995, following an unsuccessful couple of years sharing with Maidstone, the former Football League club, which folded in 1992. Maidstone's ground is now an MFI. Dartford have reformed and joined the Dr Marten's Southern Division. Armitage folded in 1994, Sudbury Town, unable to keep up their ground, were voluntarily relegated in 1996. Leicester United folded after only four games of the 1996–97 season.

'Most clubs are finding it very hard,' says Strudwick. 'The Lottery has hit them all badly, and attendances have been damaged by Sky's blanket coverage. The League's fund-raising generally has been very badly hit.'

A century of history, of football at all levels, labours of love and commitment, testaments to survival, are being laid casually to waste. This coincides with huge wealth at the top, indeed the poverty is accelerated, deepened, by the uncaring attitude of the rich. The Premier League can call the tune, and the tune, from its plcs, is to act only in self-interest. They have finally considered it in their interests to support the Football League, seeing that a few million on youth development might reap dividends for them in future. But there is no will to knit the wider fabric. These are the inevitably unequal extremes of 'market forces'; emerging 'consolidation', the soulless glitz at the top creating a mournful, losing battle below.

'It is the loss of a very important part of British history, of British life,' says Kath Marah, chairman since 1994 of Darwen, the first professional football club in the world. 'Actually,' she smiles, 'it is believed that Turton may have been paying players before we were. But we were the first to get caught doing it.'

Darwen, like Northwich, were a big club in football's early years and founder members of the Football League Second Division. Like Northwich, though, the smallness of the town caught up with it, making it impossible to keep up with the Liverpools, Manchester Citys and Woolwich Arsenals which emerged with their larger catchment areas at the same time. Darwen lasted six years, leaving the League after finishing bottom in 1899. They suffered three 10-0 defeats that season, but went out with pride; in their final game they beat Newton Heath, known now as Manchester United plc.

Kath Marah grew up steeped in football: 'I was born in the town, I have always been involved in football. I love the history of this club; the old newspaper cuttings about the club's matches. I have to be dragged out of the library once I get going in there.'

She loves the story about Darwen's FA Cup third-round tie on 9 January 1932, away at Arsenal, who had long before dropped the Woolwich and become a giant. Darwen had to hold an appeal to raise the train fare to London. The working-class Lancashire men made the most of their one-off opportunity to visit London: the local MP took them round the Houses of Parliament, and they met Gracie Fields. They also lost 1-11. It is still Arsenal's record cup victory. 'Our club didn't care,' Kath Marah laughs. 'They built a new stand with their share of the gate.'

The club, in the ever-longer, corporate shadow of neighbours Blackburn Rovers, whose blue glass is nearly visible from the ground, cannot now afford to pay players at all. It is struggling to maintain its status in the North-West Counties League Division One. Money is tight; in addition to the problems of Lottery and television, Darwen have been unable to find a sponsor in the last four years. Since, in fact, the beginning of the Walker era next door. 'We used to find a local firm prepared to do it before. Now they all want to be associated with Blackburn Rovers, who do plenty of corporate deals. And, let's face it, they get more kudos taking their clients to Ewood Park than sponsoring us, or paying a few hundred pounds for an advertising hoarding.'

Keeping Darwen going is a labour of love. Kath Marah's running of the club, helped by half a dozen volunteers, involves serving in the snack-bar, cleaning out the dressing-room, washing the kit. They struggle to make ground improvements; currently they're short of a few hundred pounds to repair the gents toilets. They suffer badly from vandalism. It would surely be a gesture, from Uncle Jack or someone else, to fix Darwen up with some infrastructure, put something back into the community. It is the smallness of the sums for which the grass-roots struggle which make the fat cats seem so shameless. But Darwen too have to pin their hopes on the answer to everything, the replacement of the spirit of human giving and public provision, the turgid, chancy rigmarole of Lottery application. 'We're perilously close to pub football, but it'll happen over my dead body,' she says.

I asked her why it was important, to maintain the club's existence, to keep fighting the losing battle. 'Why? Because football is very important to a lot of ordinary people, who love the game, who want to play and watch it. We're providing a good standard of football for people to participate in. For every kid that makes it there are 5,000 who don't. And where are they going to play if clubs at our level die?

'And, I tell you what, the best football is played now at the grass-roots. My lads might not have the skill of the professionals, but they play with passion and spirit, they give everything, and that's more than you can say for the professionals now.'

When she gets into her stride, Kath Marah shows contempt for the greed allowed to run rampant in football, maddeningly justified as necessary market forces, a recipe for ruination against which the Victorians guarded from the first day. It is so glaring, and so undeserving, personal fortunes being made at the top while the fabric of football, patched out of love, grows threadbare for the lack of small sums of money. But she believes something deeper and more fundamental is happening: 'The Premier League is run by accountants and City whizz-kids. They're not interested in football. The football is just incidental to them, it's a commodity, a product. They've taken the heart out of it, the lifeblood. Money has taken over from passion and love, which is what kept football going.

'Money is important, you have to get the books to balance. But that's a means to keeping the football club going, not the other way round.

'I'm not saying I want to be like the fat cats, I just want to keep a football club going in this town. That should mean something to the people at the top of the game, with their fortunes in shareholdings, they should want to do it. But they don't. They should be filtering some of the money down, a proportion of the television money. That would keep clubs going, maintain people playing and watching football. They're destroying the grass-roots of the game. The Premier League clubs are just the apex of the pyramid, which has a wonderful history, the result of great games and a hard struggle. History is a part of us, isn't it? It's part of the present. It makes us what we are today. Without football's history, the grass-roots, you wouldn't have a Manchester United. They have to be made to understand that, and to do something about it.'

They should bring the accountants and whizz-kids up here. Perhaps they could bring their chequebooks. Spare a thousand pounds maybe. But football won't even do that unless it is forced to. It has embraced the god 'market forces', that lying phrase, justifying with pseudo-economics the lack of restraint on greed, the delivery of all the riches to the few at the expense of the many. They will laugh, no doubt at a woman in Darwen, working every spare hour, believing the existence of her football club is more important than making money, worth nurturing for its own sake. The army of people, generations, who have worked their souls and bodies to give football life, who created the game and its population of clubs, are dismissed now as sentimentalists.

The Premier League, that arrogant name, must be made to give some of it back; its fortunes are too obscene, seen alongside committed people struggling for pennies to keep the game alive. The Drill Field should be a tourist attraction, a living museum, a place of national celebration, not a ramshackle scrap of property, clinging perilously to its future, at the back end of Kwik Save.

16

WITHER THE GRASS-ROOTS?

Spend too much time with the money men of the Nineties and it is possible to be seduced by their market-driven view of life. Sit in warmed boardrooms, flattered by airless pot plants and gentle watercolours, filter coffee clicked for and brought in on trays by tidy Essex girls, and it is tempting to want to believe that the world is a simple place, human life not varied and complex, but reducible to one principle: the rich should get richer. This was essentially the message promoted for football in February 1997 by Singer & Friedlander, the 94-year-old merchant bank tucked down a side street opposite Liverpool Street Station in the centre of the City. Alan Hansen, being paid £10,000 by the bank as 'specialist adviser', appeared at photo-calls and in adverts inviting football supporters to sink their cash into S & F's 'Football Fund'. Tony Fraher, chief executive of the bank's investment arm, did all the marketing for the fund, which promised a return for investment in 'football related' companies.

Football, Fraher argued persuasively to an impressionable sporting media, was an industry like any other and the pursuit of profit was self-evidently the best way for it to be run. The flotations would force clubs to manage themselves properly. 'The market' would decide whether any restructuring of the game was needed; the top clubs would take what they wanted from football's pyramid and develop it, leaving the rest to their own devices. Fraher even felt qualified to talk about development of young footballers. 'The logic of financial discipline will force clubs to get their finances right, and that will involve establishing youth policies.' Growing your own, in other words, was cheaper than buying from a dealer, and 'the market' would force clubs to act accordingly.

The answer to all this is simple and practical: people should get out more. Those who believe that the whole country and its national game should be decided by the accumulative calculations of boys in the City should leave Liverpool Street Station in the daylight occasionally. They need not go far, only to inner-city West London perhaps where, in the windswept lee of the A40 flyover, they will find seven floors of grey breezeblock which house Paddington Upper School. Odd flat scraps of grass band-aid the building, serving only to highlight the predominance of grey, of concrete, in the cityscape. Outside the entrance to the school is a foundation stone salvaged from a building formerly on the site, bearing an inscription: 'These Alms Houses were built in AD 1714 at the expense of the inhabitants, for the poor of the parish past their labour.'

This, for the past 20 years, has been the place of work of John Morton, president of the English Schools Football Association. At reception, they told me John was 'just sorting out a problem on the seventh floor', and they put me to wait in the head's office. It felt good to be grown up; in the head's office, but only as a visitor, able to look calmly round the room, basking in the freedom from adolescent dread. It was a gloomy room, brown and grey, with a triple lock on the door. On the desk was a pamphlet: *Here Today, Here Tomorrow: Helping Schools to Promote Attendance*. A watercolour of a rural scene decorated a wall, an A-level entry by one of the pupils from 1985, peeling slightly off its backing. Outside in the corridor, the kids shuffled home across the lino to the sound of tannoy announcements: detentions and commendations in equal measure.

'Sorry I'm late,' said John when he arrived, a brisk, cheery man, a chink of humour in his eye, 'I've been troubleshooting all over the place.'

John Morton is a senior teacher, with a pastoral, supervisory role at the school. He teaches some PE as part of his working life, but much of his spare time, always, has been devoted to football. He was a good player in his day, goalkeeper at non-league Dartford, and is an irrepressible enthusiast for passing the game on, for coaching kids and getting them playing, running school teams. Like many who love football, Morton believes its importance extends beyond fun; it is also a training, a precious game to be played and nurtured in the right way, a metaphor for life. He works at the grass-roots of the game and so it is from him that you hear the extent of its decline.

Sport's central place in British school life is unique in Europe. At the turn of last century, before education was free and compulsory, sport, especially football, was offered by British schools as a selling point to attract children. It was promoted in the belief that it was good for physical and moral health, particularly in the crush of inner-city life and the clench of poverty. Since then physical exercise has been an important part of a child's all-round education in Britain, included in the curriculum. On the continent this never happened. The school day finishes earlier than here, and sport is played in clubs afterwards and at the weekends. This is one of the reasons why European football clubs, the likes of Auxerre and Ajax, have developed exemplary youth systems – they are able to spend a great deal of time working on the techniques of their young footballers. Here, schools have traditionally been places of sporting nurture.

The English Schools Football Association was formed in 1904, a national body independent of, but affiliated to, the Football Association. The ESFA developed a membership of most schools in the country, organised competitions between them and established representative sides at district, county and national level. It is the ESFA Under-15s which is known as the England Schoolboy side, playing high profile international matches at Wembley and featuring, over the years, many who have gone on to become professionals – Charlton, Wilkins, Venables – alongside, realistically, many who have not.

Most people in Britain play their first football at school, the few who get picked off by professional clubs, and the 99.98 per cent who never so much as speckle the lens of a scout's spectacles. Many children resent compulsory sport, suffering at the hands of the cold-shower generation of PE teachers, but many love it and have gone on to play all their lives. The Fifties and Sixties were the heyday, when the post-war consensus on how to run a decent society provided, for the age, relatively good facilities. Schools were well-funded and thousands of teachers freely gave their time to run teams out of school hours. Schoolboy internationals drew crowds of 100,000, and the ESFA filled its coffers splendidly from the gates. When professional clubs plucked out the boys they fancied, they would give a donation out of courtesy to ESFA district associations which did not really need the money.

Changes in society, diluting this fanatical interest in football, caused some diminution in the wealth and influence of the ESFA into the Seventies, but school sport remained a thriving, well-funded part of school life until the Eighties. These grass-roots were watered because at national and local government level they were recognised to be important. Funds for pitches, equipment, kit, transport and maintenance were delivered to schools without question. Then 'market forces' arrived in education, the dogma that financial competitiveness would ensure greater 'efficiency' in the allocation of resources. Over the decade of Conservative rule, the budgets given to local councils, which mostly stayed resolutely Labour, were successively cut. In 1985, as the councils sought to make good the shortfalls by raising the rates, the Government introduced ratecapping, which meant that local government could not spend money where it identified local need. At the same time, councils were forced to contract out nearly all their services: educational, transport, street-cleaning, maintenance of parks – the fabric of everyday life, put out to tender. There had, of course, been some waste in many councils, but these policies hacked at the very principle of local government, of collective provision of services to an area.

The financial squeeze on schools inevitably meant that the first budgets to be cut were those for activities outside the curriculum. From the mid-Eighties' all extra-curricular life, the traditional seedbed for much of British sporting and cultural development, has been continually trimmed. When schools and teachers have protested at this growing deprivation, their voices have been drowned in a deluge of dishonest argument. Teachers themselves have been relentlessly criticised. As extra-curricular work, including team sports, has always been unpaid and reliant on teachers' goodwill, the vilification has not been good for games. And particularly powerful, resurrected again by John Major in August 1997 in a row over Labour's plans for the national sporting academy, has been the persistent tabloid myth that somehow 'left-wing' thinking has been opposed to competitive sport.

The reality is that the Conservative Government, led first by

Thatcher and then by Major himself, while espousing the traditional values represented by such things as games in schools, set about agonisingly ruining it. In 1993, the Government further extended education's budgetary squeeze by introducing Local Management of Schools (LMS). Masked by the rhetoric of 'giving schools more autonomy', in fact LMS further eroded the role of local authorities in providing educational services to their communities. Now, 85 per cent of an authority's education budget has to be handed straight through to schools which, many with businessmen on their boards of governors, look in 'the market-place' to do deals for the things they need, to buy paper and books, to find the cheapest meals, cleaning, maintenance, transport.

This dogma, separating 25,000 schools into individual units instead of making the most of pooling resources, cloaked and justified further annual cuts in central government's grant to local government. Most councils, told continually they are 'inefficient', are in fact stripped to the bone, having to raid other budgets just to keep up basic levels of spending on education. The decay in school buildings, the leaking roofs, crumbling walls, outside toilets, use of portakabins, has become a national scandal. In 1996, local authorites calculated that they were short of £3.3bn over five years, needed just to keep buildings in use, to replace temporary accommodation and outside toilets and build halls in primary schools large enough for 30 children to do PE. Of this shortfall, Nick Tricker, a senior builder in the Association of County Councils, estimated at least £255m related to maintaining gyms and school playing-fields.

In 1994, a survey by the Secondary Heads Association (SHA) reported patchy provision even of PE, compulsory under the National Curriculum. Seventy-five per cent of 14–year-olds in state schools were doing less than two hours a week. Average time had dwindled to barely 60 minutes. Seventy per cent of state schools reported a decrease in PE activity at the weekend, citing financial constraints and the lack of available facilities. Teachers' workloads have increased dramatically since the introduction of the National Curriculum, which was said by 78 per cent of schools to have led to a decrease in teacher time being devoted to sport. The constant public criticism of teachers, says the ESFA, has further depleted the stock of teachers willingly giving up their time to sport. Individual teachers, the SHA survey found, were coaching five or six teams. There was, it said, 'an urgent need for more help'.

John Major's Government finally admitted in 1995 that it had overseen a decline in school sport. Without explaining why this had happened, Major proposed to solve the problem with another in his famed line of hollow initiatives, this one ranking in the memory some way below the cones hotline. He arrived at Millwall Football Club in the summer of that year carrying his trademark smile and *Sport: Raising the Game*, a pitifully thin brochure making an impossibly grand claim, a promise to 'put team sport back at the heart of school life'. It was supported by a round of 'initiatives' and 'charter awards', but almost no new money. 'Not every problem requires a financial solution,' Mr Major smiled.

'Sheer hypocrisy,' fumed Graham Lane, chair of the Association of Metropolitan Authorities' education committee. 'John Major's own policies, particularly LMS, are destroying what little sport we have left.'

John Morton, in a hard-up school in a poor borough, can tell you how this has happened at the lino-and-concrete sharp end. To get a game on for his school or the West London District Schools side, he has to make meagre resources stretch, hustle for cheap footballs, kit, look for sponsors, try to persuade the local sportsground not to charge for school matches. Parents need to back him up with lifts and money wherever possible. 'I'm a teacher,' he sighs, 'I should be spending time teaching and coaching, but I have to wheel and deal.' Four years ago his district schools FA nearly folded. 'Only enthusiasm is keeping it going now. But it's hand-to-mouth stuff.'

Morton remembers halcyon days, before dogma, dreamt up in political offices with their own bitter rationale, ate into the solid, accepted necessities of day-to-day life in schools. 'There was that myth,' he says, 'that somehow left-wing councils were against school sport. It was absolute nonsense.' The Inner London Education Authority, slated as one of the loony leftiest, was always absolutely committed to providing a range of sporting opportunity, and fresh air, and green grass, for the children of inner-city London. Through the Fifties and Sixties, ILEA had bought and tended 13 large sports centres in a wide ring around London. The authority devoted a massive budget to sport, for maintaining the fields with crews of groundstaff, providing equipment and a fleet of coaches to ferry schools to and from the grounds. Morton's school used to use Barn Elms, opposite Fulham FC. He'd ring ILEA and they'd send a coach to take the children there.

'These complexes were Meccas for sport,' he remembers. 'ILEA provided the transport and they maintained the places immaculately. To kids from my area, these were precious experiences, and very good for sport itself.'

In 1990, ILEA, politically unacceptable, yet another enemy of the free path of market forces, was completely abolished. From then, inner London had no unified education provider, and the collective provision of sports facilities collapsed. The 13 sports centres were allocated to the boroughs in which they were situated. These councils did not have budgets to run or maintain them, and, in the age of LMS and contracting out, had, far from providing the transport and maintenance, actually to charge schools to use the grounds. The squeeze on education funding meant that schools could no longer afford it. Almost immediately the complexes fell into disuse. One, Priest Hill near Epsom in Surrey, was bought by a private company eyeing the green land for development. It became almost a post-apocalyptic vision of its neat sporting past – the pavilions wrecked and smashed, groundsman's house burnt down, circuses, fairs, even go-karting on the site.

'In some ways,' says John Morton, 'the history of the education policies of the last 20 years can be traced through the decline in schools having anywhere to play sport.'

The children of Paddington Upper School never play football on grass any more. The money is not available to pay for transport to grass pitches or to meet the cost of hiring them. The council has agreed not to charge the district team for playing on the astroturf at the recreation grounds nearby. In Camden, whose council inherited five of the old ILEA sites in North London, there is practically no demand from local schools to use them. Janet Wallis, head of Haverstock School in Camden, says her school's budget is far too pressed to spare money to ferry children out to the playing fields. The school does its best for sport with two gyms, each the size of a single badminton court, and two tarmac hard courts. The football team never plays on grass. Camden council is now considering selling four of the old ILEA sites.

The effect of the squeeze on education and local government has been devastating for many areas of civic life. School football, the game's grass-roots, is only one victim. But alongside the huge wealth pouring into football since 1992, the inequality is stark and shameful. While chairmen of football clubs have talked 'market forces' and begun now to talk about building 'academies', many of Britain's schools struggle desperately for the most basic footballing commodities: kit, balls, nets, transport, a place to play. Hardly a penny has filtered down. The volunteers who nurture childhood talent, keep the game going out of a sense of its value, are fighting sad losing battles for the lack of small change. The Victorian pioneers provided sport to civilise and counter the poverty and inequality caused by untamed market forces. Local authorities gradually adopted this duty themselves, just as they took over the running of schools themselves, libraries, parks and other philanthropic gifts of the time. Now, in the Nineties, committed teachers, after lifetimes of work, have been thrown back a century, keeping sport going only with the strength of their own belief.

In Manchester, the local council used to provide for extra-curricular school activities in the whole city via a small department called the Games Federation. It had begun as a charity in 1890, to pay for inner-city Manchester children to play football and athletics. Recognised to be of benefit, the foundation was taken over by the local council in 1923. They kept it going for 70 years, funding it without a doubt as to its necessity. In 1993, when yet more budgetary cuts came, and LMS, the council was forced to raid further its non-statutory expenditure to devote money to core responsibilities. The Games Federation had a budget of some £24,000 and it lost out in the squeeze. It was abolished. Now, only four years on, given the every-man-for-himself brutality of English life, the Games Federation handbook looks like a museum piece, a relic from a more responsible age. It notes that Manchester City Council was providing the funds and facilities for proud inter-school societies; football, rugby, netball, gymnastics, chess, even a folk dance society.

Retired junior school headmaster Des Murphy, secretary of the Manchester Schools Football Association, says half these associations have folded, deprived of any funding when the council abolished the federation. His association had been able to put some money away over the years since it was formed in 1894. After the funding dried up, Murphy has had to dip into these savings to pay for kit, balls, trophies for competitions and, most expensive of all, transport for the Manchester district teams to get to matches. The savings, £28,000 garnered shilling by shilling for over a century, have dwindled now by £10,000. If it carries on like this, he thinks in three years the Manchester association will go bust.

Murphy sits in his living-room talking mournfully of impending collapse. He works almost full time, completely unpaid, trying to stave it off: 'Sport is a very important part of education. It teaches youngsters how to work together, rely on other people, how to win – how to lose, that's very important. It's about comradeship, being a team. And football's also a great pleasure; you don't have to be the best to enjoy it. But children are being deprived of it, in one of England's great sporting cities, for the lack of a few thousand pounds. It's ludicrous.'

On his sideboard is a picture of the victorious 1989 Manchester district team. On the back row is a thin angular youngster called Ryan Wilson. His surname is now changed to Giggs. Such is the inequality lancing football at present, young Ryan could probably rescue his old association from bankruptcy with a single visit to the cashpoint.

The grass-roots of sport can only be replenished with genuine national will, backed by huge investment, part of rebuilding the general infrastructure of education and social life. But football is itself swollen with astronomical amounts of money at the top, and the lack of distribution of any of this money to its parched grass-roots comes close to obscenity. The ESFA, for offices and staff, a national network of inter-school competition and the running of the England schoolboy teams, subsists annually on £250,000, raised entirely from sponsorship and gate receipts. Malcolm Berry, ESFA chief executive, fights a lonely battle for funds from his office, squashed above two estate agents off the main street in Stafford. He has become an accomplished diplomat, employing a patient determination when negotiating with the self-interest of football and the hypocrisy of Government. Only occasionally, encountering some recent display of indifference, does he allow his fury to show: 'You could call it a national disgrace, couldn't you?' he let himself say once. 'The lack of basic provision in our schools. But there is no publicity for it. The newspapers talk to the wrong people about the grass-roots, people who know absolutely nothing about them. In fact there is a desperate need to rebuild school sport. If just a fraction, a tiny percentage of the television money, were earmarked for schools, then at least they could buy some equipment, some footballs.'

Instead, the new satellite-fuelled millions have been injected into the pockets of Ravanelli, of Sir John and Eric Hall. Gordon Taylor, chief executive of the PFA, who speaks supportively of the ESFA, earns £300,000-a-year, more than the ESFA's entire annual budget. The Premiership talks grandly about 'academies' and youth development, but on the ground it shows little but disdain for the grass-roots. Clubs still give the customary donation to district schools associations when they sign a young player, but the payments have not kept pace with football's inflation. When Manchester United plc, the £460m merchandising and software corporation, signed full-back Philip Neville as a professional footballer in 1994, they wrote a cheque to his old school FA, Bury. Secretary Alan Smith, whose biggest annual fundraiser is a hotpot supper, was pathetically grateful for the money. It was £100. When United signed Nicky Butt, trained and provided with football by Manchester Schools FA, they sent Des Murphy a cheque for £200. 'Typical stories,' sighs Malcolm Berry. 'Clubs pay massive transfer fees and obscene salaries, but schools, who nurture players for years, get next to nothing.'

The logic of 'market forces' football is to find kids as cheaply as possible, then try to turn them into multi-million pound assets. Children are now picked for professional clubs' schools of excellence, training for an hour twice a week, from the age of nine. Every year until age 16, children are rejected and new ones taken on. Voluntary youth teams who, like schools, have provided football for these young players, are commonly given nothing.

Redheugh Boys Club is famous for having given Gazza his footballing education. The club is a charity, 40 years old, providing football as part of its overriding purpose of helping children in inner-city Gateshead. Paul Gascoigne was born in Pitt Street, 50 yards from the club. Treasurer Evan Bryson remembers Paul at eight and nine years old, coming every night to play football at the club, a haven from his poor and chaotic home life. 'We helped to stabilise his life,' says Bryson. 'I believe we did that for Paul, up to the age of 15. Many of Paul's problems since then have come from the professional game, throwing millions at him.'

When he made it, Gascoigne bought Redheugh a minibus, which now bears his name. Bryson defends Gazza, feels for him, believes he has a good heart, that he is a victim of an industry which now knows only greed and selfishness. From most professional clubs, who pick up boys in Redheugh shirts, the club gets not a penny. 'It is the only industry,' says Bryson, 'which expects to get its raw materials for next to nothing.'

Hartlepool is Redheugh's favourite, for having sent £1,000 on the sale of Redheugh old boy Don Hutchison to Liverpool for £175,000 in November 1990. The other clubs, though, have been content to sign kids for free, more than they need, and to throw them back if they do not make the grade. 'It's a callous business,' says Bryson. 'They should be ashamed of themselves. They've floated these clubs on the Stock Market, and they're looking at little lads, thinking how much money they can make out of them.'

The youth clubs, and the schools, say that at this time of Sky plenty, with public provision in such decline, the cash-wallowing Premiership corporations should put something back to the grass-roots. Inevitably, though, their needs come a poor third to the twin footballing imperatives: greed and politics.

The man at the FA with responsibility for youth development, with whom the ESFA had to deal for 15 years, was Charles Hughes. When, in 1986, Hughes allocated £600,000 annually of the precious FA coaching budget to establishing a National School in Lillieshall, Malcolm Berry voiced his steady disapproval. The school was to take 16 boys in each of two years – over half a million pounds on 32 lads. It was a waste, said Berry, who argued that the money could be better spent on regional centres, giving more boys access to quality coaching. The ESFA has always argued that it was a misguided, archaic approach to introduce a boarding-school, taking children away from home at 14, to make them into footballers. They also pointed out that the unpredictability of how 14-year-olds will grow, physically and emotionally, made the selection of 16 boys as future internationals impossible.

The record of the school in its 11 years has supported the ESFA view. The player most fancied in the school's first year, Rod Thomas, was released at the end of 1996–97 by Michael Knighton at Carlisle United. He has since been picked up by Orient. A precociously talented young player, Thomas is thought to have been badly handled, and given too much pressure and fame too young. At Lillieshall they admit the school was inadequate in its early years. 'At the beginning,' says the school's physio Craig Simmons, 'we didn't know what we were doing. Nobody had worked with kids full time.'

Berry accused the FA of treating the youngsters as 'guinea pigs'. The ESFA makes the same cautionary response to the current move by the Premiership plcs to build their own 'academies'. The FA's school is to be abolished in 1998 in favour of the academies, as proposed by Howard Wilkinson. Its record will be judged in future years largely on the numbers of its old boys coming through to the top ranks of the game. Sol Campbell, one of headmaster Tony Pickerin's most fondly remembered ex-pupils, looks like he might become the first regular England international. Other high profile names are Ian Walker, Nick Barmby, Andy Cole, Garry Flitcroft. But many populate the lower divisions and some are out of the game altogether.

Pickerin, a man with extensive experience of teaching in the state sector, was brought in as headmaster in 1990, working hard to make the best of his inheritance. The school has tried to devise a means of judging boys according to potential, to avoid rejecting as too waif-like lads like Steve MacManaman who missed the cut in his time. Philip Neville is one of only three to have been offered a place and refused it.

Berry's arguments made the ESFA an enemy in Charles Hughes just as the grass-roots were beginning to wither. For a decade, Berry fought a long war of attrition, arguing that school sport represents an enviable framework for football, and trying to persuade Hughes to work with them. 'Here it has become accepted to knock teachers, to criticise school sport. Everyone talks about Ajax, and Italy and France, when it comes to youth development. Technically, in terms of believing in and developing a coaching culture, we have a lot to learn from them. But youth coaches from the European countries we play tell us they are jealous of our tradition of school sport. We have a marvellous advantage, having sport embedded in education, so that all children have the opportunity to play in the best possible environment. We should build on it, in partnership with the

265

governing bodies and the professional game, to ensure that the interests of all are properly looked after and sport thrives.'

For many years, Hughes disagreed, and the truth is that there remains antagonism, Lancaster Gate identifying another body as an administrative rival. The ESFA found itself at loggerheads with Hughes throughout the Eighties and into the Nineties, with schools becoming ever more starved of cash. This was a frustrating, desperate time, another insular turf war fought from the Lancaster Gate bunker.

Malcolm Berry pursued his argument that schools provided a ready-made, enviable infrastructure for the coaching of young players, those who might be professionals, and the vast majority who would not, but would retain a love for the game. The ESFA observes that European countries absolutely believe in coaching, improving techniques from an early age, while here there remains a belief in 'just going out there and giving it a hundred per cent'. Keen footballers can have played all their lives in Britain to a reasonably high standard and never have had the benefit of so much as a moment's real coaching. The schools criticise the lack of coaching culture, which extends to professional level. They laugh when they see Terry McDermott made coach at Newcastle, without coaching experience, because Kevin Keegan thought he would perk up the dressing-room, and when Everton try to turn Andy Gray into their manager after five years as a television pundit. The ESFA worries about the quality of coaching delivered to young children at professional clubs' schools of excellence, and is particularly critical of YTS schemes, which they believe have tended, with exceptions, to brutalise players, prepare them for the 'man's game'. The likes of Berry and John Morton hope the example of Arsene Wenger and Roy Hodgson will persuade English football that coaching is a discipline and skill in itself, related only partially to a man's former prowess as a player.

Ultimately, the argument to work with schools began to win Hughes over. There was, given the length of school hours, no alternative anyway. Hughes developed a plan to encourage football in primary schools, which have suffered a decline even worse than secondary schools. But by now English football's politics had become further complicated by the formation of the Premier League, the new, ring-fenced body formed on the We-No-Share-Anymore principle, which now holds football's purse strings. Hughes went garnering contacts in the Premier League, hoping to get money for his scheme from them. I interviewed him in May 1996, when he told me he was expecting to announce a £4m funding package, he hoped from the Premier League, before Euro '96.

It never happened. Five years have rolled on from the first £305m Sky deal, football clubs have floated to make fortunes for their owners, and schoolteachers are grubbing ever more desperately for a few quid for footballs and kit. Hughes was left dangling for a year, finalising a paper on the proposed initiative, when suddenly, after 18 months of publicly looking, in February 1997 the FA announced the appointment of the new FA 'Technical Director', Howard Wilkinson. What happened next was classic Lancaster Gate: mean-spirited, brutal politics. Hughes was on holiday in January, expecting to return and see out another couple of years in the bunker. He was notified by the FA that he would no longer be required. That was it. His staff still thought he was coming back. There was to be no dinner, no dignified farwell. Charlie was out, after 33 years. He was asked to clear his desk for Howard, and to drop off the keys to his FA staff Peugeot. Legend has it he turned up to drop the keys off in a Rolls-Royce. He was the man responsible for the FA backing the Premier League, but it is believed the Premier League would not work with him: 'The Premier League's all about the smile, the PR, the hype of football,' said one insider, 'and whatever Charlie was, he was a PR disaster. The way he went? If you play politics, rather than football, that's what you get in the end.'

The small group looking to appoint a technical director had been Jimmy Armfield, Kelly, Bert Milichip and Rick Parry. Parry's presence is most signficant; the £4m Hughes had hoped for was still being talked about as available for the grass-roots. The Premier League was going to fund the new appointee's proposals, so they were to approve the choice. When Howard Wilkinson was appointed, the newspapers and the professional game were ecstatic. 'Finally our own chairman holds the reins on the development of youth football throughout the country,' said John Barnwell, chief executive of the League Managers Association. 'It is a giant step forward in the recognition by the FA of the professional side of the game.' But the reaction to Wilkinson at the grass-roots was more guarded. Their experience of the Premier League so far has been of shameless money-making, grabbing the best kids without putting a penny back into a system descending into crisis.

Wilkinson came into the job with a brief depressingly similar to Allen Wade's in 1963: to develop a coaching structure and culture in this country. He has said he is committed to the grass-roots, but his emphasis from the beginning has been on the tiny proportion of young footballers who might make it to Premier League status: 'The aim is to work with all the relevant bodies which history has given English football, to ensure that the best young players have access to the best coaching.'

In May 1997, after a hundred days in the job, Wilkinson announced his 'Charter for Quality'. 'The Charter is radical, even revolutionary,' said the FA's publicity. As expected, though, much of it proposes only to deliver the power over youth development to corporations dedicated to profit. Under Wilkinson's charter, if it emerges unscathed through committees and council, the Premier League will run 'academies'. Professional clubs will be allowed to take 40 children per year aged under 9 to under 12, 30 players per year aged under 13 to under 14, 20 players per year aged under 15 to under 16 and 15 players per year under 17 to under 21.

These 'academies' will be allowed to have the children four times a week from the age of 12. Strictly, they will only have access to children who live close to them, but this may still allow clubs to set up boarding-type set-ups of their own. The children will go to local schools, but be taken completely out of any school sport, from the age of 12, other than football for their academy. The Premier League academy teams will play each other to a maximum of 30 games a season. The international schoolboy teams are to be taken away from the ESFA, and schools and junior football are to be 'subject to new quality controls'.

There is no proposal by the FA of money for grass-roots football, although Wilkinson has talked of it, mentioning the ghost of Charlie Hughes' £4m. The ESFA has many concerns about the programme. 'Obviously there are a lot of good things in it,' says John Morton. 'He's talking about new coaching courses, a new coaching culture, and youth development in the professional game to the age of 21. That can only be good to take our technical game up to the standard of other countries.

'But what concerns us is that Howard Wilkinson is not going to be controlling this, the Premier League is. And we are concerned that the academies will in fact amount to a massive trawl of children, at a very young age, to evaluate who might be likely players. There will be 40 in a year. What opportunity will these kids get to play football? And how many rejections is it going to involve? Ultimately there are only 11 players in a first team; if one or two make it out of a year, that's a great result, a big saving to a Premier League club.

'Our concern is that the FA is running scared of the Premier League, and that money is driving it all. Ultimately it has nothing to do with football, it's to do with how much the Sugars and John Halls and other individuals can make out of the game.

'Very few of these clubs have had any commitment to youth; at Newcastle the likes of Lee Clark have been pushed out by all the foreign signings. It is ironic that just after this charter was announced, the top clubs went out on a frenzy of buying foreign players.

'The Premier League clubs are desperately scared of losing their status in future, and this may just be a minor safeguard to them, making sure they don't miss any good kids. There is a danger that these academies will be inadequate – who will they find to staff them who know enough about young people? We are not seeing a commitment to grass-roots football, which will really raise the level of all children's ability.'

Morton's fears are based partly on the traditional underbelly of 'youth development', which has long been a ruthless business. Stories of clubs illegally paying fathers to sign their kids over have whispered through football from the beginning; but now, with the stakes so high, the rumours are louder and the figures enormous. Jim Cassell, former head of youth development at Oldham, now at Manchester City, who won his case against Manchester United over the illegal approach to David Brown, says that payments are rife, but more above board than they used to be. 'The age of the brown envelope is gone. Players are allowed to sign a contract at 17, it's all legal now, although the player is not supposed to be promised money before that. I heard of a player recently, a 15-year-old, promised £175,000 by a club to sign at 17.'

Many people are certain that illegal payments are made, although it is almost impossible to prove because neither the club nor the parent will admit to it. Fathers who sign their boys to schools of excellence are said to be rewarded, some of them, with cars, holidays. Mortgages are quietly paid off. Some argue there is nothing wrong with this: why should a Premier League corporation not pay a parent for a child who might someday make millions for them?

The worry, though, is more about the principle at the centre of it; that the grass-roots of football are becoming merely the raw material of avaricious corporations. The idea that it is good in itself for children to play and enjoy football, which produced the spectacular popularity and widespread love of the game in generations past, is now being disregarded. The worry at the grass-roots is that the Premier League now wants wholly to control youth football, not out of a spirit of giving something back, of encouraging mass participation then providing excellence at the élite end, but to trawl for the best at the age of nine and leave the rest to wither.

'The Premier League thinks that the grass-roots is hunting for star players,' complains Malcolm Berry. 'We say it is hard work, to repair the damage done to the fabric of our game by years of cuts, enabling all children to have the right to play. Our worry is that the academies are there to unearth the one star player, the rest can go to hell.

'The Football Association has a responsibility in this country to look after football at all levels, but at the moment nobody is speaking for the grass-roots.'

John Morton is clear about the answer: 'Fund school sport. Then everybody plays; we can rebuild the grass-roots, and the clubs can have their academies, properly run, or centres of excellence. There has to be some sense of community, of society, of sport for all, not just the few.'

Football's decline at the grass-roots is only a small vein in the general decay of the body of civic life in this country. Health, education, social services, parks, sport, everything is driven by a dogmatic, blatantly incorrect belief that if the rich are freed from all regulation or sense of duty, to get as rich as possible, somehow everybody will benefit. It is the blind simplicity of boys in the City, who need to get out more, see what has happened to the game they played as youngsters, provided plentifully in more communal times. Perhaps they would then not give the same advice to the Premier League, to look at the innocent scurryings of nine-year-old children with an eye only to the share price.

It is seen as somehow idealistic, fantastical, simply to argue that a large proportion of football's great new wealth must find its way into the suffering body of the game, not the pockets of the already very rich. The Premier League faces no real pressure to do so; it spends its time in cushioned offices considering ways to make even more money; about making fans pay per view, about having no more relegation to the Nationwide League, about paying less for players by introducing 'academies' stuffed with 40 nine-year-olds. The greed of the City is driving football now, not tempered by simple common sense, human thought, the benevolence of a more civilised way. John Morton, who runs and coaches teams, and heads the association struggling to keep football available in our crumbling schools, has received not a penny from the Premiership Age. He, a senior teacher, in love with the game and believing in its inherent value, has to spend his time scouring West London, searching for a cheap deal on footballs.

17

DAMN THE GRASS-ROOTS

In 1996 Manchester United plc completed their £18.65m, three-level North Stand, whacking an extra tier on all-cantilevered Old Trafford to embrace 55,000 people into a range of corporate entertainment luxury. Two miles away, along a straight road east, squats Chorlton Park, a windswept, barren scrag end of ground, containing five sets of haggard goalposts. If Old Trafford is the Theatre of Dreams, then Chorlton Park is the Community Hall of Despair. It boasts every conceivable impediment to a decent game of football for the amateur teams who are cursed with it as their home ground. The pitches are small, tight, faintly marked out, lined so closely by trees that the branches overhang and get in the way of throw-ins. Half the trees are horse chestnut, the conkers fall on to the wings, the prickly shells staying for months, decaying in piles. Chorlton Park seems to have no friends, barely a groundsman ever comes to visit. When the leaves fall off the trees, they are left to go brown, fester and rot in the wet Manchester gloom. In the corner of one of the pitches, a tree root, thick and solid, lurks for an unsuspecting knee to crash down on it. Behind the goal of the middle pitch is some burnt-out, graffiti-splashed wreckage, a building formerly known as changing-rooms.

Today, Rusholme Argyle are fighting a tough battle with The Station, in the Manchester Publicity League Division Three. Rusholme, a young, nippy team in Aston Villa colours, are finding it impossible to score against the rugged pub-side defending of much, much older men. Rusholme hit the post, the bar, an old bloke on the line, they skid the ball determinedly through the leaves, they head it, they shoot, they place it, still they can't score. Then a grey-haired bloke in a faded blue shirt, sponsors' lettering peeling off his chest, passes to a bald bloke who runs unstoppably up the field and blasts a stunning winner. Station win, 2-1.

Drama, commitment, squalor. The heart and soul of football. Hundreds of thousands of people, men mostly but a growing number of women, play every weekend on municipal mudbaths like these, purely out of love or habit or because they have grown up with the game. In the last few years, though, each set of playing fields has competed with the other to provide the most degrading conditions. After the game, Rusholme's lads, for the lack of changing-rooms, get changed outside, without a shower, in the biting Chorlton wind, cowering behind the leafless conker trees.

Chris Winne, 31, a postman, has been manager of the team since it started. The lads, when they were 15, used to knock a ball about every Sunday in a school playground in Rusholme, south Manchester. One of them knew Chris and they'd asked him to sort them out into a proper team and be the manager. The first year they'd gone into an Under-18 league and been hammered, '20-odd nil'. 'We did win one, but we finished bottom. Anyway, we wanted to build the team, and we've carried on from there.'

They are close-knit, there are two sets of brothers, John, Des and Pete Liston, Pete and Charlie Alaimo. The lads, who do all kinds of jobs, from waiters to computer programmers, are friends, they stick together, go for a drink afterwards. They have been going six years now, improving considerably. This year they're neat and tidy, a good passing side, top of the third division. It costs, Chris reckons, £700, all in, with kit, nets, balls, referee and league fees to keep a team going. For the privilege of changing out in the open and playing on a shitheap like Chorlton Park, they pay Manchester City Council £200. 'It's very bad really, terrible conditions to play in. Money needs to be spent at this level to provide decent facilities,' says Winne.

The plight of Manchester's parks and playing-fields points up the madness of the funding strait-jacket into which dogma of the Eighties and Nineties forced local government. When councils first protested about cuts and ratecapping, they were told by the Government to make up the shortfall by selling some of their assets. At a time of rising property prices, playing-fields, a feature of British municipal and philanthropic life built up painstakingly over more than a century, became one of the Peters, robbed to pay Paul. Since 1981 an estimated 5,000 playing-fields have been sold nationally, gone forever to housing developers and the inexorable urban colonisation by the supermarket.

'We described it as a crisis in 1989,' says Don Earley, deputy director of the National Playing Fields Association (NPFA), a charity dedicated to protecting Britain's play areas. 'Since then even more land has been taken.'

What is worse than a crisis? A disaster? A catastrophe? A national scandal?

In 1994, after 13 years of unmonitored sales, a national register of playing-fields was produced. It found there were 77,946 pitches in England, almost half, 39,000, for football. London had the worst squeeze on fields: 1,950 people to every pitch, while the East Midlands is best served: 820 people to a pitch. Only half the sites had changing-rooms. In Greater London, 263 sites, 16 per cent, were subject to applications to allow them to be built on. Outside London, 227 sites, 1 per cent, were due to be developed.

Of the fields which remain, the mess of Chorlton Park is not at all exceptional. The SHA survey of schools in 1994 found that 56 per cent of pitches had drainage and maintenance problems. There are no national figures for pitches in the community at large, but amateur footballers have experienced a dismal deterioration of facilities.

'The problem,' says Jean Wenger, NPFA technical director, 'is largely the result of ground maintenance being contracted out by local councils. Previously, local authorities or schools employed groundstaff themselves who would tend the pitches. And they would train the next generation of groundsmen. Now, one team, usually the cheapest bid, gets the contract to do all a council's pitches. They end up racing around in a van, marking out once a month, cutting once a week, doing five sets of pitches in a day. No long-term quality work is being done. A pitch can look green but if the necessary feeding, seeding and maintenance isn't done you get disease. One heavy rain could put some of our pitches out of action. At the moment the state of pitches is a disaster waiting to happen.'

Councils, deprived of day-to-day revenue and the right to

administer it as they see fit, have instead been forced to apply for help via grants and initiatives, from Europe and central government, mostly available for individual projects or grand schemes. Manchester City Council, veteran of two failed Olympic bids, has become adept at making applications for such cash. The city is sprouting new buildings and one-off amenities: the £145m Metrolink urban tram system, £42m for a new concert hall, a £7.5m velodrome, a multi-purpose arena: £70m. Now it is preparing to build the controversial £170m second runway at Manchester Airport and a £100m stadium, with Lottery money, for the 2002 Commonwealth Games. This is a city which can now boast facilities to host a tournament for world-class athletes, yet cannot provide decent pitches and some changing-rooms for its own ratepayers.

The council admits this almost surreal imbalance exists, but protests it is only doing what it can, and succeeding more than most, in impossible circumstances. When councils were first bruised by the 1985 ratecapping policy of the Thatcher Government, Manchester's hard-left council reassessed its policies and priorities. Parks and sporting provision are discretionary, not statutory council responsibilities, and in Manchester they were the first to go. 'Criticise it if you like,' said Graham Stringer, then leader of the council, now Labour MP. 'But we had hard choices to make. Parks had to come behind education and social services.'

There is a gallows humour acceptance about the conditions in which amateur football is played in this country; always a predominantly working-class game, players have never expected too much. There were few changing-rooms at all until councils were shamed into building nasty, concrete, primitive affairs in the Fifties and Sixties, with rudimentary toilet and washing facilities. In many cases these are the ones still in use, or standing vandalised, in the late Nineties. In the age of football's boom, of satellite television, of huge money for foreign stars, this is where the 99.9 per cent of people who play football in England are expected to turn out. They have only ever paid out, never been paid, to play the game. 'We play for the love of it,' says Chris Winne, 'and the desire to win. Just to be involved in football.'

Football always was an amateur game; just about every team, ever, started out as a group of friends or workmates. Only Liverpool FC, 'the Team of Macs', and Chelsea, formed by invitation to fill Stamford Bridge in 1905, were professional from the outset. The Newton Heaths, the St Domingos, they happened to rise up and out of the general mass to become Manchester United and Everton. But they came from this great popular fabric, as football exploded with enthusiasm and passion. It was never a business, never only a business.

Football as a participation sport took off after schools began actively to promote it. Churches, in the era of 'muscular Christianity', formed many teams, alongside the other great stalwart institution of the amateur game: the pub. Local centres of communities, often with a field out the back, pubs were ideal places to base teams. The landlord used to get local kudos and a barful of thirsty men in his pub afterwards.

Sunday football had to be fought for, against the Lord's Day Observance Society, which bitterly opposed games on the Sabbath. But with many men often working all day Saturday, Sunday was the only possible day to play. Bill Quinn, a Londoner, fought a long, lonely battle for acceptance, finally starting the London Sunday Football League in 1932. He became known as 'Mr Sunday Football'. Sunday football was popular in the Fifties and Sixties, but it did not gain FA recognition until the early Seventies. The game, played by a generation of men who had played it as an integral part of their youths, in school and out, was by then astoundingly popular. A million miles, mostly, from any hope of being professionals, these were people playing the national, people's game for the love and because it was part of their culture.

The wonderfully named Ron Halfacre, 68, finished playing the game in 1954, and founded the London Sportsman's Senior Sunday League. 'I had had a lot of enjoyment from a game I loved,' he says, 'and I wanted to put something back.' Forty-three years on, he is still the league's secretary. He remembers the rudimentary improvements done to London's most notoriously barren set of pitches, Wormwood Scrubs: 'When we used to play on there at first, the only water for washing was from some horse troughs. In winter they were solid ice. The so-called dressing-rooms were ammunition sheds from World War One. People can't believe we played on there, but we did.'

In the mid-Sixties, Mr Halfacre took the chairperson of the London City Council round to show the spartan conditions of the capital's sportsgrounds. She was shocked, and new dressing-rooms were built then. They have never been replaced. Municipal leaders, and football's adminstrators, have since lost the capacity to be shocked by squalor, and the last Government had no sense of shame. All over the country, amateur football is played in the same depressing circumstances, primitive facilities which, far from having been modernised, have actually declined. Of the half of Britain's stock of pitches which have changing-rooms, many are without showers, lights, toilets.

'Part of the problem,' according to Nick Reeves, head of policy at the Institute of Leisure Amenities Management, 'is that nobody has ever undertaken a proper audit of pitches, what the demand is, whether they are in the right places. We all know parks where the goalposts have simply been thrown up, but the pitches are unused. What we need is an overview, a concentration of facilities, perhaps fewer pitches in certain areas but of much better quality.'

The match in a mudbath, without a shower, provides tales of endurance which give post-match pub conversations their camaraderie, but in fact it is no laughing matter. In European countries it has been seen as important to fund public sports facilities. Trips to Germany, France, Spain, Holland, reveal municipal stadia, for use by all the community, which put the declining wreckage of Britain to shame. Here, sports facilities have become just one part of the general deterioration in communal, civic life caused by a destructive war waged by central government against councils who had had the audacity to be run by Labour majorities.

Despite the increasing squalor of conditions, many councils have felt constrained to put up the price of renting a pitch. A pitch, used four or five times a week at most, can never make the council a profit, but it can earn some useful revenue. In 1996–97, estimates from the Chartered Institute of Public Finance and Accounts are that £10m was earned nationally from charges for outdoor sports facilities. Not much, but money that local councils cannot afford to turn down.

In the period when Football is Coming Home, Wearing a Replica Shirt, Drinking a Bottle of Becks and Singing a Silly Song, when football is everywhere and every man-jack claims to have it in his blood, you would assume that the amateur game would be thriving. In fact it is declining. Uncared for, left to rot, increasingly Third World in the places on which it is played, the game is being quietly abandoned. Nearly all the local leagues in English cities are reporting falling membership. The Liverpool and District Sunday League has lost just over half its teams in recent years. Secretary Glyn Jones says that the problem is mainly cost. The council has put its fees up, and in a city of high unemployment, teams are struggling to afford to play. 'The poor quality of the facilities is a factor as well,' he says. 'Particularly changing facilities, it's driving players away.'

The London Sunday Football League, one of the greatest ever amateur leagues, folded in 1985, merging with the Combined South-East League, which itself folded in 1988. 'We were losing teams left right and centre,' recalls Fred Harris, formerly secretary of the league. 'People think football is booming, but it's dwindling at the grass-roots. It's making itself too expensive.' In London the cost of pitches has gone up drastically in recent years, reaching as much as £60 a game in some boroughs. 'The ordinary guy who wants a game of football is struggling now,' says Harris. 'People can't afford it and the facilities are awful. And you see all this money in football at the top, none of it is coming down to the grass-roots. Even 1 per cent of the money from Sky TV, 1 per cent, would make such a difference to the grass-roots.'

Ron Halfacre says that undoubtedly cost is the main factor: 'You've got boys leaving school with no job to go to, they can't afford to play any more. Then they get a job and it's stacking shelves in the supermarket, the cost is still too high. It's a very great shame. Leagues are dying fast.'

Mike Appleby, membership secretary of the FA, confirms that there has been a decline in adult amateur football in recent years. The FA has for the last two years been promoting women's football, and a few hundred teams have now sprung up. Youth football is on the increase, believed to be partly because it is now being seen as a potential career for their sons by thousands of soon-to-be-disappointed fathers. There is a great tail-off at 16. Appleby is not sure of the figures, but he thinks probably several thousand teams, out of a high of 43,000 nationwide, have folded in recent years. One of the many genuine football lovers who do good, unglamorous work at the FA, both centrally and at county level, trying to promote grass-roots football, Appleby is another who believes football's inequality to be a matter for shame.

'It would be nice to see the Premier League share the wealth lower down. We make them fully aware that they'd be well received if they're seen to chip in to the grass-roots. We've said they can donate money on their cheques, we'll administer it, have photo-calls to show it being handed over. I don't understand why they don't. Imagine if local playing-fields were given superb new shower blocks, bearing a plaque, "Donated by Arsenal", or whatever, the clubs would get so much good will. People wouldn't see them so much as greedy corporations. But once they go public, these clubs lose control, they can't do anything which means less money for shareholders.

'My worry is that one day television is going to drop football like a stone in a pond, once it has had what it wants from it. And what will we have to show from this time of unprecedented wealth? Nothing at the grass-roots, just more deteriorating public facilities.'

Fred Harris, who has played and organised football all his life, watches the decline of the amateur game with dismay: 'If the Premier League wasn't making all that money you wouldn't feel so let down. There's a lot of money in football, but it doesn't come down far enough. If you don't have grass-roots where do you get your players from? It's only one in a thousand that makes it as a pro. The rest just want somewhere decent to play, and to enjoy it.'

You would think that Manchester United would want to renovate the changing-rooms in Salford, or Stretford, or Manchester, for a few thousand pounds. Or back a splendid new municipal facility, as a gesture, for a drop in the ocean of their unimaginable revenue, as thanks to the city which has made the Edwards family its unimaginable wealth. But, dreaming of superleagues and how to make the populations pay to watch football on television, they probably never think about the squalor in their own neighbourhoods. That is the way, the wilful obliviousness, of Britain in the Nineties. And the football business, belatedly, has become one of its greediest new industries. Somehow, of all the obscenities, of great wealth going into individual pockets from the people's game, this is the greatest injustice of all. The fact that two miles away from the self-styled Theatre of Dreams, which used to be home to a football club, grown men playing the game for love have to pay to change outside in the rain after a match on a compost heap.

'It's a joke,' says Rusholme Argyle player Steve Liston, cowering behind a conker tree on the Community Hall of Despair. 'It's an absolute disgrace.'

18

THE COCK-UP THEORY

For some time, thinking about the way football had become a commodity to make a few people rich, I nursed a feeling that it could not really be true, that it could not have so blithely handed itself to a 20-club élite to run the game purely for the profits of their shareholders. I looked carefully at the politics of how the Premier League had been formed and at the people involved, and managed to construct an alternative view. I began to imagine that perhaps the FA recognised all the problems in its game, the inequalities, and in fact far from having abdicated responsibility for them, it was engaged in a patient, long-term plan to benefit the game as a whole. Many who know Graham Kelly say he is wrongly maligned as the product of a charisma bypass, negotiating Lancaster Gates's committees but providing the game itself with no leadership. They say he's all right when you get to know him, that he loves football, that he has a dry sense of humour.

Looking objectively at his career, I constructed a view of him as a shrewd, strategic thinker, working from a deep understanding to bring about eventual change. This interpretation goes as follows: Kelly worked at the Football League's Lytham St Annes bed and breakfast accommodation for 20 years, rising to be League secretary. He had therefore incomparable knowledge of the politics of the Football League, knew them to be unworkable; the big clubs always at loggerheads with the small, fighting for more money, threatening throughout the Eighties to break away. In 1988 Ted Croker retired and Kelly became chief executive of the FA. The following year was Hillsborough. Kelly was at the semi-final that day, it was to him that Chief Superintendent Duckenfield lied about the exit gate having been forced by Liverpool fans. Liverpool supporters say Kelly was sympathetic to them there, at least at first.

The Government had made its call for unity after that but, so my interpretation goes, Kelly knew from experience that unity was impossible within the Football League. His backing of the Premier League was a risky gamble, but necessary – initial bloodletting to break the stagnation of the professional game. The FA would become rightfully the dominant administrative body, although for a time the big clubs would dominate. Gradually, though, Kelly would work to bring football together. His appointment of Howard Wilkinson had built another bridge between the FA and the professional game, and eventually it would all be unified, out of disharmony, under the auspices of the Football Association, his historic employer, which gave the great game to the world. Then the game could be run in the interests of all, not only the rich, who would be required to filter money down. It had to be this way, surely, or at least along these lines.

Kelly kindly agreed to see me at Lancaster Gate, through the reception with its silver, pewter and cut-glass ceremonials and picture of the Queen. The bookshelves in his office proudly hold a full collection of Charles Hughes' books – bought at a discount, one hopes – two books about Blackpool FC, whom Kelly supports, and a copy of Greville Janner's *The Complete Speechmaker*. Photographs of Bobby Robson's 1986 England World Cup team smile from the walls, together with Graham standing in a team photo of his own, looking, from his tracksuit, as if he is the sub. A replica of the World Cup sits on a table, and a single international cap. His office irresistibly evokes the bedroom of an unhappy schoolboy, bored with homework, who would much prefer to be outside playing football. Some kit – tracksuit top, socks – is strewn all over the floor.

I put to Kelly my questions about how much was accident, cock-up, his coming over to the FA after 20 years at the League and immediately challenging his old employer with the rich man's breakaway, and how much was shrewd planning. Kelly wastes no time in completely destroying the idea that there was the remotest hint of shrewdness, in blowing my optimistic interpretation out of the water.

No, he says, he took the job at the FA in 1988 simply because he was offered it: 'It was a career move at the time, a change of job.' They hadn't, at the FA, thought of backing a Premier League at all, he said, until David Dein and Noel White came visiting in 1990, following their breakaway dinner with Greg Dyke. Kelly and Charles Hughes had already started working on the *Blueprint*, following the League's publication of *One Game One Team One Voice*.

Was it Hillsborough, I asked, which prompted the *Blueprint*, the major rethink for the future of football? 'Hillsborough had a major effect. But it wasn't the catalyst or the prompt for the *Blueprint*.' Erm . . . 'The Football League were wanting to play a bigger role in the overall administration of the game. They wanted equal shares at the FA and we couldn't countenance that. David Dein and Noel White approached us about breaking away from the Football League and it coincided with what we were doing.'

So you were, after all, just trying to smash the Football League? There was no higher purpose than that? 'Er . . . I wouldn't put it as bluntly as that. We wanted to work closely with the top clubs, for our clubs to be successful – and to resolve some of the issues which were around at the time.'

Expanding, he says the FA Council contains 93 members, from the County FAs and representatives of other areas of football. The Football League, in *One Game One Team One Voice*, was proposing a joint board to run football, five people from each organisation, plus the chief executives. The FA council saw that as their own extermination: 'It was the old cliché; turkeys don't vote for Christmas. The FA Council said at that time: we don't interfere with the way the Football League runs its business, why should they want to share power in this way?'

It seems unthinkable that the man with the top job in football really backed a rich man's breakaway, before a massive TV deal, allowing the clubs to keep all the money, actually to avoid a constructive suggestion for unity. Why, I asked, couldn't the FA have regarded *One Game One Team One Voice* as a starting point, for discussion, negotiated on it, argued the Football League down, say to seven from the FA, three from the Football League, or whatever, as the first step towards unity?

' . . . (pause) . . . I don't think it was very realistically argued.'

But, I said, what happened was that instead of working towards a more unified approach to football, you've actually created another body, the Premier League, with yet another separate set of interests.

'Erm . . .' he said, 'created a more . . . erm . . . yeh, I suppose you're right. I can see that . . . but we've also created a more . . . erm . . . streamlined approach between the FA and the Premier League. No, I can see the point you're making . . . there's another hat in the ring, as it were . . .'

And what is the relationship between the FA and the Premier League?

'Erm . . . fairly good . . .'

No, I didn't mean that, I mean in terms of what you get from them. You run their disciplinary and refereeing systems, what do they give you?

'We work with them on many things. On the appointment of Howard Wilkinson, on the National Academy, hopefully on the World Cup bid.'

But you never asked them to share any of their money with the rest of football?

'I don't think there was any intention to take a proportion of their revenue.'

But what about the wealth gap? Between the Premier League and the rest of football?

'It depends where you're looking. Obviously for some clubs, like Brighton and Exeter, Darlington, it's a struggle to survive. But you have to look at the running of those individual clubs. They haven't necessarily been disadvantaged by the Premier League. They may just have got themselves into debt. That's not the result of the Premier League not sharing its television money. And the Nationwide League is now getting its own money from Sky. But if you look at the grass-roots generally the game is very buoyant.'

But that isn't true, I say. Schools and the amateur game are struggling for money in an age when football's incredibly well off.

'. . . Well, erm . . . I don't think it should be true. I'm not quite sure where the need is.'

It was extraordinary.

Well, I said, you've got schools which would bite your hand off for a free football or a bit of kit, their playing fields might have been sold off, schools aren't exactly over-resourced these days. And yet the 20 Premier League clubs have made a billion pounds in the last five years. That's pretty stark inequality.

'... Erm ... yeh, erm ... maybe we will attack some of that money and get it down to the very grass-roots ... You're saying there is still a need ... it's something we'd need to look at, we'd need to address ...'

What I don't understand, I say to Kelly, in the very top job in the governing body of the billion pound, most fantastically popular, game of English football, is why the Premier League was allowed to break away from having to contribute at least some of its money to the smaller Football League clubs, that you freed them from that responsibility, yet you did not tie them in to any kind of payment whatsoever to the FA, even though they bear your name, they've moved in next door, you do all the donkey work for them ...

'Erm... it was never envisaged that the price of their freedom would be a levy ...'

But, although obviously many good things have happened since the dark days of Hillsborough, and the game's better off since then, there's such massive inequality. I would have thought the FA's role would be to get hold of some of this money that is sloshing around and make sure it is spread.

'... Well ... maybe that's a new role for the FA, to do more redistribution of income ...'

It was scary. It was like he had never thought about it before, what the FA's job is. He just likes football, apparently he has a good sense of humour once you get to know him, and he is obviously good with committees. What do you think, I asked him, about single individuals making £100m from floating their football clubs on the Stock Market?

He gave a sort of snorting, silent chuckle: '...Well ... I won't say as Alan Shearer said when modelling the new England strip: "That's life" ... [*chuckles again*]. But that is the market economy, isn't it, it's the free market ...'

Yes, I said, but all markets, even in this country, have regulators. Even the privatised industries have regulators. Oftel, Ofgas, Ofwat. All those. And their jobs are to make sure that prices stay affordable, that excessive profits aren't made and that money is ploughed back in investment. And that seems to be precisely what has happened in football: increased prices and excess profits, not enough investment in the long term. And in this industry, you, the FA, the governing body, are the regulator.

'. . . Aah . . .' he said. He looked wounded, tired, upset. As if he is always being asked difficult questions when he just loves the game. 'No, I don't think, being honest, it was on the agenda at the time . . . I can see what you're saying. But it wasn't on the agenda at the time.'

He hoped, he said, seeing me out, that I would not be too cruel to him in my book.

It was much more depressing than I expected, even after seeing his performances on television, the top man in English football inviting Peter Osgood, or Johnny Giles, at the draw for the FA Cup, to 'push the button please'. He seemed not to have given much thought before to the FA's role as governing body. It seemed as the worst interpretation suggested, all about protecting the position of the FA as a body, nothing really to do with football. Just preserving the institution as it has always been. Schools and amateurs are forever banging on the FA's door, pleading for some money, the ESFA had fought a war of attrition with Charles Hughes for a decade, yet Graham Kelly said he knew little about their needs, he said the grass-roots were 'buoyant'. There had not, he made it emphatically clear, been any long-term vision behind the backing of the Premier League.

He had never thought of asking the Premier League to contribute to football's well-being. The smart Eighties men, coming down to have 'a quiet word' with the FA after dinner with Dyke in 1990, must have smiled all the way to the Stock Market. All this at the governing body of the game, with genuinely the most distinguished history.

It was the FA's responsibility to safeguard football, to insist that the new television money and Government money be spent wisely, to rebuild the whole of English football after its disgrace and disaster. So that it was spent on the long-term fabric of the game, that the most was made of the opportunity, and the best was done in memory of the dead. To ensure that prices were kept affordable to the ordinary football lover. That the historic, incomparable love of the English for the game of football which they gave to the world, was nurtured, treasured, not exploited, stretched, tested, weakened, cheapened.

But the FA has not done that, and there has been no long-term plan. The FA did not want to share with the Football League. And . . . that was it. Like many governing bodies in an age of triumphant 'market forces', it has lost sight of its role, come to believe it is there to help the rich get richer. Not to preserve the integrity of its game in the face of its various challenges. There are 93 people on the council and 130 staff, many of them football-loving people who do a good, unsung job. But English football, under them, has become a free-market business, without a regulator.

19

TO THE MILLENNIUM

If nothing changes, the future of English football is entirely predictable. And it is infinitely less interesting than its past. Some people seem to find it fascinating, the 'issues facing football', which are entirely based on making money for the top clubs: whether and when pay-per-view television will come in, whether and when there will be a European Super League. But the truth is that the future is certain. The future of football will follow the course of every 'industry' which has been subjected to the divisive acid of 'market forces', guided by no more human force. The result is 'consolidation'.

Every decision will be made solely on the basis of whether it will make more money for the already rich. Pay per view will make more money for the already rich, and so it will certainly be introduced. It will force loyal supporters to pay to watch their teams on television match by match. Nobody will ask the spectators if they want this, because they are almost certain to say they want at least some live league football on ITV or BBC, where it used to be, because it can be watched free by a mass audience. For that, they will even be prepared to put up with Jim Rosenthal. Instead of consultation and in the absence of regulation, the clubs will introduce pay per view against the supporters' will, and price it at the absolute maximum that the fans will bear.

A European Super League will come in at some stage. This will not be because any supporter wants it; indeed the majority are probably against it, preferring the parochial rivalries built up over a century, with European competition a knock-out treat. The super league will come in because the television revenues to the clubs from such a competition will be Europe-wide, not restricted to the 'domestic market'. In other words, it will make very much more money for the few clubs which go into it and as individuals and plcs they will be unable to turn the money down. The rich clubs will get richer.

Football will continue to present itself as 'entertainment' and to take for granted its loyal adherents, treating them as a 'captive market'. Increasing numbers of people, imbibing their football via Sky and its attendant gloss, will not support a club for the traditional reasons of family or where they live, and therefore stick with it, 'in the blood', all their lives. Instead, like any entertainment, they will consume the product of highest quality. The same teams will constantly be on television, aggressively marketing themselves, through merchandise and publications, as the 'brand' of preference to all 'customers', wherever they live.

If nothing changes, therefore, three or four or five football companies will dominate English football. They will enjoy full stadia which will be choice tickets for corporate entertainment, and legions of the excluded will pay to view. At present, the most likely companies to dominate the 'industry' in this way are Manchester United, Newcastle United, Arsenal and Liverpool. They will make a very great deal of money. Barely any of this money will go anywhere except to the players bidding up increasingly obscene wages, and to the owners and directors themselves.

All other professional clubs will jostle into destinies of relative inferiority. The effects will not be seen for some time, and the boom will no doubt continue in the short term, fuelled by hype. Some clubs will shortly float on the froth of the City's superficial interest in the game, and make big money in capital gains for their current owners. More in doubt is the quality of what they are handing over. After a time, the inferiority of the rest of football to the handful of big clubs will begin to matter. If a European Super League is formed with room for only three or four English clubs, all the rest will then be by definition second rate, as the Nationwide League has been since the formation of the Premier League. A new generation of football consumers will not see the deeper point in supporting a team which has no hope at all of ever winning a trophy, let alone being the best.

As the years pass, football will test the loyalty of the 'new' fans, on whom it will dawn that their clubs keep not winning anything. The new supporters may well change clubs to support whoever is the current champion, or get bored with the game altogether and find a more gratifying entertainment.

No governing body will impose any more substantial sense of direction and there will be no regulation. Prices, to get into matches and to watch telly, will continue to rise to 'what the market will bear', driving out some lifelong fans who have, however deep their attachments to these avaricious plcs, a limit to their funds. Football companies may even encourage this in the boom because the poorer fans will be replaced by those who can easily afford the higher prices.

The lower-division clubs will require exceptional leadership and strong strategies if they are to survive and their only chance is to embed themselves in their communities. Without an overall framework to encourage this, and without distribution of any of the wealth at the top, survival will be difficult. Over the years, some of these clubs are likely to go part time, or go bust. The lower strata of the game will be maintained only as far as the Premier League companies see it as in their interests to do so, to have suppliers of talent. Feeder clubs may turn out to be a chosen route – consolidation by acquisition.

The non-league 'pyramid' will see many clubs and possibly whole leagues fold under intolerable pressure and the drift of support away from the grass-roots towards television consumption of the top clubs. These agonising deaths, local tragedies, the despair of local committed people, will be noted hardly at all in the City. If the City flickers, it will be to note the beginning of consolidation, the efficient working of 'market forces'.

School and youth football might receive a little money from the top clubs, enough for them to keep going to provide very young footballers to be trawled by the Premier League clubs. These clubs will have 'academies', of variable quality, which will have enormous failure rates, paving the pathway to a professional contract for the few with the broken dreams of the many, at young ages. These academies will, however, not stop the top clubs continuing to sign foreign players.

The amateur teams will not matter, as they do not matter now. By the time a player hits his teens, he is a reject anyway, sentenced to a life on the quagmires, changing in the rain. There is little currently in prospect which suggests there will be any improvement in the degrading conditions in which amateur football has to be played.

Football will gradually become much less a participation sport, much more a form of mere television entertainment. The Football Association will continue to see its role as helping the rich to get richer. At the top, football will create more multi-millionaire shareholders, directors, players and agents. A generation of couch potatoes will be their gift to the country, people paying to watch a handful of teams on telly in their own homes. Fewer and fewer people will experience the joy of playing the game, according to their preferred or natural level.

This may seem a profoundly depressing prospect to many, but many others will see it as the desirable future, the one to which they are currently working. Mostly the rich will want it this way. It is what boys in the City, who know only money, the current breed of short-term bottom-line merchants, call 'consolidation'. It is the only language they understand, and they will continue to be listened to because they offer money to people who seem never to be able to have too much of it.

The future of football is therefore much like that of every other industry governed solely by the free market, lacking the redistributive hand of regulation. Like the retail food industry, which now, across the country, has four superstores where everybody does their shopping, from which the poor and the carless are generally excluded. The banks; once there was one in every town, now there are four major ones with some minor players. Cinemas – a few multiplexes. Clothes – a handful of chain stores.

This is the inevitable, provable, logical consequence of allowing anything to be run solely according to who can make the most money out of it. The Football Association knew that in 1863. But years of dogma have made them forget what it was once widely known, that there is more to life than money. In football there used to be custodianship, passing the beautiful game on to the next generation, but now it appears not to believe anything is more important than money. Football has lost its confidence, its heart, and, despite the current boom, the atmosphere of the game, the participation, will dwindle. It will make a few people very rich, and lose its soul.

But it is not too late for the obvious alternatives to be imposed on unwilling entrepreneurs. The Labour Party came to Government with a Charter for Football. In it, it said that it did not believe that football has moved in the right direction, specifically citing escalating ticket prices, restrictive TV coverage and the precarious position of lower division clubs. 'Labour,' it says, 'rejects an excessive reliance on market forces.' It promised a task force to look into football and legislation to put right its injustices.

As soon as Labour came to Government, it appointed Tony Banks as Minister for Sport. The instructions from Prime Minister Blair to a man who never dreamt he would have any ministerial responsibility were 'to shake things up a bit'. He certainly did that. Banks appeared not to have read his party's own charter, to have no idea there was any serious job to be done. Known as a wisecracker and campaigner on single issues such as animal rights, Banks spent his first weeks trumpeting his credentials as man of the people, which he thought he was expressing by shouting about his support of Chelsea Village plc, which has recently put prices up to £50. After some off-the-wall outbursts, Banks then mercifully stayed out of the limelight, but he returned in late July with a bombshell. First, he had read the charter. He had realised that Labour was supposed to be forming a task force. Second, he was appointing as its head a former Tory minister in the Thatcher and Major administrations, who had played a significant role in driving the free market to be the defining force of all British life: David Mellor. Incredibly, Tony Banks seemed to believe this was a popular choice, because so many people telephone Mellor's phone-in programme on Radio 5.

So the man who has refused to allow politics to be discussed on that programme, who was a rising figure in right-wing politics before his downfall, who has a string of corporate directorships to his name, is now to head the force looking at the effect of excessive market forces in football. The terms of the task force are narrow, although it is to look at the effect of flotation on football clubs, at ticket prices and at racism. But The Football Association, which, for better or worse, is the governing body, was barely consulted. The Premier League is to be represented, in the formidable form of Professor Sir Roland Smith, chairman of Manchester United plc.

One of Banks' justifications for appointing Mellor was that Mellor has experience across the relevant areas. 'We needed someone who would not be afraid to confront authority and yet retain an awareness of what it is politically possible for the Government to do.' This is a fantastic statement. In Britain the Government can do anything it likes. David Mellor knows this as well as anyone. The Government can privatise publicly owned utilities, it can impose a poll tax, it can close all the coal mines down. Yet here the Labour Government, finally with an opportunity to put right some of the inequalities in football, needs the advice of a former Conservative minister as to what it is 'politically possible' to do. It seems prudent not to expect very much from the Mellor-led task force.

The task force idea was a promising one, although the scale of the greed which has overtaken football suggests a more robust procedure, such as a public inquiry, with the right to call witnesses and hear their evidence on oath, might have been necessary. The time is long overdue and the opportunity perfect for 'the fullest reassessment of policy for the game', called for by Lord Justice Taylor. The inquiry could have taken place in his memory, and begun with his own recommendations, as to price, as to caring for the grass-roots supporter, as to removing from directors the opportunity for 'wheeling and dealing', which they chose to ignore, using his report instead as a commercial opportunity for themselves. The Premier League, and the FA, want Government help and money to support the World Cup bid, as well as Lottery cash. They have said so themselves and they are always looking for it. This gives the Government an even stronger hand to legislate for football.

It is not my place to present a set of proposals for necessary reform. That should be done by democratic process, and at least in the task force room has been made for supporters organisations who will make suggestions in the interests of those who are being alienated. I make only suggestions about some aspects which must be considered. It is not too difficult; football is not a complicated business, it is a game, not a 'product'. It should be watched and played by as many people as possible. It does not have to be run in the interests of the few, it can be organised as people want and believe it should be.

Professional clubs need to make money; they always have had to, but they should have to work carefully, hard and fairly for it. Not to turn up for their television money every few years, whack their prices up, then pour all the money out into personal pockets. Surely this orgy of personal moneymaking has to stop. Under David Mellor it is impossible to imagine a tough approach being taken against this, and already the issue of flotations is being couched almost in academic terms. But the Labour Government does not like companies which make excessive profits out of their monopoly positions. It has already proved that it is politically possible to impose a windfall tax on companies which do so. All the dire pre-election warnings of legal actions if the Government dared to impose a one-off tax on the privatised utilities came to nothing. The Government can do anything and it duly imposed the tax, with massive public support. A confident sports minister would be looking closely at football's excessive profits and its lamentable record of investment, and looking carefully at the possiblity of a windfall tax.

This could be done by slicing the Premier League's television income, the £670m over four years due to be troughed by only 20 football companies. A large proportion of this money could be spent on repairing the wider fabric of football, perhaps of sport at large, on building decent, proud local sports centres for communities which have seen facilities crumble over the last two decades. As the Premier League companies have not seen fit to share any of the combined turnover of £1 billion in their first five years, the Government might decide that 70 per cent would be an appropriate figure for taxing the next one. This would still leave £200m for the 20 Premiership clubs over four years, which seems quite enough to be going on with. The rest, £470m, could replenish the grass-roots.

The Government could also have a look at a windfall tax on the club-companies themselves. Alternatively, it could look at a windfall tax on the excessive capital gains of the owners themselves. A wealth tax. If this could be done, 70 per cent might not be thought enough. John Hall's company, for instance, has made a capital gain of around £100m in five years out of the ownership of Newcastle United. If the tax were only 70 per cent, the Hall family would still have made £30m from five years involvement in the club. Some people might regard this, still, as an excessive return from the Toon Army, from the people's game.

But reform must go further than ensuring that the phenomenal money at the top of football is distributed for the health of the wider game. The ownership of football clubs must itself be looked at. There was never any intention when the clubs were formed that they be speculative ventures, making money for their owners. They were clubs, formed to play football, and that is still how most supporters regard them. Even the new owners profess to believe that their clubs 'belong to the fans'. Some way must be found to force clubs, all of them, including the plcs, to widen ownership and to introduce real democracy, with clout, into their running.

At present this is happening in a tiny minority of clubs: Northampton Town and Bournemouth, small clubs, saved from going out of existence by supporters' trusts. Football supporters must take some responsibility on themselves, not hail every swooping millionaire as their messiah. Supporting can become a more active part of life than passive consumption. Barcelona, the biggest club in the world, is run like this, by membership. It means that the clubs are not 'investment vehicles', opportunities to fleece their public to make money for the owners, but football clubs, dedicated to being good at football and serving their communities well.

Much of this is accepted absolutely in Europe. In Italy, the owners of clubs have never been permitted to take money out of them. Yet this is shortly to change, because the likes of Silvio Berlusconi have seen the money to be made from flotation, as in the Premier League. We go to Europe to learn about coaching, how to play and pass on the game. They come here to learn about realising their assets. It is currently our example to the world.

In June, two Norwegian businessmen bought Wimbledon Football Club, a former Southern League club, from Sam Hammam for £30m. They came to England because the rules of the Norwegian FA forbid the commercial takeover of clubs. In Holland, many sports clubs are run by major corporations, but without the accent on profits, and they plan for the long term. Almost all football federations redistribute television money throughout their pyramids, and build substantial coaching infrastructures. They have concentrated on developing systems for running a sport. We have fractured our system, because we forgot, at the crucial time, that it is a sport at all. And that there is more to life than making money.

Football must remember what it is for; it must have a soul, a sense of itself. The Football Association as presently constituted has proved itself to be manifestly not up to the task of defining football's purpose and governing or regulating the game to that end. Reform of the game's administration is vital. It requires unity, a single governing body, to run the whole of football for the common good. This would seem most obviously to require a mix of trained, tough people, with a management board of only 10 or 12, directing the lovely, replenished pyramid of a healthy game. This requirement has not changed, only become more urgent, since it was rejected by the FA in 1990.

Unity would extend to the professional leagues. They can call the First Division the Premier League if it satisfies their ego, if 'First Division' does not flatter enough. But there surely is no justification for the continued separateness of the Premier League from the body of football, taking the money and draining it out. The Premier League must return to the body of the game, perhaps as the apex of a trimmed and restructured pyramid, pruned carefully and mercifully for its own overall health. 'Market forces' has no idea how to do this except by putting cherished institutions completely out of business, and glorying in doing so. Any restructuring according to long-term modern needs requires careful planning, with respect for all levels of the game, and for the people giving their time out of love.

A strong governing body would also be a regulator. Its role would be to protect the supporter, the consumer, from exploitation. This would include regulating ticket prices, and introducing policies to ensure that football is available as a pleasure to as wide an audience as possible. The question of television coverage will be decided on this basis, according to football's own demands for the good of the many.

A regulator would also ensure and supervise constant investment in the long-term health of its sport, at youth and school level, in the smaller clubs, league and non-league, and amongst the amateurs. It would be proud of the unique, original, historic, comprehensive framework of football which was bequeathed to the current generation as a life force by the previous passion of very many people. And it would also see that a healthy grass-roots can only be good for the apex at the top of the game.

Football could look to become much more actively involved with the local community in a number of ways. The big clubs which claim to be 'adverts' for their poor towns could actually do some advertising, genuinely helping the towns to market themselves, rather than expect favours simply for existing. All clubs could introduce much greater, properly funded community programmes, allowing public use of facilities, coaching and outreach sessions, including community service by the players, doing some wider work in return for their million pound salaries.

Football could join with local authorities to bring the standards of municipal sports facilities up above those of degradation. The lottery cannot do this, because it cannot plan, it has to wait for bids, and it cannot allocate according to a national pattern. Coaching qualifications could become extended, compulsory even, for the managers of every club, professional and amateur, as is the case in many other countries, so that everybody is given the opportunity to improve themselves, and players' enjoyment of the game will be enhanced by an appreciation of its subtler patterns.

The game would be kept under constant review, as to how to improve it, strengthen it, to build on the joy and love it has produced, naturally and spontaneously, in so many people since the moment of its inception.

'The fullest reassessment of policy for the game' never happened and is long overdue. The Premier League chairmen should be forced to come to a public forum and explain their conduct and future plans, justify their lack of investment in the fabric of football, their breakaway from it, their outrageous fortunes and how they propose to spend them. Everything ought to be up for discussion and up for change, because everything is possible.

It may be that when this reassessment of policy takes place, people will decide that in fact they like the 'free-market' model of football. They might think it right that only a few clubs will dominate, that pricing policy should be ruthless, that supporters should be treated as a 'captive market'. They may decide that human beings must not stand in the way of 'market forces', and that cherished institutions should be allowed to die. 'Consolidation', they might decide, is preferable to variety and soul.

Or they might decide the opposite. That making money is an important activity for football, but only if it is to be put to constructive use. That money is a tool, not an end in itself. People may decide that it has all been a strangely paralysing dream, this handing everything to the rich, and remember that human beings can organise their own societies and institutions. They may decide football must be run in a businesslike manner, to guard against the shame and tragedy of the past, but that business alone does not preserve history, magic, soul. Indeed they may see that it necessarily destroys, drains miracles of their splendour, turns them inevitably into mere commodities. People may rediscover an ethos to sport, to football and its institutions; they may find a higher pleasure and satisfaction to be had there than mere consumption. They may decide that football is a beautiful game, and things of beauty need careful preservation, not remorseless exploitation. They may find, on the fullest reassessment, that for some inexplicable, elemental reason, sport has a soul, and football the heartiest one of all. They might, after proper reflection, decide that football is a greater, more wonderful thing than merely a business. And that it needs to be reclaimed, before it is too late.

BIBLIOGRAPHY

History and Football History

Bennett A., *The Card* (Penguin, 1975)

Butler B., *The Official History of the Football Association* (Queen Anne Press, 1991)

Dunning E. and Sheard K., *Barbarians, Gentlemen and Players* (Martin Robertson, 1979).

Harding J., *For the Good of the Game: The Official History of the Professional Footballers Association* (Robson Books, 1991)

Holt R., *Sport and the British* (Oxford University Press, 1995)

Inglis S., *League Football and the Men who Made it 1888-1988: The Official Centenary History of the Football League* (Collins, 1988)

McCord N., *North-East England: The Region's Development 1760-1960* (Batsford Academic, 1979)

The Naldrett Press, *The History of the Football Association* (1953)

Vamplew W., *Pay Up and Play the Game: Professional Sport in Britain 1875-1914* (Cambridge University Press, 1988)

Walton J., *Lancashire: A Social History 1558-1939* (Manchester University Press, 1987)

Walvin J., *The People's Game* (Mainstream, 1994)

Football General

Ball P. and Shaw P., *The Umbro Book of Football Quotations* (Stanley Paul, 1993)

The Football League, *One Game One Team One Voice* (1990)

The Football Association, *Blueprint for the Future of Football* (1991)

Fynn A. and Guest L., *Out of Time* (Simon & Schuster, 1994)

Hopcraft A., *The Football Man* (Simon & Schuster, 1988)

Hornby N., *Fever Pitch* (Victor Gollancz, 1992)

Hughes C., *The Winning Formula* (Collins, 1990)

Hugman B. ed., *The 1996-97 Official PFA Footballers Factfile* (Queen Anne Press, 1996)

Inglis S., *Football Grounds of Britain* (Collins Willow, 1996)

Pickering D., *The Cassell Soccer Companion* (Cassell, 1995)

Rollin G. ed., *Rothmans Football Yearbook 1995-96* and *1996-97* (Headline, 1996)

Soar P. and Tyler M., *The Encyclopedia of British Football* (Marshal Cavendish, 1977)

Hillsborough

Scraton P., Jemphrey A., Coleman S., *No Last Rights: The Denial of Justice and the Promotion of Myth in the Aftermath of the Hillsborough Disaster* (Liverpool City Council, 1995)

Taylor R., Ward A., Newburn T., *The Day of the Hillsborough Disaster: A Narrative Account* (Liverpool University Press, 1995)

HMSO, *The Hillsborough Stadium Disaster, Inquiry* by Lord Justice Taylor, Interim Report (Cm 765, August 1989)

HMSO, *The Hillsborough Stadium Disaster, Inquiry* by Lord Justice Taylor, Final Report (Cm 962, January 1990)

Business and Biography

Evans E., *Good Times, Bad Times* (Phoenix, 1994)

Shawcross W., *Murdoch* (Pan, 1993)

Thomas D., *Alan Sugar: The Amstrad Story* (Century, 1990)

Tomas J., *Soccer Czars* (Mainstream, 1996)

Football Biography

Clayton R., *A Slave to Soccer* (Stanley Paul, 1960)

Clough B., *Clough: The Autobiography* (Corgi, 1995)

Dalglish K. and Winter H., *Dalglish: My Autobiography* (Hodder & Stoughton, 1996)

Graham G., *The Glory and the Grief* (Andre Deutsch, 1995)

Keegan K., *Kevin Keegan by Kevin Keegan* (Arthur Barker, 1977)

Lawton T., *Football is my Business* (Sporting Handbooks, 1946)

Liddell B., *My Soccer Story* (Stanley Paul, 1960)

Matthews S., *Feet First* (Ewen & Dale, 1948)

Milburn J., *Golden Goals* (Stanley Paul, 1957)

Moore B., *My Soccer Story* (Stanley Paul, 1966)

Pringle A. and Fisher N., *Where Are They Now?* (Two Heads Publishing, 1996)

Seed J., *Soccer from the Inside* (Thorsons, 1947)

Shearer A., *Alan Shearer: Diary of a Season* (Virgin Books, 1995)

Wilson R., *My Life in Soccer* (Pelham Books, 1969)

Clubs

ASTON VILLA

Ripon A., *The Aston Villa Story* (Breedon, 1993)

BLACKBURN ROVERS

Francis C., *History of the Blackburn Rovers Football Club 1873-1923* (Geo. Tolmin & Sons, 1925)

Jackman M., *Blackburn Rovers: The Official Encyclopedia* (Breedon, 1994)

EVERTON

Clegg B., *The Man Who Made Littlewoods: The Story of John Moores* (Hodder & Stoughton, 1993)

Keates T., *History of the Everton Football Club 1878-79–1928-29* (Thomas Brahell, 1929)

Platt M., *Everton: 'School of Science'* (The Bluecoat Press)

MANCHESTER UNITED

Crick M. and Smith D., *Manchester United: The Betrayal of a Legend* (Pelham Books, 1989)

Dunphy E., *A Strange Kind of Glory* (William Heinemann, 1992)

Tyrell T. and Meek D., *The Hamlyn Illustrated History of Manchester United* (Hamlyn, 1996)

White J., *Are You Watching, Liverpool* (William Heinemann, 1994)

Wyke T., *A Hall for All Seasons: A History of the Free Trade Hall* (The Charles Halle Foundation, 1996)

Young P., *Manchester United: The History of a Great Football Club* (William Heinemann, 1960)

NEWCASTLE UNITED

Joannou P., *Newcastle United: The First 100 Years and More* (Polar Print, 1995)

NORWICH VICTORIA
Edwards K., *A Team for All Seasons: A History of Northwich Victoria FC
and the Story of the Drill Field* (Cheshire County Publishing, 1992)
TOTTENHAM HOTSPUR
Davies H., *The Glory Game* (Mainstream, 1990)
Scholar I., *Behind Closed Doors* (Andre Deutsch, 1992)

Newspapers

The Guardian, The Independent, The Times, The Daily Telegraph, The
Daily Express, The Sun, The Mirror, The Sunday Times, The Observer, The
Sunday Telegraph, Independent on Sunday, News of the World, The People,
The Sunday Mirror.

Local Newspapers

Evening Standard, Manchester Evening News, Liverpool Echo, Liverpool
Daily Post, [Middlesbrough] Evening Gazette, Newcastle Evening
Chronicle, Newcastle Journal, Lancashire Evening Telegraph.

Magazines

Business Age, FC, FourFourTwo, Goal, Total Football, When Saturday
Comes.